Fragments

by Graham Spaid

Disclaimer

The events in this book are my memories from my perspective. Certain names have been changed to protect the identities of those involved.

CONTENTS

The big, bad teacher

Monica

The pink pen and pencil set

I tutored Monica for two years. It's a long time. Parents normally give up, or the child does. She was nine when we began. We prepared for the 11-plus, the entrance exam for secondary school, the so-called 'best' schools. Parents are keen on these. I often have pupils. They normally fail. I don't tell parents that. In our two years, off and on, I asked Monica if she remembered our first lesson. She either said nothing or "No," but she liked to say that, and everything she told me wasn't true.

At the start, we met once a fortnight. For lessons, you need somewhere comfortable, without distraction. Daddy suggested the dining room table. We tried it, but the light was poor. He said he'd buy a reading lamp. In the meantime, we could use the sitting room. There was a huge TV on the wall. When I walked in, the screen was black, but it hadn't been for long. I could hear its cooling clicks, soft and private. The screen still glowed. Monica glowed too, but she always did. I relaxed on the armchair in front of the screen. The seat was warm. She'd been sitting on it, watching television. There are secrets like that, which you learn without even trying.

As soon as daddy left the room, Monica sniffed. She did it several times. I found myself waiting for the next sniff. When one didn't come, I said, "Sniff," but she wouldn't. She didn't say no. She just didn't sniff.

"Have you had a tutor before?"

"Yes, but he didn't know anything. Daddy told him not to come anymore."

Below the TV screen, there was a mantelpiece with a few photos, one of which showed a small girl and an old man. He looked jovial. He had a red suit and a long beard that was so white it didn't seem real. Judging by her grin, the girl was thrilled. She may have been on his lap.

"I see you took a photo before you sacked him. He was very hairy."

In another snap, Monica was by herself.

"Who's that pretty girl?" I asked.

"It's my twin sister."

I believed her. It *was* the first lesson. It was her first fib, too. When she saw I believed her, she confessed.

"I believed you!" I whined, like a child. "You shouldn't be able to trick me. I'm the teacher." Pause. "Are you sure you won't sniff? Otherwise, I won't hear you. Either you'll be better next time, or I'll get sacked and won't come anymore."

Once again, she didn't say no. (It *was* the first lesson.) She just didn't sniff. She was right, in a way. Children aren't meant to sniff. Teachers don't like it. They don't like being coughed on, either, or farted at or clung to by nose-pickers. But it still happens.

We must have done some work. I just can't recall what it was. Monica sat on a giant cushion, one meant for sitting, with a low table to write on, drawn up in front of my chair. She had a new pen and pencil set, the sort of thing a girl buys for a new tutor. It was so new she hadn't opened the packet. There was a biro (the kind you press at the top), two pencils, an eraser, a sharpener and a short ruler, all of which were pink, the same shade exactly. She took the pen out first and dismantled it carefully but dropped some bits and couldn't put them back together. I found the spring on the carpet and held it out to her like a lost jewel.

"Are you going to sniff for me now?" She looked across solemnly but didn't answer. "I found your spring." Pause. "Are you going to?"

"I just did."

"I didn't hear you. Do it again."

I heard this time. It doesn't take much to please me. I wasn't sure about daddy. At the end of the hour, when he came in, I pointed to the remnants of the pen. It was all there, just in the wrong order.

"I found the spring," I said, "but we left it for you. I didn't want to waste time."

Daddy smiled and nodded.

"I won't be in next lesson," he said. He did business overseas and had to travel. He was Nigerian. "My partner will be here. I'll introduce her to you."

He called out like summoning a child. Immediately, a woman stepped in. She'd been waiting. He must have told her to. Smiling shyly, like a child, she stopped in the centre of the room, wiped her mouth with the back of her hand and lowered her eyes.

There's no money

Next lesson, there was no daddy, just as daddy had predicted. There was a new lamp on the dining room table. He'd said that, too. The lamp had a long, silver neck that you twist around to suit you. It was so bright I turned it away. I called it my hair dryer. The first time I said it, Monica laughed but only the first time.

Her mother wasn't home, not bad news in itself, though daddy said she would be. Auntie opened the front door. When Monica and I were alone, she said straightaway, "There's no money."

Daddy had not mentioned this. A lamp is one thing, abundant light, but you can't live on that. Auntie should have told me when I got there. *She's spineless*, I thought. I looked at the little girl.

"It's not your fault," I said. There was no money; it was a problem, but she was nine. It wasn't her job to tell me. I remember thinking, *This child is worth more than her adults*. In all the months that followed, I never changed my mind.

At the end of the lesson, auntie came in. She looked as if she didn't want to.

"Her mother didn't leave any money," she said then turned to Monica and frowned. "Why didn't you tell me?"

It happens now and then, no money at the end of a lesson. Mostly, I assume it's not on purpose, and go back. But it was two weeks until the next lesson. They'd forgotten once. They could forget again. When I rang the bell, they might not answer. That's happened too, more than once, with other people. On the bright side, as it were, they had bought a lamp. It shed a ray of light on the future. There'd be work at that table, lessons even. On the other hand, they mightn't involve me.

I decided to go back, if only to collect the money they owed me. I could sack daddy later. That's how I view quitting when I don't like a client. I'd done it to other daddies, but sacking him would mean sacking Monica, and I was fond of her. It was a bad start, though. Mother had only had two tests, and she'd failed both of them. In the first few months, she failed the money test several times. I kept count for a while. When I reached six, I told Monica. She didn't speak; she just lifted her little hand so the fingers showed, and hid the thumb. I kept going back. I got paid in the end.

Their house is up the road from mine, three bus stops away. It was convenient – another reason to go back, if I needed one. Occasionally, I saw Monica on the bus. The first time, it was Sunday, the one after the lesson with no money. I'd been shopping. I was on the 145, sitting near the back. She got on. When she caught sight of me, she grinned and sat across the aisle. Her mother was with her, and her four-year-old twin brothers. They took the seats behind me. They'd been to church and were in their best clothes. Monica was holding a special bag.

"What's inside?" I asked. She opened it. When a girl lets you look in her bag, you feel you know her better. Mother ignored me. I thought, *OK*, but it was odd. She apologised in the next lesson.

"I didn't recognise you!"

"I'm glad," I joked. "I get recognised everywhere I go."

We laughed, but for mother, it was another test failed. She let Monica speak to me when she thought I was a stranger.

Moneyca

Monica, lesson three. I rang the doorbell. It wasn't an ordinary bell, just a metal rod which you push and pull, like poking someone. I always did it twice, as if that made an answer more likely. It grated noisily. However many times I went, it surprised me, a bit like Monica.

The curtain swept aside, and there she was in the window frame, a live picture. I told her more than once, "I know what you'll look like when you're sixteen." She didn't mind, until I added, "You'll need a good tutor."

As soon as I walked in, mother paid for two lessons: the one she'd missed and the current one. Too quick, I thought; she was proving something. The twins were on the staircase, one at the top, one at the bottom.

"I'll eat you later," I said. Monica was jumping up and down.

"Fizi's upstairs."

As in *fizzy*.

"I don't believe you."

"Technically, it's true."

"'Technically'? Do I say that?"

"No, I do."

"It's a big word for a little girl."

She may have got it from the TV. *My Little Pony*. One of the boy ponies, a show-off, said it all the time. I asked if she watched it. She didn't want to answer. She said she watched it with her brothers.

We all show off. She did a cartwheel on the dining room floor. Her feet just missed the light.

"Careful," I said. "If you break that, I mightn't get paid."

I mightn't anyway.

Another cartwheel.

"I saw your tummy."

In the middle of the lesson, I asked, "What do you think is more important to me, you or money?"

She thought for a moment then answered with a firm voice.

"Money."

I nodded.

"Can I call you Moneyca?"

"No."

She had an old notebook with her and was reading a page. I tried to look, but she wouldn't let me. It was personal, she said. She'd been feeling sad back in Year 3 and written about it. A short silence.

"I need a pen. I've got one upstairs."

She stood up, opened a drawer, put her notebook in, closed the drawer decisively (she didn't have a key) and left the room. The air went heavy. I could feel a girl waiting, but I couldn't see her. I tiptoed to the drawer. She gave me enough time then stepped back into the room. When she saw me at the drawer, she screamed, one of those spine-chilling screams from a horror movie. Then she grinned.

"I knew you were there," I said. "I wouldn't have touched it."

When she screamed, no one came. She went upstairs for a few minutes and returned without a pen.

"You just went to see Fizi, your imaginary friend."

"She's not imaginary. I couldn't find my pen."

I gave her mine. She let me read the secret notebook. After that, we did some scrambled words. *Amphibian* came up. I stressed the 'fib' bit. It was true, though, about Fizi. On a pretext, she came downstairs, another sweet Nigerian girl, a year younger than Monica.

"I know all about you," I said.

Monica pointed to an empty chair. I looked at Fizi.

"I wish you could stay, but you can't."

At the end of the lesson, Monica held out my pen.

"Technically, it's mine, but you can keep it, Moneyca."

She raised a finger to her lips and gazed at me mournfully. There was disappointment, too. As I got up, she slipped the pen in my bag. When I'd said to keep it, she hadn't believed me, or it wasn't the right thing to do. I put it on the table.

"You can give it back next week."

But she'd moved on already.

"Look, I can do the splits."

"No, you can't."

Fizi was in the sitting room, watching TV. I peeped in on the way out.

"Can you do the splits? Monica can't."

"No, but I'm double-jointed."

She tucked her ankles behind her head.

"Wow. I can't even cross my legs."

I walked down the road, thinking about splits and knots and the eight-year-old who wrote when she was sad.

Girl spray

When I got to Monica's and pressed the bell, the door seemed to open by itself. "Hello, ghost," I'd say pleasantly and walk in, as if I wasn't expecting a human. Then Monica showed her face. One week, she looked different.

"Are you Fizi?"

"Fizi doesn't like you."

"But you do?"

It was only half a question. She seemed older, prettier. I asked when her birthday was. She gave me her reproving look.

"I know I've asked lots of times. Write it down so I won't forget."

She took a sheet of paper and wrote *Monica's birthday: 2 August* in big letters. She got the apostrophe and colon right. I placed the sheet in a folder in my bag. Months later, when I came across it, I handed it to her. She said the date was wrong, tore the page in half and handed it back. I still don't know her birthday, but I've kept the page. It has more meaning now, though I'm not sure what that is, either.

"My brother calls me Moneyca."

"Oh, no! How could he?"

"He heard you."

"How is that possible? He's always outside during the lesson."

"He must have been listening."

I thought of all the silly things I'd said. If the boy had heard, mother must have too or auntie. Somehow, I hadn't been sacked – unless Monica was fibbing.

"What language does your family speak?" She told me. "Say something for me." She did. "What did you say? *You're a smelly old man?*"

"I don't know the word for *smelly.*" Pause. "What's your surname?" I told her. "Mr Spaid is a poo-poo head."

She was getting naughty.

Daddy asked me to come three times a month instead of two. I spoke to Monica about it.

"Are you free on Tuesdays?"

"I'm not free."

She was sniffing again and sneezing. After one sneeze, she waved the tissue in front of me. It was very wet.

"That's girl spray," I said.

She leapt up from her chair. It crashed noisily on the floor behind her. She picked it up, sat down and did the same thing again. There was another noisy crash.

"Shush!" I whispered. "Your mother will hear."

She did it once more. Mother put her head around the door. I said Monica was excited when she got the answers right; she was keen to learn. I finished with a warm smile, "She's only nine!"

Mother smiled too but walked in and fingered a few pages of her daughter's book like an inspector. At last, she left the room. I remembered the pen I'd lent Monica.

"Where's my pen?"

"I took it to school and put it in the pot on my table. A boy stole it."

"Boyfriend?"

"That's disgusting!"

"No more disgusting than a snotty tissue."

She had to do an exercise on synonyms.

"If I get the answer right, I can put spit on you. If I get it wrong, you can tickle me."

"I hope you get it wrong." When she did, I pointed out, "We had a deal."

At the end of each lesson, if there was money, Monica went and got it. This time, when she came back, she was holding her hands out in front of her, a wet tissue spread across the palms.

"There's no money," she intoned, like a funeral service, and slowly shook her head. She looked miserable. Suddenly, she grinned and peeled back the tissue. The money was underneath. If I wanted it, I'd have to take the wetness, too.

"I never thought you could be so wicked."

"I don't like you."

"I lied for you."

"Fizi *loathes* you."

"We had a deal."

On the footpath, I turned my head. Monica was at the window. She grinned and waved. She must have run to catch me.

You should've told me

Before each lesson, I reminded Monica's parents. I texted them – daddy, the day before; mother, in the morning. It didn't make much difference. Sometimes there was money, sometimes not. Today, there was not. At the end of the lesson, mother came in, followed by auntie.

"You should've told me," she said to Monica; to me, "I forgot. It won't happen again."

"It won't happen again," said auntie. As a rule, I didn't see her. She was upstairs. When the ceiling creaked, Monica told me what room she was in.

Mother peered down at the table. Monica had escaped but left her book open. The work was messy. Mother didn't like it. Neither did auntie.

"It's all right," I said.

"Can you read it?"

"Can you read it?" said auntie.

"I don't usually look. She just tells me the answers."

"Can you give her homework?" mother asked.

"Homework," nodded auntie. It was the summer holiday. A girl had time to spare.

The adults disappeared, and Monica returned. I left some photocopies stapled together. There were lots of examples but few questions.

"It's not as long as it looks," I said. "Your mother'll be happy, but it's not much work, really."

"I'll tell her you said that."

As I walked out, I wondered, *Will she wave at the window?* It's something children do but not forever. I was on the footpath now. I turned my head. She wasn't there. I could feel her, though, behind the curtain. *She's playing with me.* I took three steps then looked back, and there she was, laughing, waving.

Next lesson, at the start, Fizi wandered in with a plastic bottle.

"Do I know you? Are you Fizi?"

She nodded. She was very quiet. I'd heard her speak only once.

"You look different," I encouraged. "Your hair's changed, and you weren't carrying a bottle." Pause. "I didn't know you were here." I turned to Monica: "You didn't tell me!"

Monica wasn't listening. She was searching for her homework.

"Are you sure you did it?" I asked.

Fizi slipped out in her soundless way then came back a minute later, holding the homework like a treasure. She put it on the table and left again without a word.

"That's amazing," I said. "Whenever I need something, Fizi will know. She'll be there, waiting." Pause. "Does she have a tutor? I'll give her my business card." I reached for my top pocket then stopped. "I don't have a business card."

Monica made one for me from a piece of paper, the right size and shape, put my name on it and wrote *Fish* underneath, like a job title.

"What's your phone number?"

"I don't think Fizi's mummy will want her to have it."

Monica made up a number and read it out.

"Is it like yours?" she asked.

"Very."

She let me see the card. There was a mark between the *F* and the *i*. It looked like a *j*.

"It says *Fjish*."

"Fjish!" Monica repeated then went to find Fizi. After a moment, the little girl appeared ahead of Monica, clutching the business card.

"Why did you send me a card with *Fish* on it?"

It was only the second time she had spoken to me.

"Monica did it. She wrote *fjish*."

"Fjish!" Monica repeated with a grin. Fizi went out again with her card. I had some paperclips. Monica took a pink one and twisted it out of shape.

"It's a heart," she said, showing it to me.

"It's a bit squashed. You can have it. A memento of the lesson."

"What does *memento* mean?"

"Something you keep to remind you of a precious time." She threw the paperclip across the room. "You'll come across it later and think of me."

"Wimp," she said, as if it was me that she'd tossed away.

The hour was over. The homework sheets were loose.

"What happened to the staple?" I asked.

"I'll do it," she said. She had her own stapler, a tiny, pink one. When she'd finished, she passed the sheets to me.

"They're in the wrong order," I said.

"You should've told me."

I love you more than money

Monica's exam was coming, the great 11-plus. After years of work and a thousand pounds of tuition, it was probably our last lesson. Daddy hadn't told me. I hadn't asked. In fact, I didn't want to know, not beforehand, before the last lesson.

"Every year, a thousand girls do the test for that school." I was talking to Monica. "Less than a hundred get in."

"You sound as if you expect me to fail."

"I don't. You're good enough to go. If you don't pass, I'll still think you're clever."

I told her a story about a girl I'd tutored, same test, same school. The girl's mother was confident. The first time I went, she smiled knowingly, brought her hand up near her cheek and said, "She's *very* clever." At the word *very*, she squeezed her thumb and forefinger together, as if to pin it in my mind.

"Did she pass?" inquired Monica. She liked to hear about my students, especially the ones her own age.

"She came equal 800th."

At the end of the lesson, as usual, Monica went to get the money.

When she reached the sofa, she cartwheeled onto it and stayed there, upside down, with her feet against the wall. That wasn't usual. She was facing me. She was just upside-down. I thought, *She doesn't want it to end*.

We kept on talking.

"I haven't got change," I said.

"Liar."

Each week, when they paid me, it was always in notes. I tried to bring change. That day, I didn't have any.

"I love you more than money," I said.

"No, you don't."

"It might be our last lesson." She knew already. "You have to beg daddy to let me come. I can prepare you for your Sats exams in Year 6. Tell him."

"No."

"Do you remember our first lesson? I saw your photo on the mantelpiece and asked who the pretty girl was. You said it was your twin sister. Do you remember?"

She didn't speak. She may have nodded, but it's hard when you're standing on your head.

"You used to wave through the window when I was going. Do you remember?"

She'd gone solemn, or I thought she had. She was still upside-down.

I got paid. For once, they had the right money. They didn't need change. There'd be nothing to sort out in the next lesson. In the past, exact payment would have pleased me, but right now it felt like an omen. There'd be no next lesson.

On the footpath, I turned my head and looked for Monica. I thought she might be there at the window, one more time, because it was the last, but I couldn't see her. I walked on three steps then turned again. No Monica. *She might be there behind the curtain. I just can't see her.* But I couldn't feel her, either.

The day before her exam, I sent a text to daddy, wishing good luck.

At the end, I added, as I used to, "See you Monday," though I meant Monica – I didn't see much of daddy – and this time I didn't much believe it. A text came back a minute later from Lagos or London or Dubai. It was two letters long.

"OK."

There are letters like that, rich as silence.

On Monday, when I got to Monica's, I found her in the passage where it turned the corner into the dining room. The lights were off. She was standing by herself in the semi-darkness.

"Did you do the test?" I said in a searching voice but softly so the adults wouldn't hear.

"No."

Good old Monica.

"They didn't register you in time."

I said it flatly, as you tell someone what you had for lunch or how old you are. She smiled.

I still love you; a bit less, maybe

"A dog bit me in the face when I was little."

Monica was chatting. It wasn't all true, as you know. I watched her to see if she was blinking. She told me she blinked when she lied, though I wasn't watching when she said it. Maybe she blinked, but even then, I wouldn't know the truth.

"Did you go to hospital?"

"No."

"Do you have a scar?"

"No."

"Are you fibbing?"

"No."

Pause.

"I sometimes forget you're a child. Have you ever been bullied?"

"Yes. A boy was mean to me at school. He was mean to everyone. He had to leave."

"What did he do, bite your face?" Grave silence. "I just bullied you." Her right eye was shinier than usual. I leaned closer. "Is that a tear?"

It was, a true tear, somewhere in her eye. She hadn't released it, that's all. She smiled. You can hide a tear, a scar, but I didn't know a little girl could do it and smile.

I ask too many questions. A while ago, I asked a teenager why she hadn't sacked me. She didn't answer, but her father stopped the lessons two weeks later. With Monica, I said annoying things, like "I know all about Year 6s" and "Boys are intelligent." She'd be cross, but she didn't sack me. I told her about a boy I'd tutored for the 11-plus. We did an hour a week. His mother stared at us the whole lesson. In twelve months, his level went up two years. His mother still wasn't happy. When she showed me his school report, she wailed, "A year of tuition, and this is all he got!"

"She was thinking about the money."

"Why didn't you stop going?" asked Monica.

"I was thinking about the money. I went on so long they had to sack me. I hope he failed."

Monica leapt off her chair.

"I'm going to ring daddy right now and tell him!" Pause. She sat down again. "My mother doesn't spy on us."

"She does. She looks at your book when you're not there. This is her."

I took a page by the top corner, as mother did, turned it suspiciously, like a dirty ear, and looked underneath.

"I told her, 'It may not seem very much, but we've worked hard.'"

Monica gazed at me. I saw amusement, wonder, wickedness – the perfect mixture in a girl's eyes.

"You need to write more," I said. "She might sack me." Monica smiled and put her pen down. "That's not very clever." Pause. "Who's the cleverest child in your class?"

"A boy. He was dumb at first. Then he got a tutor. Her name's Mirabelle. She tutors eight people in my class. She gets very good results. She's older than you."

"She must be very old."

"She's more dedicated."

"Dead-icated."

"You're jealous."

"Yes." *Mirabelle* – that's a good one. As for the boy, "Ask him what rotund means."

"He won't know."

"He will. Is he fat?"

"No."

"So, you can ask him. You can call him rotund because he isn't – when your teacher's not around."

"She won't understand."

"She will."

"She won't."

At school, Monica remembered the word. She asked the cleverest boy what it meant, then told me in the next lesson.

"He said, 'Fat and round.'"

"Is he handsome?" She didn't reply. "I'm going to make you into a young lady, someone who doesn't spit or pick her nose."

"I don't really want a tutor."

"Yes, you do."

"I don't."

"You do."

"I don't."

Pause.

"I still love you; a bit less, maybe."

"You don't."

"Is it opposites day?" Pause. "You're right. I don't love you less." Pause. "You'll have lots of boyfriends in secondary school."

"I won't."

"You'll go to milk bars and movies."

"I won't."

After all the teasing, she was still calm, still certain, still beautiful. I once wrote, *This child is worth more than her adults.* She was worth more than me.

I'm going to slap her

Once when I arrived, mother was in the passage. She saw me standing with Monica.

"Put a jumper on, and socks," she said. Lesson time. The girl was a little bare, but she always was – at six o'clock on Monday, anyway. Mother hadn't noticed before. She rarely saw us together. If she was about, the child disappeared.

Monica. I've started calling her *child*, partly to remind me, as she's looking older, and partly to annoy her. We converse in adult fashion. We tell each other things "man to man." It's just the sort of phrase which annoys her.

"Are zebras white with black stripes," she asked, "or black with white stripes?"

"I've no idea, child."

I told her an anecdote. I was on a crowded bus. I wanted to get past a young woman and said, "Excuse me."

"You should say, 'Excuse me, *please*.'"

Nowadays, I'm not often surprised. I examined her.

"'Excuse me' is enough for most people. All right. Excuse me, *please,* with cherries on top."

She said something rude.

"That was rude," I replied. "Someone got out of bed on the wrong side."

She said something ruder.

"That was even ruder," I replied. I thought she was going to burst. I added, to Monica, "You know how annoying I can be."

Monica had listened politely, but she wasn't smiling. Sometimes, I made her laugh.

"I heard a man say "Bisquits!" in the supermarket. He was by himself in the dairy aisle. That's all he said."

"Bisquits!" she repeated with a giggle.

I told her about Bizz in Year 4. His family, like hers, was Nigerian. I asked him if Bizz was short for something that he didn't want me to know. He nodded sombrely. I couldn't help guessing.

"Bizzopolis?" He looked at me. "Bizz-pants-on-fire?"

I expected Monica to laugh, but she didn't play with names, except her teachers'.

"That's not funny," she said.

"Bizz didn't think so either."

One lesson, she wasn't there at the beginning. She'd never been late before. She was at a friend's house, auntie explained. Someone was driving her home.

"I told her to be back on time. I'm going to slap her."

She said it in a cold voice, as if she meant it. We sat and waited. The TV was on, though neither of us watched, and we didn't talk. No Monica. After a few minutes, auntie repeated, "I'm going to slap her." She may have said it to impress me, to appear strong. Perhaps she didn't mean it; she wouldn't slap Monica at all. But I didn't like it. I said, "She's just a child. She's not responsible for what the adults do."

Auntie didn't reply. She sat there, squinting at the new idea. We kept an eye on the street. Eventually, a car pulled up. It was like a tank in size. Monica got out. She looked small – her thin body – next to all the metal. Auntie went to get her. I couldn't hear what she said, but she was still cross. They had to pay for an hour, and it was almost half over.

I asked Monica if she'd been with Fizi. She wouldn't say. She didn't seem happy. She was in trouble. I found the sheet she'd torn in half, the one where she'd written her birthday. I showed it to her to cheer her up or something.

"It's Fizi's birthday, not mine."

"I don't believe you." Pause. "Auntie said she's going to slap you. I defended you. I said you weren't responsible for what the adults did."

She sat there in silence, a bit like auntie.

I didn't stop at the normal time. I went on teaching sad Monica for almost half an hour. I hoped auntie would notice. Next lesson, I asked, "Did she slap you?"

She shook her head, but you know Monica.

I'm ringing daddy!

Mother put her head around the door.

"Did Monica say there's no money?"

"No," I replied. "I was talking about daddy. I saw him on the street."

The week before, mother hadn't paid the right money. She had forgotten again. She owed me eight pounds. The next day, I dropped in to get it. Still no money.

"Her father's coming," she said. "He'll pay you."

She didn't know when exactly. I walked to the bus stop, the same one as ever, without the same money. I felt stupid. While I was waiting, a car pulled up. Daddy got out, hand in pocket. The car crept forward. I pointed to it. I thought there was no one in it. There was. Once again, I felt stupid.

"Shall I pay for two lessons?" He held a roll of notes in the air. "When are you coming next?"

"In two weeks."

He thought for a second then closed his fingers around the notes, put them back in his wallet and gave me eight pounds in coins. It didn't make me feel any brighter.

Monica had her own anecdote. She giggled when she told me. She was with a friend outside a supermarket. A homeless man had asked them for money. The friend's mother offered to buy him food. He said he wanted Macdonald's.

"In a way, it's funny," I said. I talked a bit, finishing, "It could have been me if there's no money."

Monica asked me for past exam papers. Auntie had told her to.

"Not to do with you," she explained. "To go through with auntie."

It's my teaching material, I thought. *If auntie wants to tutor, she can get her own.* But she'd blame Monica if I didn't bring something. I said I would, then I realised: *Auntie...past papers...I won't be needed anymore.* Too late. I'd promised. Next time, I gave her a paper.

"You brought it!" she cried. She'd forgotten or didn't think I would. It was an old maths test, the first few questions, the easy ones. It hadn't printed well.

"I need a colour cartridge," I explained, "but I don't want to buy one."

"Skin-flint!"

Say that to auntie. Mother put her head around the door; she was popping out for a moment to the cash machine. She'd forgotten my money again. Monica grinned. Auntie was upstairs. The lamp was too, the one daddy had bought for the lesson. It was auntie's now. Soon, she'd have my questions. When mother left, I stood up.

"I'm ringing daddy!"

Monica started miming. I don't remember what, but she was animated, a one-girl band. She gesticulated, sitting next to me, and jumped about, which meant banging chairs. She'd never been cuter – or noisier.

"Sh!" I said. "Auntie will hear!"

She stopped suddenly and said in a measured voice, without looking at me, "It's our last lesson next week. You're getting sacked." She glanced across to see what I'd do, then looked down. "You'll have no more money."

"I don't believe you. They wouldn't tell you now."

"I overheard them talking."

I sensed a fib. Her parents weren't good at next day, let alone next week; they didn't focus, not with her education. They'd forgotten the 11-plus. They'd forgotten to pay me ten times over. Still, her exams would happen whether they remembered or not. Summer would come. Why have a tutor? They'd ask themselves sooner or later. Next year, Monica would be in secondary school. I'd helped her in primary. I belonged to the past already.

"Look." I put a finger to my eye. "There's a tear."

If there was, she didn't see it. She kept her face down, studying her book like a good girl. The sentences she'd spoken, they were too easy. She was fibbing. I was almost certain.

"You'll learn lots of things at secondary school, how to make boys suffer, twist them around your little finger." I smiled. "The way you do with me."

Missed the tear, missed the smile – they mightn't have existed. She took pity on me.

"It's not our last lesson."

Tickle the boxes

The Easter break was here. Mother said they were going away. I suggested she write down the date of the next lesson. She had forgotten once, the lesson after Christmas. I didn't mention this, but I thought it might happen again.

"I won't forget," she said.

She didn't either. She remembered enough to cancel. There were no lessons for the whole of April. When I finally saw Monica, it felt awkward. Her exams were starting. Next week might be the last lesson. When the hour was done, on the sixtieth minute precisely, she stood up. We had always finished late.

"Don't go yet!" I complained. She had gone already. She was in the doorway, pulling faces.

Next lesson, when I arrived, she was in bed asleep. She'd had her first exam, English comprehension. She came down at last. It was a Monica I didn't know, a grumpy one, without the glow. She never quite woke up.

Afterwards, her mother asked, "Are you coming next week?"

She was checking daddy's schedule. Usually, we had three lessons then missed one. The next, on the 15th, would be the third for May.

"Yes," I replied. "There are always more exams. I'm a secondary teacher. Secondary."

The following week, when I turned up, there was no car in the drive. It wasn't a good sign. Auntie opened the door. No Monica. She wasn't home. I had to wait. Auntie didn't explain. Five minutes later, mother appeared, wearing a dressing gown.

"I'm sorry. I was asleep. Monica is out with her dad."

Auntie should have told me. Another five minutes. No Monica. Was auntie going to slap her? Another five. There was a noise at the front door. Monica walked in. She was dressed in boots and jacket like a young lady, not my pupil. She was reserved, too, like a young lady who'd been out with daddy. They'd been shopping. Monica frowned.

"I didn't get everything I wanted. We had to come back for your lesson."

Mine, not ours, not anymore. Her exams were over; she didn't need a tutor. She must have thought that.

"Did you tickle the boxes?" I asked.

The Monica I knew would have smiled. In arithmetic, she had missed four questions. Two pages were stuck together. She hadn't noticed till it was too late.

"You would have got it all right. Did you cry?"

"No." Still her best word. "I was upset, though."

She wasn't upset now. She waved her travel pass. It was laminated, like a credit card, with her photo and date of birth. I asked to see it. She dropped it on the table beyond my reach. She did it several times. I had to try and get it. Toss the Travel Pass, a new game; the last, probably, if this was the last lesson.

"It always falls face down. I was doing it at school."

She dropped it again. It bounced over. I could have reached. She snatched it back and held it up for me. I could see the photo – it didn't look like Monica – but her thumb was over the date of birth, conveniently. I asked when her birthday was. She said October 15th.

"I'm eleven already."

The last fib.

The lesson was almost over. I wanted to end it myself before she ran out. She used to like it when I mimicked her parents. Hoping she'd smile, and I'd feel clever, I came up with this.

"When daddy sacks me, I'll say, 'I'll think of Monica on her birthday, October 15th.' He'll say" (in daddy's deep voice) "'October 15th? No, August the 2nd.'" She smiled, and I smiled back. "I'm just happy I'm here."

"It's our last lesson."

A short silence.

"You said that before."

Her voice was different now.

"I asked daddy in the car. He said, 'Probably.'"

"I don't believe you."

"It's true this time."

A man with a tie

Bussing, the old 1-2-3

The 123 is not as simple as it sounds. It's slow, even for a bus. Occasionally, it doesn't come at all. It has a timetable of its own. For years, its paintwork stayed yellow when other fleets went red. Now, it looks like them. It couldn't hide its blushes any longer. From Wood Green to Ilford then back again, through Walthamstow and Tottenham, it lumbers along over twenty hours a day – in other words, almost all the time – through the heart of riot land, loot 'n' burn. The heart is a complex thing. I try not to catch the 123, but sometimes there isn't any choice. Grab what you can.

On a fresh afternoon, when the wheels are turning and it's not crowded, the 123 is like a normal bus. You enjoy the ride. But it can still take you where you're not expecting. A boy and two girls got on and stood at the front near the driver. They were about thirteen and looked south Asian; south of Naples, anyway. They spoke Italian like a mother tongue. They were in school uniform. Don't ask which one, but the jumpers were green.

The boy's stop was coming. He went "Ciao," wrapped his arms around the slimmer girl (she was very pretty) and kissed her on the lips. A long, adhesive kiss. Grab what you like. The rest of us watched – old boys, old girls, a man with a tie and the other child – passengers. Ciao a tutti. It was cinema on wheels, the famous smooch that Clark gave Vivien in 1939, summer of love, though the kids used their tongues and didn't stop to chat in the middle. *Buss.* It's another word for kiss. It really is. You can look it up, along with the jumper.

There were two old ladies in the front row, watching. You can't blame them. They were sitting in those seats when the kids got on. Once the show started, it was too late to move. If they did, they'd have to get off the bus. They couldn't just shift to another seat. Everyone would know they were embarrassed. They couldn't even turn their heads away. The passengers behind them would have seen. Stay calm, sit it out. Anyhow, it was hard not to watch the children kiss.

But it did go on a while. I began to feel uneasy. When was it going to end? The other girl, the not so slim and pretty one, the one not being kissed, was worried too. She turned her head abruptly and stared down the aisle. *Yes, young lady, we're still here.* I thought she was going to run. But you can't get off a moving bus, and you can't abandon friends. All she did was blush then face the front, trying to conceal it from us. She put a hand near her cheek and fluttered the fingers like a beating wing.

Suddenly, the girl who was being kissed put her palms on the boy's chest and tried to push him away. It surprised me after all that kissing. She'd had enough, but she didn't have the strength to push him off, and he wouldn't stop. He was looting kisses now. She pushed again, with violence this time. He let her go. She straightened her jumper, as a cat licks itself, and announced in Italian that he was too thin. When she saw the other girl, the crimson cheeks, she said, "Che c'è?"

The G-spot

I was covering a Year 9 computer class somewhere in London. A couple of the girls were giggling, skittish, like a cat with the wind in its tail, as my grandma used to say. They were sitting close together and made a unit the way girls do. When one of them spoke, it was what both were thinking.

"What's the G-spot?" Kayleigh asked me.

"You'd better ask your science teacher."

To be honest, I wasn't sure, and they were in that mood. I sensed they knew as much as I did or more and were being silly.

At that moment, the class teacher came back to get something. Immediately, the same girl fired the same question at miss, who wasn't a science teacher but who knew more than I did about the female body. She stopped in front of the girls and answered with a schoolmarm's confidence, in a matter-of-fact tone, as if she was explaining how to save a document. The girls squirmed. It was fun to watch – for me and perhaps for miss, who must have seen their embarrassment but ignored it and went on in her schoolmarm voice, rather idiotically, I thought, unless she wanted to prolong the squirming. *If you can ask a question, girlie, you can hear the answer.*

Miss went out again. I sat on the chair behind her desk. Most of the children were working, even the boys. It felt strange. Boys in far corners aren't usually so engaged. There was a printer in front of me. People printed on it from computers around the school. Every now and then, a sheet would slide out like magic and drop into a metal tray under my nose. It was satisfying. I couldn't help watching. One sheet had the photo of a naked woman, a girl, really, in the late teens. Her whole body. She was lying on her back. I glanced at the boys. So quiet there. Filling in some gaps in the old man's knowledge? I looked at the image again. For once, they had done their best, the distant boys, but if miss was right, the G-spot wasn't showing.

The prettiest girl in the school was in that class. I'm being subjective, and beauty shouldn't matter, but we all know it does. The boys were happy. She was much loved. On the other hand, among the girls, she was much despised.

"Where's your family from?" I asked.

"I'm French-African," she replied with a flashing smile. I improvised.

"French people are very elegant."

Another girl glared at her accusingly.

"You're blushing!"

It was true. The pretty face had changed colour. It was now a Haut-Brion Rouge. She was thirteen, remember.

"Oh, I've been blushing all day," she said. I improvised again (the best teachers do).

"Your father must love you very much."

"Yes, he does!"

I got up and moved around the room. You check the screens, look as though you're working. When I reached the other girl, the pretty one's accuser, she said in a soft voice, but everyone could hear, "You smell of pee, old man."

Good friends and laughter

I cracked open a fortune cookie and read what was on the slip of paper: *You will soon be surrounded by good friends and laughter*. Great, I thought. But whose friends? And what will they be laughing at?

Year 10 maths. I walk in, surrounded by good friends and laughter. I know the class already. Charlotte is standing on a desk, airing the contents of her little skirt. It isn't even her desk. I write the lesson objective on the board. Charlotte sits down. A couple of children start work. There's a break in the noise. Tommy says, "Wanna shag Charlotte?"

He thwacked it at me from his bunker by the window. No warning, only instinct. I didn't answer. He reflected for a second then improved the offer.

"Would you like to have sexual intercourse with Charlotte?"

When he said "sexual intercourse," he slowed down and pushed his lips around in a rubbery way. I gave his style some ironic praise, then Charlotte called out, "Do you want to fuck me, sir?"

She always called me sir.

"Charlotte, that's worse than anything Tommy said!"

I had one more lesson with that class. Charlotte asked me when my birthday was. I told her, adding, "I want a card."

She tore a piece of lined paper out of her notebook, did a sketch and handed it to me. It was a girl with stick limbs and Goldilocks hair, a bit like Charlotte, and a generous salutation. I pointed out the skinny legs. Her face fell. I still have the card, preserved in a folder along with other documents, like the apology from Sammi-Jo – 'I'm sorry for being a pian in the backside' – and the huge, crayon heart, anonymous, with a sword driven through it to the hilt.

I'm in the staffroom now. It's lunchtime. Exhausted already, I close my eyes but only for a moment. Something hits my ear. A screwed-up ball of paper. I push it away, surrounded by good friends and laughter.

Susan and the donut

For a few months, till mid-May, I had a private student called Susan. She was in Year 11. I tutored her in English at her home every Saturday. She attended a Catholic girls' school, had a friend called Bethlehem and went to church with her family. On Saturday, both parents were usually out, which meant I was alone with Susan. When I saw the mother, she addressed me warmly, ending with the phrase *God bless*. They gave me a box of chocolates for Christmas. I don't get many presents these days. It all harked back to another time when the world was nicer, and you could trust people. *Susan.* The name itself is old-fashioned. This girl would be dependable and well-behaved. I thought she was shy. She was certainly quiet, answering little and volunteering less. But don't forget why I was there. She wasn't very good at English.

The Lord giveth…

Arriving for tuition was like stepping into a cave. The dining room curtain was drawn and the window shut. The place stank of bad air, old food. There was rubbish all over the table, chairs and floor. I could see what the week's snacks had been, and the week before. It was impressive, in a way, like those modern sculptures which are real heaps of rubbish. An art gallery cleaner threw one out once. He thought it was some rubble left by builders. Unlike that piece, which was finished, Susan's evolved. When I came, she started poking at the rubbish. Not before. Maybe I wouldn't come. She didn't want to tidy up for nothing. In terms of cleaning, Susan was a virgin; hesitant, unconvinced, as if it was something she wasn't used to doing or didn't want to or both.

Unsure about the cleaning, she didn't trust the old man, either. My jokes are sometimes funny, sometimes not, but they make girls laugh. At times, I suppose, the giggles are polite. I can annoy people. Susan was one of these. I asked her if she had a pet name. Pause. Then she said Susanna. There's an Old Testament story. Susanna, a young virgin, is set upon by two old men. I mentioned it to her. She would have known the story. No answer. I called her Suzy. No answer either. Whatever I said, she never laughed. She just looked uncomfortable or else replied, "That's a weird thing to say."

When she turned sixteen, I asked her if she had a boyfriend, an admirer on the bus to school, someone. She gave me a coy smile (the closest she came to laughing) and shook her head. She may not have broken the seventh commandment, but the eighth was showing cracks.

…and the Lord taketh away

One lesson, at the end, Susan said she didn't have the money to pay me. I said I wasn't leaving without it; I didn't mind waiting; she could make some tea. I spoke pleasantly.

"You make tea, don't you?"

"Can't you get it next week?"

"We won't be having a lesson next week, will we?"

She didn't reply. She rang her mother, repeated what I'd said, except for the tea, and listened to the answer. Then she hung up and pulled the cash out of her pocket.

Of all the garbage piled on Susan's table, the donut container was the best, a big, plastic box from a supermarket. Thirty-two donuts, but only one was left, unwanted, like a failure. For weeks, it sat there beside me, a sweet little thing with a hole at the centre.

A girl called Kamaica

I knew a girl called Kennifer – that's her real name – but I'm not going to talk about her. I'm going to talk about Kamaica. That's an alias. Lots of things about Kamaica weren't real. For a start, she had a range of ailments to avoid work, depending on what she had to do: stomach ache, arm hurt and (my favourite) foot pain. Everything seemed OK, then suddenly she was in front of me with sorrowful eyes, nursing a body part.

If she couldn't escape a task, she'd simplify it. When the children had to write a diary entry for a character from their story book, she merely copied the first page and converted every *she* to *I*. It took me a couple of sentences to cotton on.

A Caribbean girl can brighten up the dullest lesson. With a friend, Kamaica did some artwork for me. They both drew people, but Kamaica did a bare chest and nipples, which she pointed out in case I missed them.

"It's a boy," I said.

"No, it's a girl," she smiled cheerfully. She was in Year 5.

"Can I keep it?"

"You'll just throw it away."

"If you sign it, I'll keep it forever."

The girls signed their drawings and gave them to me. One girl put her real name. The other put *Kamaica*. I knew a girl called Precious; a Lovely, a Pretty. A Jihad. Now, there was Kamaica.

It was time for shadows. They're a problem, aren't they? Poetry is littered with them. But this was science. We had to understand how shadows change position as the sun moves across the sky. A child's notebook was brought in from another class where the lesson had been done already. It was a model for us all. There were three suns arched across the sky, shining down on a solitary human figure. The shadows for sunrise and sunset were fine, but midday, when the sun was above him, had deceived the little Newton. The shadow was the same length as the others. It just pointed down. Even the class teacher had missed it. She may be good at poems.

The children started work in their notebooks. I walked around, looking over shoulders. Each child drew a different kind of sun: three plain discs with lines poking out; three smiley faces with curling, golden hair, and so on. Then I got to Kamaica, who was for once in perfect health. With her own strange poetry, she reversed the metaphor and drew three sunflowers in the place of suns, with petals and a stalk and leaves.

I write *but* a lot. I got it from Kamaica. It was her favourite word. One day, she said it too often. I called her the "but girl." Everybody laughed. I didn't mean it that way. The class has left now, gone to secondary school. I have the drawings, though.

Counting candles back from zero

"They won't understand that."

It slipped out. It can happen in the morning. My morning. Too much coffee for breakfast, a sweaty train ride then a crackpot lesson plan, all stuck under my nose, one after the other. The young teacher tightened her jaw.

"I want them to do it."

Did she mean, 'There's nothing wrong with the plan. You have low expectations of the children'? Or 'I know it's too hard. I don't make the plans, do I?' Or something in between. She could have said, "They have to do it," instead of "I want them to." But she wished to appear in charge. And if she agreed it was too hard, she would have to modify it. However, that morning she was out of class. She had better things to do.

Year 3 in October. The little creatures have just crawled out of Year 2. They are scarcely evolved. The lesson today was about the Olympic Games. There was a slideshow on the interactive whiteboard. Teacher told me that the children needed to get the hang of the BC/AD business. While she was at her computer, I checked through the rest of the plan and saw that one page had BC/AD, another BCE/CE.

"I don't want to be annoying."

It was not completely true. I pointed out the discrepancy. She said the children wouldn't notice. I agreed. She had said something clever at last. The whole lesson was too hard. If you can't see the hippo, you won't spot its ears.

The school bell rang. It was strident. Not all schools have a bell, but when they do, it's rarely so loud. Such clarity and purpose, the sound was a metaphor, describing what the lesson should be like, not just when it started.

The pupils filed in. Most had heard of the Olympic Games. I showed the slides. The first was a timeline of key dates, starting at 776BC and ending at 2012AD. There were illustrations, like baby Jesus, away in a manger, fully-clothed. He was smack on zero. We (the seven-year-olds and I) now grasped the origin of the Western calendar and the maths involved in counting back from zero. Some pillars, far left, even meant that ancient Greece was clear.

"AD comes from Latin," said the classroom assistant. Every face was glowing.

He might as well have said Luton. Time and Space, two cheeky ones, were acting up again. One child thought that Greece was part of London. Somebody said that Christ was born 12,000 years ago. Another could not tell me his own birthday.

THE AUTHORS!
In an adventure with TEACHERS

You know the expression, *Children should be seen and not heard*. Well, writers should be read and not seen; some, not even read.

It's common here in London for children's authors to visit primary schools. They come to do a 'workshop' with a class or two and put a story together. It's meant to inspire children to write. It's really a marketing trick, part of the author's contract with the publisher. After school, they try to sell their books. I remember one author. He was by himself, sitting in the corner of an empty hall, behind his stacks of unwanted titles.

One day, I got my own author. I'd never heard of him, and I don't remember his name. He was middle-aged. He'd set his books up on the teacher's desk. They were tempting. Each cover had a different, candy colour. He was waiting next to them like a shopkeeper when I came in.

"Hello. Sorry we're late," I said brightly. No answer. The Year 4s followed me in. "I'm not the normal teacher. I do supply." No answer either. Our champion of literature, if not the spoken word, surveyed the children, who had sat down on the carpet. They asked things first.

Their questions were predictable, but he wasn't the Archbishop of Canterbury, who once came to a school where I was working. At each commonplace question, the churchman paused gravely as if it was important, as if it was something he needed to think about. Our author didn't have that dignity or that patience. He had the look, rather, of a man who wished he was somewhere else.

"How many books have you written?"

"Around twenty, but they weren't all published. Some are better than others. My publisher only picks the best ones."

I wanted to put my hand up. I wanted to ask him what 'the best' meant. Plot? Style? Characters? Earning potential? He didn't say it, but he let the children think, as everybody does, that the best books are always published.

The workshop began. It produced all the clichés in children's fiction, except the fat boy with glasses. The author suggested a girl who didn't like sport, but on the whole, he let convention lie. Soon, the children wished they were somewhere else too. If you're a child and you want to get out of class, there are lots of excuses you can make: the toilet, you feel sick, are injured, need to fill your water bottle, find your jumper in the playground or give something to a teacher in a different room. I usually say no, but today the reasons seemed genuine. I allowed each child to go, one after another. Some, I evicted. Fooling around again! Meanwhile, our hero did his workshop. Or tried to.

"No more distractions now."

Before he left, he read out a passage from one of his books. Two boys, aged nine, were talking about a teacher. When one was scornful, the other replied, "He's a supply teacher, and you know what *they're* like."

Hardly the words of a nine-year-old. Of all the middle-aged dialogues in all the pretty books on display, the author had chosen that. A girl I'd just punished turned to me and grinned. Revenge is sweet.

Throw some sharks in

"You've got white hair. That means you'll die in a minute."

The little girl spoke to me with confidence. It was almost time for drama. One day, she'll be a fine actress. She was already an excellent human being.

A specialist drama teacher took the lesson. He soon had the six-year-olds believing he was stuck in a bucket. You drama professionals are nodding, but it was new to us. There was a real bucket and lid. The teacher stayed out of sight behind a cupboard, crying for help. Two girls held the bucket. However hard the poor man cried they wouldn't let him out. They wouldn't take the lid off. The rest of the class was laughing wildly. The more he pleaded, the more hard-hearted the girls became. One of them struck a ruler on the side of the bucket. She did it repeatedly. Imagine the sound in his ears! The audience laughed even louder. The other girl raised the lid an inch or so, just enough for the class to see, but not enough for a man to escape. She lowered her mouth to the opening and whispered very sweetly, "I'm going to throw some sharks in," then banged the lid shut and listened to the cries. They were pitiful, but she ignored them. We knew she would.

She had a little smile on her face. The man was nearly sobbing. To make it worse, she waited a few moments before she threw them in.

Children keep the best cruelties for each other. Once, in Year 5, I had to fill in ten minutes at the end of the day, so we did 'pay a compliment.' In this exercise, everyone says something nice about a different child in the room. For this group, it was not an easy task. They started to fall back on sir. One girl liked my eye colour. A boy praised the shape of my head. Another girl picked a child who was not in class that day.

"I compliment Malia for being invisible."

There's an ant on your tit

A five-year-old, a boy I once tutored, had an interview for admission to a private school. Yes, an interview for a five-year-old. It was a lovely day. The school had plenty of lawns. The kind lady suggested they sit outside. She probably thought it would help put the little chap at ease. She knew how stressful interviews could be.

They sat on the grass in the shade of a nice tree. While she was talking to the boy, an ant crawled onto her hand. She didn't notice. He watched the little chap as it hurried up her arm, moving with purpose, as ants do. He didn't say anything. He didn't want to interrupt the kind lady. The ant reached her chest. The lady stopped and smiled at the boy. He saw his chance.

"There's an ant on your tit."

She ended the interview. She wasn't cross with the ant. You can't blame ants for much that's wrong with the world. They behave inappropriately without even knowing.

In fact, the little chap – the boy, I mean – was too young to know what an interview was. He had no idea about private schools. If the weather had been wet, he'd probably be studying there today. If the kind lady had seen the ant first, he'd probably be studying there to-day. If she understood children, he'd probably be studying there today.

Faris from Paris is my name

How sweet

Faris was in Year 6. For a month or two before Christmas, I prepared him for the 11-plus. His mother was aiming for a top private school. She said he was good at all his subjects except English, so I helped him with that. The first time we met, I got him to write a paragraph. To make it seem longer, he left every second line blank.

"How sweet!" I said.

"It's not sweet!"

He was turning eleven and objected to *sweet*, quite naturally – sweetly, in fact. He wasn't being rude, not in the first lesson, He didn't know me well enough. It was, all the same, his first act of defiance.

There were other sweet things. In his room, where we had the lessons, he kept a stash of goodies. Drinks from Algeria in strange-looking bottles, lolly-coloured water without fizz or any that I could see through the cloudy glass. Grandma brought them when she came to stay. There were fruit gums as well from a local shop. And cakes from Paris, thanks to Auntie, who was also staying. Half a dozen delicate things – the cakes and the people. They were a gentle family.

His goodies were in a big, plastic box. He didn't get up to open it.

He didn't need to. He just reached over. The lid made intelligent sounds: *I'm full of sweet things!* when it snapped open, and *Stay away!* when it snapped shut. His stash was hardly a secret, but he liked to pretend it was.

Each lesson lasted two hours, though he usually stopped trying after one.

"How many push-ups can you do?" It was my question. It was that time of lesson. He jumped up and did a few but scarcely bent his elbows. I told him to jog to the window, do five push-ups, jog back again and do five more then go back to the window. He did what I instructed, but somehow finished up beside me.

"You got it wrong," I said. "You need to make three trips and end up at the window so I can relax over here by myself." With my right forefinger, I drew the three journeys in the air, zigzag, like the sword of Zorro. "You have to do it again."

His room had a wooden floor, so I added, "Don't tread so loudly this time. Your mother can hear."

He grinned and did it all again, just as noisily, then waited at the window and looked at me. It was another sweet thing. When I let him back, he showed me a certificate with his name in Arabic. Then he opened his wardrobe. Another store of treasure.

"This is my Eid suit."

He held it up. It was black and very small. It looked like the costume for a large toy.

Before the end, his mother came in. She knocked first – the power of a closed door, even in your own home.

"I'm always on the phone," she explained. "I didn't say hello properly."

It was true. When I arrived, she was chatting to someone. But now she said what she had really come to say.

"Is he being good?"

She said it doubtfully. I leaned back and smiled.

"Two hours is a long time."

I love my tutor

"Hello, Graham," Faris said, with meaning, when I came for the next lesson. He was in the front garden. "I've got everything ready."

He had. In his room, pens and books were lined up. He'd organised the chairs. He'd closed his curtain to thwart the neighbours. When I sat down, he shut the door. A toy helicopter was also on the desk on his side. It was what he'd really meant by "everything ready." A birthday present, with remote controls so he could fly it. He spent a while whizzing it around, especially at my face. I had to dodge. There were two sets of blades, at different levels, to stop it tipping over, I suppose. I thought the extra blades looked funny. I didn't tell him, though, and they didn't stop it crashing. By the end of the lesson, it had hit the floor loudly several times. I wondered how long it would last.

"Will you tell my mother I've been bad?" Faris said when the lesson was over. He put his head down and pretended to cry.

"No."

"Promise?"

"Yes."

There was no need to tell her. She could hear for herself each time the helicopter crashed. But he hugged me with both arms.

"Are you fond of me?" he asked.

"Yes."

There was a little box on his desk. It had been there at the start, like the helicopter, but he only showed it to me now.

"Is that your ear stud?" I teased when he opened it.

"It's Auntie's, for a locket. She asked me to look after it when she goes back to France. It's very precious."

I picked up my bag.

"I'm Faris from Paris," he chanted softly as he left the room, holding his helicopter. He'd said it before, once or twice, his little rhyme, or "Faris from Paris is my name." He had lived there, too.

I was still fiddling with my bag. On the landing, he called out, "I love my tutor!" to no one in particular, to the staircase, to the wall in front of him. It was the push-ups that did it in the first lesson. The playfulness. It can steal a heart, for a week or two, anyway.

When we were both downstairs, Faris told his mother, "He said he's fond of me."

She looked up.

"There was a context," I said. "I don't remember now. I didn't just blurt it out."

In French, she asked Faris about the noise. He replied in English, saying I'd done it; I was having trouble with my chair. It was partly true. I'd injured my ankle more than once and made a noise on the floor. Then she asked me how he'd been. Fine, I said. She looked doubtful, but she wanted to believe me. I was the teacher, after all, and he was her son. She didn't know about the promise and the hug. Apart from that, I would have looked stupid if I'd complained about him just because she asked. But there's one more reason I agreed with Faris. He had answered her in English because he wanted to be sure I understood. He wasn't daring me to snitch. He was inviting me to lie. We were now conspirators.

He put the helicopter down, got two apples off the table and cracked them together like little skulls.

"You'll bruise them," I said. He did it again immediately.

"Faris!" mother said but only because I'd spoken. It's not the worst thing he's done, crack a pair of apples together.

"That gave the worms a headache," I said.

She chuckled politely. Faris returned to his helicopter and buzzed it around the kitchen rather wildly.

"Be careful with it, Faris! It was expensive."

A new toy – you mess around a while, until it breaks or you get tired of it.

A happy house

"You told your mother I was fond of you," I said a week later. "It was a bit embarrassing."

"I won't tell her things anymore," replied Faris. He understood embarrassment. He showed me the back of his hand. There was a pattern on it, drawn with henna. In London, *mehndi* is popular with south Asian girls. I'd never seen it on a boy. He looked sad.

"Auntie did it for me. My friends laughed when they saw it."

Auntie was still staying. She was a young woman. She smiled when we first met. The second time, she offered me her hand and left it in mine for a few moments. Afterwards, I said to Faris, "I get goose bumps when people speak French." We continued working. "Your auntie likes me. I could marry her, and we could live here together in the spare room. I could give you lessons every day."

"Oh, no!" he cried. "You shouldn't say things like that. You're married already!"

"If I wasn't married, I mean."

He was wearing a bright, woollen jumper.

"My mother made it. Her boyfriend has one the same."

"Could she make one for me? Auntie might like it."

His parents were separated. On a shelf near his bed, there was a photograph, a recent one, taken at a theme park with his father. They were sitting in a giant teacup with another boy, all wearing Algerian football shirts, looking at the camera. There was a woman, too. I didn't spot her at first. Her face was turned away. Faris said he didn't know her. I don't think he wanted to, either. He asked about my wife, if I had a picture of her. His last question was, "Is it a happy house?"

During the second hour, he went for a toilet break. When he came back, he was walking very slowly, as if something terrible had happened.

"My father died. My mother just told me."

He stood with his head bowed, as a boy might if he was grief-stricken.

"He did not," I said. I was used to his little stories, sorting the real sadness from the false.

"A friend believed me once when I told him."

We did a comprehension. A carriage was crossing the moors with a young girl inside. It was night time, and she couldn't see anything. She felt anxious. In the last question, Faris had to continue where the extract left off. He produced a gunshot in the far distance (his phrase), killing both horses. A single gunshot. I pointed out that, from a far distance, a single shot was unlikely to kill one horse, let alone two. You'd have to line the heads up together, like a selfie, and hold the barrel next to them.

"That's violent!" Faris said, but he looked as though I'd called him stupid.

"No more violent than a distant gun shot, just more believable."

"Lining the heads up is worse!"

Sometimes, the heads align themselves. He'd been at the swimming pool and met two twelve-year-old girls. While they were splashing around, one of the girls pointed at the other and said to Faris, "She likes you." When he was going, she mouthed the words, *Call me*. At the same time, she raised a hand to her cheek, the thumb and little finger in the shape of a telephone, like an actress in a movie. He showed me with his own hand.

"Did she give you her number?"

"I'm going to see them again next week."

"Are they pretty?"

"Sh! My mother might hear."

"Do you like girls?"

"Sh!"

"Thingummies. Is that your first romantic experience?"

"Stop! That's why I never tell people things."

"I won't do it again."

So, that was the lesson: sex, violence and embarrassment. The following week, I asked about the thingummies. He had lost interest.

"The first time, they were in the water. I just saw their heads."

He didn't go on.

"Were they fat?"

"Yes."

He hadn't wanted to say it.

Quality time with my sister

I was late for a lesson. When I arrived, Faris was agitated. Our lessons were too long already, in his opinion, and he was right. Starting late would make it even longer: two hours, plus the time he'd waited. Five minutes before we normally finished, he said I should go; he had to watch *Sherlock Holmes*. I guessed it was on later and said, "Stop lying."

There was more bad news. His toy helicopter was broken. He had crashed it too often, the final time just before I came.

"If you hadn't come late, it wouldn't be broken!"

"You said you loved me," I reminded. "You called out on the stairs."

It didn't help. He had to write another story ending, his least favourite task. A girl was locked in a tower by a river. One day, she heard someone singing. She looked out and saw a young fisherman on a boat floating past. She was captivated. What happened next?

Faris, same as anyone, imagined her escaping from the tower. In his version, though, she made a steel staircase. He was serious. It wasn't his revenge for starting late. That would have been clever. I gave him some advice.

"If you're making up a story, avoid logical flaws. Don't say things which can't be true or can be proven false. A young girl can't lift steel girders and weld them together, even if they happen to be lying there conveniently on her bedroom floor with all the equipment she needs. And remember, she was in a tower. You can't build a staircase from the top down; you have to be on the ground, but if she was, it would mean she was out already and no longer needed to escape. Still, if she did somehow manage to build a staircase, it would take so long, the fisherman would have floated away."

This didn't help either. I had made him feel stupid again. But I was teaching him how to lie, effectively, I mean. He needed help with that.

"You have to go." Faris was still trying to get rid of me. "I'm missing quality time with my sister. I could be downstairs now, playing with her."

It was cleverer than *Sherlock Holmes*, something I couldn't disprove, however unlikely: a boy's urge to bond with his sister. She was two. The only time she kept quiet was in front of the television, in her high chair, with something to eat in her hand. The light from the giant screen flickered over her.

I still refused to go. He tore a page from his notebook and screwed it up.

"I'm sick of writing. I need to do grammar."

"If we start doing grammar, you'll say you're sick of that."

"I'm a kid," he replied in a lighter tone. He wrote in his book *Faris is stupid* and *Faris is very stupid* several times. When he finished, he read them out to me.

I got up to go and nearly did. He knew I meant it.

"Don't go!" he said. He meant it too.

At the end of the lesson, he played his cello for me. It was real quality time. He played superbly. As for the bad behaviour, he begged me not to tell his mother. He swore he'd work next week, "On my mother's life. On the Quran."

Next lesson, as soon as we sat down, he apologised. I think he'd been waiting all week. He still misbehaved, of course. I hadn't told on him. He would have misbehaved anyway.

He took a pair of scissors and cut a lock from his hair, at the front, above the forehead. It was jet black. He put it on a small piece of paper, which he folded carefully, like collecting evidence, like Sherlock Holmes, then gave to me.

I unfolded the paper and felt the lock.

"It's woolly, like a sheep," I said. "Hello, sheep."

"Don't call me that."

Faris from Paris is my name.

My mother's a lady

"Bring me some stomachs next week."

That's what I thought Faris said. It was Starmix, a packet of sweets. He was updating his stash of goodies.

"Does your mother let you have them?"

"Yes."

"OK, I'll bring some."

"They make me hyper."

He held his arms out like a zombie and quivered then mumbled something about a lesson at school.

"What?" I asked. I was having trouble hearing that day. He mumbled again. I got it the third time. "Oh, intercourse!" I cried happily.

"Sh! My mother's a lady!"

It was something else embarrassing, the mechanics of sex, as simple, really, as eating, but at his age, complicated.

Early December. Faris had to do a 'pre-test' before he could sit the main exam. Another £200. Schools have a sense of humour. His mother thought he'd pass.

"I'm 99% sure."

In general, mothers think their children are clever. His was no different, but at least she understood the concept of failure. There was one more lesson before the pre-test. She said to him in a quiet voice, "Next lesson might be the last."

She was caring for him. She'd heard his declaration of love. The whole house had. Goodbyes can hurt. He walked into the next room. I could see him through the doorway with his sister, washed in the flicker of the giant screen. Mother turned to me. If he passed the pre-test, she said, we'd carry on preparing the 11-plus. If he failed, I could come back in January and prepare for his Sats exams. He needed help in grammar. She'd let me know on Wednesday, when the results were out. She asked for my number again and saved it on her phone. She even rang to be quite certain. She was caring for that, too.

I called out to Faris, "I'll see you again for Sats."

His mother blanched – because I thought he'd fail the pre-test, or she wasn't going to ring me if he did. Both, probably.

The next lesson, I brought him his packet of stomachs. He said, "I didn't know if you would," stepped forward, hesitated then hugged me, saying, "I'll do you proud."

"Are you sure your mum won't mind me bringing you sweets?"

"I'll tell her it's a leftover packet."

"There's no need to show it to her. Don't lie unless you have to."

Maths was his best subject. We hadn't been practising it. His mother said to do a bit now. In a sample paper, he got stuck on question two. If 1/3 is 0.333, what is 1/30? The easiest questions are at the start. He refused to continue and sat there tapping his pen.

The front door banged.

"It's my stepdad," Faris said. "They think you're an excellent tutor. Please say something nice about me!"

When the lesson finished – the final one, maybe, and all that – there was nearly another hug. It became a high five. A boy knows why. Downstairs, I mentioned question two. Mother was horrified.

"Have I left it too late?"

Stepdad asked about behaviour.

"I'm very fond of him," I said. "He's an angel."

The adults were pleased, but they didn't believe me.

Faris failed the pre-test. I assume he did. His mother didn't call. She didn't have to, though she said she would. She didn't ring in January, either, to arrange grammar lessons. I called her, and she didn't answer. I received a text three days later, at one in the morning. I was glad when I saw her number, but the text ran, "I'm sorry I missed your call. I don't know who you are. I lost my contacts. If you reply, I'll get back to you."

I did as she said, and that was it.

A solid address

Henry and ANNA

An afternoon in early summer. I had a new lesson. The address was a leafy street in central London, away from traffic. I remember walking down the road, the quietness, the sunshine, the patterns of shade. It was an end-of-terrace house but not the cramped sort you find in the suburbs. There were three floors, built with great blocks of stone. The whole row looked like a palace, an extra-wide one, a few steps from Paddington Library and, on the other side, Royal Oak station. As solid an address as you can find. Every August, on bank holiday, Notting Hill Carnival arrives. It winds along not far from their door – very close, in fact; they must hear it. Yet the exuberance passes them by. I'm guessing, though. I wasn't there in August. The lessons didn't last that long.

Mrs M. wanted a tutor for her son. He was sitting the 11-plus. The first day, when I knocked, she opened the door. It was the only time. After that, the nanny always did it. Mrs M. had a Greek surname, but when I saw her, I thought, *She doesn't look Greek*. Her husband did. He was at his desk, a large, wooden thing; solid, like the masonry. He himself was heavy. He was also cross. He turned around slowly and stared as if to say, "I'm too important to talk to you."

The boy's name was Henry, a famous one in English history. It was the only imposing thing about him. He was ten, to begin with, and small for his age. He seemed anxious. It *was* the first lesson. It got worse. No sooner had we sat down at the dining room table than father came in and stood over him, a huge frame next to the thin body. Henry didn't look up. At first, the man was silent, a cross silence for at least ten seconds. He stared down at the little boy the way he'd stared at me, an annoying stranger, as if he didn't like him or was accusing him of something. When he spoke, his voice was cold, like the stare. He told Henry to work hard. As far as boys go, I've never known one who worked harder or was more good-natured than Henry, to the point of blandness. Father must have known that too, but there he was, like a sovereign smelling betrayal. Was he trying to impress the boy? Or me? I just thought, *This man's a bully.*

I don't remember anything else about that lesson. The following week, Henry wasn't in. Mrs M. asked me to teach her daughter instead. In future, she said, I could teach both of them, two hours altogether. Anna was seven. She wasn't there the first week. In a tactful way, Henry had warned me about her.

"She's different from me," he said without explaining.

"Perhaps she'll be scared of me."

I held up my tie and wiggled the end. He smiled weakly. When I saw her, the first thing she did was speak sharply to the nanny like a cross parent.

"What are you doing?"

She sat down, picked up a pen and said, "I'll show you my handwriting." She wrote for a moment then pushed her notebook across. "It's an Arabic word."

Squiggles, certainly. She signed it ANNA. The capitals made her name more important, like pillars, Greek ones, I suppose. They spelt her opinion of herself.

"Don't write on your forehead," I said. I don't remember why. Perhaps I could see some ink. Perhaps there was no reason; I said it to surprise her. With girls like Anna, the ordinary doesn't work. Anyway, as soon as I told her not to, she did it.

"Apart from that," I went on, "you can do anything except kick me."

She kicked me. Not hard; to make a point. There was no song and dance like a girl at the carnival. That lesson (the only one with Anna), she was polite. She tolerated me, like her father.

I thought you hated me

When I arrived for the next lesson, I saw Anna first. She was in the passage. I said hello.

"Ready for the lesson?"

She stared back angrily. Her mother was in the kitchen and hadn't seen, so I told her. It was just a point of interest. I wasn't upset. Neither was Mrs M. In fact, her face brightened.

"Did she do that?" she asked, as if her daughter had curtsied. She was marvelling, almost admiring. She explained that I wouldn't be teaching Anna anymore, just Henry. I had come for two hours, but there was only one. It was a problem, the kind of thing which irritates a tutor. She hadn't told me beforehand. Perhaps she didn't know. Anna probably refused when I came. Why refuse earlier? I mightn't come. I couldn't blame Mrs M. Nonetheless, she didn't apologise. Worse, she didn't see the need. Anna was being Anna. There was nothing anyone could do.

Mrs M. was being Mrs M. She had a uniform. She worked for a bank or something, a place that valued rules, where authority was respected. But things didn't bother her when I thought they should, and bothered her when I thought they wouldn't. What I said could leave her tongue-tied, like a seven-year-old (an ordinary one). I mentioned the library, which was virtually next door.

"Handy for books," I said encouragingly. Books, children, mother – I couldn't go wrong. Her face froze, and I knew they had never been.

During Henry's lesson, I sensed someone moving behind us. It felt surreptitious. I said, "Spies will be executed," then turned around. It was Anna, fortunately, not a parent. She was holding a piece of glass with a snail on it. I realised she had brought it to show me.

"I thought you hated me," I said. She came closer silently, focused on the snail so it wouldn't fall. "When you get sick of it, don't throw it out the window." We were on the first floor. Silence. "What's its name?" Silence. "I'll call it Anna."

"When mummy calls me, it won't know who she means."

"That's true. We can still call it Anna. You can be Anna 2." We were wasting Henry's lesson. He didn't seem to mind. "She loves me, she loves me," I chanted quietly. To Henry, I said, "It's a joyful thing when a girl loves you. You'll find out one day if you haven't already."

"I don't like you," Anna said decisively.

There was another child, Max, who was five. He walked in and asked me like an adult, "What's your name again?"

"Graham. What's your name, Max?"

"Max."

Mrs M. had two sets of children: Henry, Anna and Max, and two grown up girls, university students by the look of it, from a former husband. I'm guessing again. She never explained. I saw the big girls once. They had the feel of visitors. I don't think they lived there, not during term, anyway. Mrs M. had a 'new' family, and she indulged them. They were like a bonus at work or, at her age, retirement gifts, ones of special value, which she hadn't expected. At the same time, she was uncertain. Perhaps I made her nervous. Whatever it was, when the little ones misbehaved, she didn't do anything. Maybe she said things when I wasn't there – even punished them – but, quite clearly, she didn't want to.

After the lesson, while I was talking to Mrs M., Max came in shouting.

"He's trying to drown you out," she explained. To Max, she said nothing. She just gazed at him, marvelling, almost admiring.

The hard *g*

Mrs M. had the painters in. All the carpets were covered with sheets. The men hadn't started painting. They were preparing the surfaces, as painters say. It was that kind of place, that kind of family. You saw the cracks.

The painters were Italian, Mrs M. said. It pleased her, obviously. Italy is known for painters. The job they did on *her* house would be a work of art.

"I lived in Italy for five years," I said. Her eyes glazed. "I don't want to sound as though I'm showing off."

The little ones were being naughty too. Mrs M. had to go out. She put my money on the table. Max ran off with it. Mrs M. smiled. Anna pulled my tie. Mrs M. smiled.

"Stop being naughty, or I'll tell daddy," she said through a smile. It's hard to imagine a kinder threat.

"I wear a tie every day," I observed, in my explaining voice, as if that was the reason Anna pulled it. "Except when I'm sleeping and washing."

The smile faltered. I glanced at the table where the payment had been.

"I was never very good with money." Pause. "Max has talent. He may end up in a bank."

When Mrs M. left, Anna hugged me.

"Hello, Anna 2." She had a handful of Lego. "Don't swallow them," I said. She put one in her mouth straightaway then turned around and pretended to swallow it. I flicked her right pigtail. She froze, I did it again; still nothing, but the third time, she swivelled about, frowned and forked her fingers at me, as if warding off the Evil Eye. She did it furiously, like the wife of my old landlord in Rome – a dispute over money. This was much graver, a dispute over hair.

"Stop being naughty, or I'll tell daddy."

Anna said that. Unlike her mother, she meant it.

There were toys all over the painters' sheets. I said, "It looks like a bomb's gone off."

Laetitia, the nanny, began tidying up. Perhaps she thought I wanted her to. I regretted the bomb bit and added, "He who made the mess, or she, should clean it up. If your name starts with A or M, you should clean it up."

"If your name starts with L or G, you should clean it up," echoed Anna. She did a hard *g*.

"If you're little, you can say hard *g*. Are you little?"

"I'm seven."

"You're little."

Without a word, Laetitia went on tidying. I felt sorry for her. She was about twenty and seemed nice. We were comrades too. We both worked for Mrs M., and we were both exploited, to some degree. Mrs M. called her a nanny, but nannies mind children. Laetitia did a lot more than that. She wasn't so much a nanny as a servant. When someone knocked, she opened the front door, even if Mrs M. was home. She was a butler, a maid, a cook and no doubt other things, all the roles you find in a stately home, except the groundsman (I never saw her go outside). She didn't complain, I'm sure. She wanted the money. But the extra tasks disturbed me. Meanwhile, Mrs M., the lady of the manor, spoke to her in a hard voice. She didn't use the same voice with me. I was older than Laetitia, and my comments startled her. She didn't treat me as a servant because she sensed I wouldn't let her; I didn't care if I worked for her or not.

The biggest poo in the world

The next week, Mrs M. asked how Henry had done in the previous lesson, when she was out. She had passed on some maths questions provided by the school as a sample of the exam. They were very difficult. There was an answer sheet (the first thing a tutor looks for), but no explanations, no method. I had to work them out myself.

"There was a very hard question at the end. I got it right, though." Mrs M. widened her eyes but didn't speak. "Teachers normally prepare, to avoid looking foolish in front of their pupils."

More silence. Mrs M. was sitting on the sofa, next to Anna, who had propped her legs up, as children do. I persisted.

"Are you putting all your eggs in one basket, or are you applying to other schools?"

She still didn't speak. Silence is one thing. Mrs M. did more; she withdrew, in her mind, to another place, away from my questions, the flippancy. What could be more serious than a mother's plans, and whose were more important than Mrs M.'s? She was trying to get her son into one of the 'best' schools, yet it wasn't just my tone which grated. She thought I was hinting he might fail. In fact, I was sure he would, though I wasn't hinting. It was common sense to apply to several schools. But I was talking to Mrs M. Meanwhile, she was thinking. She grasped Anna's leg above the ankle and rubbed her palm up and down, rhythmically, over the golden curls. Anna shut her eyes. Think and rub. Think, rub. Sleep. Anna had drifted off. In a way, her mother had too. It was probably then that she decided to sack me.

Mrs M. went out again, but she promised to be back before we finished. There was a thunderstorm. At every crack of lightning, Henry jumped, really jumped, as boys would from the cane, in the old days, I mean. He was very nervous, not the type for a high-pressure school. Why should he go to one? Had his mother or father? The 11-plus exam. It's more about the parents' vanity than the child's education.

Anna, on the other hand, ignored pressure. She did what she wanted. At the end of the lesson, she parted my shirt between the buttons and peered at my stomach. She lifted her eyes and did the same for my chest, but this time she said, "Wow!" Her eyes widened, and she looked a bit longer. Then, she asked sadly, "Did you ever want to be a girl?"

"Yes, I've always wanted to be a girl."

Laetitia smiled.

"I want to be a man!" said Anna.

"We can swap."

Laetitia smiled again. I looked around. Henry had disappeared.

"Where's Henry?"

"He's having a poo," Anna said. "He does the biggest poo in the world."

I realised he'd been doing it every week, disappearing at the end of the lesson and emptying his bowels. There's an idiom for it, a rude one, which boys use about their teachers. All this time, it had been happening quite literally to Henry.

Mrs M. was late. During the lesson, she had sent a series of texts to reassure me. Now she called. She said she'd be there soon. I put the phone down. To Laetitia, I said dramatically, "I'm not leaving without my money!"

She smiled. Mrs M. called again. She was almost home; she could meet me at the end of the street, on the corner, if I left now.

"Technically," I said to Laetitia, "I'm leaving without my money."

Laetitia smiled once more. To Anna, I confided, "We're going to meet on the corner like spies. It's very exciting. I'll tell you what happens next week – if I'm not caught."

Henry wandered in. Anna turned to him.

"We were just talking about you."

Everybody loves me

"Max, do you still like me?"

When I asked, Laetitia smiled. When he said yes, she smiled again. The lesson before, he had jumped onto me. I was on the sofa, waiting for Henry, when he pushed me down and lay full-length on top of me, his chest bare and his arms around me. He was lying like this when Henry walked in. The older boy stopped and stared. He wouldn't lie in my arms even if he liked me enough, and I don't think he did. The five-year-old adored me. I'm not sure why. Perhaps, in me, he saw an adult as silly as he was.

After the lesson, Mrs M. and I had one of our conversations. It was about Anna. We recalled how she'd refused to have tuition, although she plainly liked me.

"Everybody loves me," I said. "Anna loves me, Max loves me, Laetitia loves me." I glanced across – she was smiling. Then I looked at Mrs M. "You love me." Her body tensed. "I'd better stop talking."

"Yes, I think you had."

She spoke without hesitation, the only time I remember. We heard a voice upstairs. The painters were still there. It was July.

"They're Italian," I said. "They won't work in August."

She looked at me in her old, blank way. As it happened, the work finished before then. Mine did too. Once, when I walked in, Max ran the length of the passage, a very long one, into my arms, like Hollywood, right in front of his mother.

"Isn't that nice?" she said and tried to smile, but she didn't like it. I thought, *Does he do that to his father?* It was the kiss of death, without the actual kiss. Max was a boy. He didn't do that.

The cancellation had been coming. Mrs M. had grown convinced that Henry would fail his 11-plus. She didn't tell me. I felt it. Perhaps she had always doubted him, his intellect, his stamina. She'd been a reluctant client from the start. It took weeks for her to fix the first lesson. She wanted Henry to go to that school; she wanted it very much, but if he wasn't able to pass, it was better to pull out now, before the exam. Not to save money on tuition or to spare the boy's nerves – nothing like that. Her own feelings were always more important. If she pulled out now, she would avoid the shame of failure. I had often embarrassed her. The irony, the quips, had in themselves not been enough for sacking, but when the time came, they didn't make it any harder. My sacking was revenge for all those moments she'd stood in front of me unable to think of what to say, or unwilling to speak in case what she said was wrong. She didn't want me any longer, but she still couldn't tell me. She cancelled two lessons in a row by text at late notice with weak excuses. "So sorry," each text began. Two lessons, not the whole tuition. In terms of sacking, she was silent. She hoped I'd understand and simply not come anymore. Less awkward that way, for her, at least, and that was all that mattered.

I answered the first text but asked her to confirm the next lesson, pretending not to know what she meant. I deleted the second text. It was I who didn't speak, I who stopped. In the end, I sacked myself.

Parrot

Dunno

Mother asked for an assessment of her son, who was in Year 10. He needed help in English. I arrived at their address. Most bells are unobtrusive or don't work. Not this one. There was a camera and intercom, the first I'd seen at this kind of house, a small, east London terrace. It seemed pretentious, and I was being scrutinised before the lesson started, before I stepped inside. I didn't like it. When I pressed the bell, it brought forth a series of dongs – Rudolph the red-nosed reindeer, a joyless, metallic version – so loud the neighbours would have heard. I didn't like that, either. But visitors could be important. You don't want to keep them waiting.

Mother let me in and led me to the dining room table. There was parrot in a cage but no boy.

"Peter's in his bedroom," she explained in a reassuring way and went upstairs. *At least he's home,* I thought. Boys aren't always. After a minute, she returned alone. "He's very tired."

The quiet, explaining tone once again. She was empathising – with her son, not me. There was no apology. Then she walked into the kitchen. Short of pupils, I assessed the bird. It was big, and its cage was too; taller than me, the shape and size of a public phone box, wide enough, certainly, for a bird to flap in. They must have thought they were being generous. *This is one happy bird!* But a cage is a cage, like a prison cell; however grand, it deprives you of freedom. I don't know how the parrot felt. Birds don't smile. Do they get depressed? In a boy's case, it's easier to tell.

When Peter came down at last, he was half asleep. Physically, he resembled an adult. I gave him a poem to read, in the first lesson. I don't know why. Boys don't like poems, especially when they're tired.

"Did you have PE today?" Boys prefer that. No reply. "I'm a bit tired too. If I fall asleep, you can kick me."

Peter – even his name had PE – stared blankly. I set a question, and he began to write. At one point, he stretched his legs out under the table and kicked me, accidentally, I think. Like his mother, he didn't apologise. He wrote a paragraph and read it out. It needed examples, I said then leaned back and gazed at the wall. There was a plaque entitled *Family Rules*. You know the sort, a list of sentences in fancy letters with a pretty border, swirls that show the joy of writing, the beauty of rules. Nothing about kicking. Next to it, there was a clock which had stopped, like a metaphor, a clock in literature, and there are plenty of those. This one said twenty to four, home time when I was at school. You had to stop working; you couldn't go on even if you begged to.

"Ready?" I asked, turning back to him. How long would he have waited? He nodded at the page in front of him. I was expecting examples, a few more lines of writing, but the page didn't seem any different. I looked more closely. It was, in fact, the same answer, except for a cross at the centre, a neat, little thing. He was unhappy, he explained, with the word *show*, so he crossed out the whole paragraph.

I asked another question. Silence.

"Dunno."

I gave a hint and repeated the question. Silence.

"Dunno."

There was something in his voice, and each silence was the same length. Was he counting the seconds? He said he didn't know, and I thought he didn't want to, either. I gave a more explicit hint. The answer was plain, so plain that only someone who understood nothing could fail to understand now. I paused then asked the same question again. With a half-smile, he peered at the ceiling and moved his lips, as if imploring it to fall. The excruciation of thought – nothing could have shown it more clearly. He lowered his eyes and spoke a third time, in the same voice, after the same silence.

"Dunno."

Sick as a parrot

It was Halloween and another lesson with Peter. We had just sat down. The doorbell rang.

"Trick or treat!"

Peter jumped up to open the front door. From the kitchen, gently, mother chided.

"I told you not to answer if they ring."

We were doing descriptive writing based on a photograph. I asked for his personal response.

"It's boring," he replied without the normal silence. He also yawned. His mouth opened wide with a loud noise. He made no effort to hide it. In fact, he exaggerated. Hyperbole, to emphasise something, in this case, suffering. He yawned a lot every lesson. To tell the truth, he did little more than yawn. It wasn't strange. He was a typical lazy boy. The parrot was the only abnormal thing. I won't make analogies: the schoolboy and the caged bird. Neither tried to escape, not while I was there. He was, however, doing all he could to dump me or, failing that, to avoid the tasks he found most unpleasant.

One day, I got a phone call from mother. What I was teaching was "not in the syllabus." I sensed his presence; he was standing there with her, I was certain. She was repeating his words. The lessons required "more structure." She was hesitant, trying not to offend – not easy when you're being critical. She didn't want me to stop tutoring, merely to do it better.

"I used to think I was doing the right thing."

"You were, you were."

"I mean when I started tutoring, twenty years ago. I didn't get students to write, and they didn't improve."

More structure. What about yawns? The architecture of a desperate noise.

Towards Christmas, an hour before a lesson, I got another phone call from mother. I heard a voice in the background. Peter was monitoring. The parrot wasn't well and had to go to the vet. Could we have the lesson afterwards? No, in the end, we couldn't; we had to cancel. The next week, I asked mother if we could have an extra lesson at Christmas to make up for the one we'd missed.

"I'll be busy," the boy cut in. He had never spoken so fast.

"Hang on, hang on," said mother. The old, soft tone. But there was no extra lesson at Christmas.

He was nice to me only once, when he answered the door himself. He apologised for keeping me waiting. *Is this our last lesson?* I walked into the dining room. The parrot made a noise, a deep one, not like a bird. After a few minutes, I heard the noise again and realised what it was: a yawn. More than a yawn, this was the sound of ennui. With a noise like that, you don't need a vet; you need a psychiatrist. Another yawn, and I thought of Peter. It wasn't him this time; he was writing or trying to or pretending to try, and his mouth was closed. The parrot had copied him. It's what parrots do, but why yawn now? Birds don't get bored in tuition, and it wasn't empathy – they aren't so clever. Peter may have yawned all day. The parrot was always listening; it didn't have much choice, locked in the cage. Perhaps it yawned too. I had to hear it sooner or later. But it hadn't yawned once in any of the previous lessons. It yawned now, like Peter, because it saw me. Yawns and me went together like a table and chairs, like a bird and cage. The parrot, at least, had listened; the parrot had learned.

Words in the book

Pyramidss, Shperes and Cyinders

Year 2, silent reading. A single voice piped up.

"I'm telling off you!"

Miss couldn't let it pass. The girl's tone, she said, was sarcastic and nasty. She didn't want that language in class. She didn't ask what the problem was. It couldn't have been important. Instead, she explained the difference between *off* and *on* in the phrase the child had used. In other words, she dealt with two things at once. So early in the day (I'd just sat down), but miss was on fire already. She must have thought so too because she went through the whole thing twice.

I wasn't sure why I'd been sent to that class. Normally, I fill in for an absent teacher, but miss was there, no doubt about it. Miss Times-two, in fact.

Handwriting. Some children had finished their notebooks. Miss told me to get some new ones from the stock room, which was just next door. The books had been finished the day before, but she didn't go herself. She can't have had the time. When I got back, she was at the whiteboard modelling the letter *p*, upper and lower case, coaxing out each trick and turn. I waited at the door, books in hand. She turned to me sarcastically.

"What do you think you can do with those?"

"You want me to hand them out while you're presenting the lesson?" Silence.

After handwriting, it was maths. Subtraction. The children moved to the front on the carpet. Miss thought a number line would help. They could draw one on their whiteboards. Looking good again. Very carefully, the children filled their little boards with glistening, black strokes. Lines appeared, most with numbers, sometimes more than were needed, or not enough, and not always in the right order, with upside-down digits, or fanciful things – herring bones, train tracks and millipedes – that didn't belong in maths at all. It was literacy after break. I wondered what they did with words.

On the table next to me was a pile of number lines, stiff, laminated strips The assistant had left them there. Miss told me to hand them out. Before getting up, I passed a couple to the nearest children.

"Quickly!" she snapped – at me, not the children – then snatched up the strips to show me how. She couldn't stop teaching for a second.

Everybody listening? She wrote an example on the board, 43–15, drew a number line and started counting back. She used partitioning as well. *The kids are pretty smart here,* I thought. The assistant pointed out that the plastic strips only went up to 30. It didn't distract miss. She continued just the same.

Time to put the learning down on paper. They returned to their tables. There was a textbook with questions. Different groups were given different tasks according to ability. Miss typed the group names on her computer, along with the question numbers. It all came up on the big screen: Pyramidss, Shperes and Cyinders.

The big, bad teacher

It was playtime. While the children were outside, miss stayed at her computer.

"Have you got a cold?" I asked. I had heard her coughing. A pause. She grunted. "I don't want to sound bossy; it's your room, but is it OK if I open a window?"

The room smelt, plus the germs. A long pause. I thought she wasn't going to answer. When she did, she spoke slowly, as if she was tired, and she kept her eyes on the screen.

"I open the two windows above the door."

I glanced up. The windows were too high to reach.

"I don't like to interrupt."

"Stop going on about the windows, would you!"

Nothing tired about that. I was impressed. Miss was sharp. She had seen through my fake politeness. She understood words and their real purpose. English was going to be fun.

When the children were seated on the carpet, she typed the lesson objective on the screen: WALT (we are learning to) *Descibe a character, personailty*

It had to be a character from the story they were reading. She stressed the importance of powerful language, of not repeating the same word. She gave her own example, as good teachers do.

The big bad wolf,

Whatever she was doing at playtime,

is a huge scary beast.

sitting at the computer,

He tal pointy ears

she wasn't preparing this.

always alert

She typed the words now as they came into her head.

with a long point jaw

It wasn't just a lesson in descriptive writing.

and ferocious sharp pointy teeth

It bit to the quick of the creative spirit. She didn't explain *alert*. They would have known that, the six-year-olds.

When miss finished her presentation, she sat at the table with the high achievers. She liked to inspire the bright ones. She put me with the weakest group. There was a boy who hadn't been at the school very long. Abid couldn't speak English, so I sat next to him and said some words. He was sleepy, but as soon as he saw that I was trying, he woke up. I thought we could do the date. It wasn't easy. It was taking a long time, though his face began to shine. He realised that I wasn't giving up. Miss noticed too.

"Words in the book!" she snapped.

She was right. The date was only a number. I wrote the word *pointy* and helped Abid copy. The class had got it three times over, and now so would he. Even better if he knew the meaning. I found a pencil and tapped my finger on the point. Abid watched closely. In case he thought *pointy* meant *pencil*, I drew the wolf's ears, big, pointy ones, and tapped with my finger again. I smiled. He smiled. It was clear this time. *Pointy* meant *ears*.

I started talking to another child.

"Write the question down first."

"Write the question down first!" miss repeated instantly to the whole class. Her voice was raised. It sounded strange. From miss, it was even stranger. Wasn't I always wrong? But I saw no malice, no sarcasm, and I looked quite hard. She simply agreed on certain things when I didn't expect her to. Still, I kept my voice down; I spoke as little as I could, but you can't stop talking completely, not if you're a teacher.

"Be careful with your handwriting," I whispered.

"Be careful with your handwriting!"

My words kept coming back, amplified, like a responsorio. It wasn't my last day in a British school, or I might have said something else.

Story time

After lunch, miss had an issue with Abid, the boy who couldn't speak English. There was a muddle during registration. In most schools, the register is taken twice a day. I don't know what happened that morning. I arrived late. But things are more difficult after lunch. You can't blame miss.

Each time she called a name, she said *Good Afternoon*, as if she cared for the children personally, and they said it back to her. Meanwhile, Abid sat on the carpet as he always did, among the others but apart (they left a generous space), watching the room with his wide, unknowing eyes. Then miss called his name. He was a nice boy; he tried his best, but he couldn't say *Good Afternoon* though he heard it almost sixty times a day. Miss made a comment. The fact that he had spoken at all or simply made a noise, proving he was there – not lost or kidnapped or lying somewhere mute with pain – was not enough for her, though it would have satisfied most teachers. She wasn't like most teachers. I forget what she said. Nothing too offensive, but she regretted it immediately. We might feel she'd picked on him; worse, picked on him because of his race. Whatever she felt about Abid, in the end she cared more for herself. She went on to praise him, his skill in English, his native language and his ancestry. She explained what really happened when the register got stuck. She hadn't been critical; she'd been curious. It was Miss Times-two again: the register and a lesson in diversity. Patience, too. It took a while. What contortionists do with limbs, she did with words. If politeness had fingers, she would have strangled him.

When the register was finished, she switched on the screen, superimposed a smaller one and presented the lesson. Then she sat with the top group again. Some children at my table had to copy from the screen, so I asked her if she wouldn't mind removing the smaller one.

"Why don't you do it yourself?"

Use your initiative.

The children were working quietly. To help them stay on task – they were Year 2, remember – she gave instructions in a firm voice, things like, "Try to finish before afternoon play," adding under her breath, *"Or next summer."*

It was an adult gloss, a commentary which, for the most part, the children couldn't hear or, if they did, wouldn't understand. It was cynical but fun, her way of coping with a day at school. You have to do something.

"Stop writing now. *If you ever started.*"

Three o'clock. Story time. The children were on the carpet again. Miss picked *The Gruffalo* and began reading. She was very good. I mean it now. It was her best work. She changed her voice to suit the character, high for the mouse, deep for the Gruffalo, and like an actor, gave it expression. For the illustrations, she showed each page to her left, front then right, always in that order, without haste, so every child could see and knew they would.

She didn't have to read so well. Most teachers don't bother. She did it because she wanted to. The children loved it, and so did she. But it wasn't teaching. It was hardly work at all. I sensed something else. The day was over. Seven, long hours. She was celebrating.

The telephone dance

The telephone dance

There's a little girl I haven't mentioned. We had lessons at her kitchen table. It was heavy, with a solid glass top (that's important, as you'll see), the sort you might find in a dining room.

When we sat down, her uncle wiped the surface with a damp cloth. Despite the curry stains, it was handy being in the kitchen. The little girl – let's call her Priya – could open the food cupboards and the fridge. She liked her drinks. The glasses were on a high shelf. To get them, she had to climb on a cupboard, stand on her toes then reach her hand even higher. She was small, only seven. From my chair across the room, it looked like rock climbing.

I remember one lesson. She had made her favourite drink (she mixed stuff together) and kept it in the fridge in a big jug. She had drunk almost all of it. There was enough for one more glass, but she wanted me to have it. She said how yummy it was – she said that several times – then put the glass in front of me.

"Are you sure you want me to have it?"

She nodded. Priya was sweet. I left the glass on the table. I wasn't tempting her. I thought she might change her mind.

"Sure?" I repeated. It was too much. Without a word, she reached across and drew the glass back in front of her.

At one time or other, I tutored the whole family, the child portion: Priya, who was an only child, plus two teenage cousins. They lived in the same house. In the kitchen, there were three plants, one for each child, Priya explained, put into pots when they were born. It was a nice idea and a sunny kitchen. The plants had done well, turning into trees and bushes (Priya's was taller than she was), but I couldn't help thinking, *What happens when the plants die?* I didn't say that to Priya.

"Did R– behave himself?" she asked after one of his lessons. R– was thirteen. She actually said, "Did W– behave himself?" In speech, at least, she hadn't mastered the letter *r*. It was another cute thing.

S–, the other child, had turned sixteen. Another girl. Priya came in during one of her lessons. She brought a pile of books and sat opposite me, in silence, with a pencil in her hand, looking studious.

"You're peeking," I observed. It was true. She was keeping an eye on us. She was also distracting me. "I don't want to be mean, but I can't concentrate while you're there. Please don't stay."

She picked her books up and went out obediently. At the start of her own lessons, Priya was usually asleep. When I got there, I'd find her on the sofa, out cold, at five-thirty in the afternoon. She cried when she had to wake up. She was, I think, the perfect, bawling little sister – or cousin, in this case.

Once, she fell on the stairs. They were steep and narrow. She told me when I arrived.

"Did you cry?" I asked.

"No."

"I bet you did."

She confessed. When Priya was wide awake, the fun began. There was a telephone by the sink. It rang every lesson with a cheerful melody and was very loud. When she heard it, she did a dance. "My telephone dance." She used to practise when the phone wasn't ringing, between me and the giant plants. At times, she danced on the table (she liked climbing, as you know), especially when the phone rang. There was more room, and it must have felt like a stage.

One day, R– came in late from school, looking for food. Priya was writing.

"She did her telephone dance," I said. R– didn't know what it was. "I only come once a week. You live with her, and you haven't seen her telephone dance!"

Errors that we make

Priya's family was from Sri Lanka. They were Buddhists. I liked the house, the atmosphere; it was quiet, apart from the phone and Priya, but her mother was always cross, at least when I was there. On one occasion, she said to me, "I don't know how much work goes on in her lesson."

"It's certainly not boring," I replied. I shouldn't have. We all know that lessons should be boring. If things get slow, I show off, and I did the same with Priya.

"Move on!" she'd say in a hard voice, like her mother. Or, "I don't understand you."

She'll be an imperious lover.

No matter what Priya did, I never got angry. Raiding the biscuit tin, dancing on the table. They were her biscuits; it was her table. She never did anything very bad, though her mother might not agree, and most teachers would have said something. I'm not sure if she was trying to make me angry, but she must have wondered why I wasn't and what she'd have to do to make me. Sometimes, things just happen, don't they?

S– stopped her tuition. They found someone else but didn't tell me. Priya mentioned the new tutor, then she saw my face.

"You're angry!" she declared triumphantly.

"I'm not."

It's hard to learn certain things. To learn them from a child is even harder. Harder still, to learn them casually. Priya had done it, made me angry, and without trying. She made me lie, too. It was quite a victory.

R– had stopped already. Priya was the only one left. There are other families. Priya had a friend the same age, and I tutored her as well. Priya asked, "Who do you like better?"

"Whatever I say will be wrong. If I say I like her better, you'll be jealous. If I say I like you better, it'll hurt her feelings when you tell her. So I'm not going to answer."

Time for a telephone dance. The telephone hadn't rung. She was practising on the table. After a whirl or two, she went, "Ouch!" stopped dancing and examined her arm. I forget which one. She had scratched herself at school.

"Show me," I said. She waited shyly, then held out her arm as if she didn't want to.

When girls go "Ouch!", they need something sweet. Priya did, anyway. She opened the chocolate cupboard and pilfered some. That's right, a cupboard full of chocolate. She had shown it to me in our first lesson: her treasure chest, wrappers like gold bars but in many colours. They had family in Switzerland. She ate a few pieces in front of the open cupboard then sat down with a big bit in her hand. A quick struggle. It was in my hand now. She lunged for it. Again, things just happen, like winning back a big bit of chocolate and tipping gently into someone's arms.

She had to do a story on her laptop. There was a prize at school for the best piece. She'd written a page or so, and we continued, but she pressed the wrong key and deleted everything. She wailed, a beautiful, scything wail, as if the world was over. Uncle came in, intrigued not worried, then S– like following a scent.

Noisy or sweet, the moments ran out. The school year finished, and so did our tuition. In the final lesson, Priya told me what her mother had said. We were stopping for the summer; she didn't say forever. Gutless, I thought, to make the child tell me, but worse to let her think we might continue. Like a business woman, Priya wrote my details in her book. I can hear her little voice.

"Name." Telling more than asking, the way a grown-up does. "Cell."
"Do you really think she'll call me?"
"She might."

Nunu

Before Nunu

I didn't call her Nunu straightaway. It took a few lessons. She was ten. I tutored her for the 11-plus. We got on pretty well, pretty soon, before the rupture. But more of that later.

When I first arrived, she looked ill. She was fine, really. It was seeing me. She stared at the strange man, one she'd have to sit with for an hour; one who'd tell her what to do, and make her read and write. Think of it, a whole hour, when a single minute is unbearable.

We sat at the kitchen table. I had photocopies. Verbal reasoning. Her answers were slow. She wasn't exactly rude, not in words – in syllables, in silence. The questions were multiple choice. Some answers had been circled already. Another girl had done it and kept doing it when I asked her not to. I talked about her now as if I didn't like her. I thought it might please the new girl. She didn't flicker. I tried again. Did she have a pet name? No. It was hard to believe. Girls with long names get short ones, cute things, like the girls. It's fine till they grow up or think they have. But Nunu's voice was cold. If she had a pet name, she wasn't telling.

I referred to "mummy." I don't remember why. It sounded wrong.

"Do you want me to say mummy or mother?

"Mother," she said. It was her quickest answer. No one could have answered more quickly. Names are important.

The lesson was about to end. We could do one more question. I turned to the next sheet. There was a line on it in blue pen.

"It's that girl!" I cried, as if I'd just noticed, though it had been there for years. She smiled at last – the girl who would be Nunu – not at me, at the page. But she smiled. I said, "You're the best girl ever."

The hour finished. She stood up brightly and left the room. Her mother appeared.

"I think you told her a little fib." She was hesitant. "She said you told her she's the best girl ever."

"I did. Teachers tend to lie, but there was a reason. I had a pupil once who wrote on my sheet and wouldn't stop even when I told her. Your daughter wouldn't do that."

"No, she wouldn't."

"She's very sweet."

"Yes, she is."

I was lying again. She wasn't sweet at all, not in the first lesson; she didn't want to be, and from what I'd seen, she got what she wanted.

For the first two lessons, we sat at a glass table, then a wooden one took its place.

"What happened to your old table?"

"My uncle took it."

"I prefer it. I could see what your feet were up to."

She had large feet. *She'll grow into them*, I thought, like hand-me-downs or a new tutor. For the time being, she didn't show much emotion. I was after another smile. I tried again. She had pens in different colours. She chose the pink one to write with.

"Don't waste that on me," I said. "I know it's a girl's favourite colour."

"I hate pink!" she answered, as if that explained why she'd picked it.

I laughed. She was pleased. She had made me do something. She almost smiled.

"Let's play Xs and Os," she suggested.

"I call it noughts and crosses. Why are girls always different?" She drew a grid in her book.

"Your mother'll be suspicious." She ripped the page out, and we began playing. At the end, she screwed it up then threw it in the bin. "Your mother might see it."

"She won't look in the bin!"

"Some mothers do."

I peered in the bin like a nosey mother. When I sat down, she drew a line across my sheet.

Nunu

Mother rang me before a lesson. She was concerned. Her daughter refused to write. Writing is part of the 11-plus. Hopefully, I could get her to do it. The girl seemed to like me, which should help. That's what mother said. I offered to set a question on the phone; mother could give it to her. She said no. She wanted me to do it in person. If teacher said "Write!", a child would have to.

She also said she'd bought a new notebook. Next lesson, it was on the table, waiting. Neatly placed, it looked untouched, except by mother. I picked it up. Hard cover, hundreds of pages, quality A4, thick and shiny – it would last a long time and hold lots of writing. Most important, it would impress her daughter. The writing would be quality too.

I put some work beside it, a comprehension from *The Secret Garden*. The girl read for a moment.

"I know this!"

She had seen a film version then borrowed the book from her school library. It was upstairs. She asked if she could get it. When she returned, she held it out proudly. I almost liked her.

"You need a pet name," I said. Her real name had four syllables. *Nu* was the second. "I'm going to call you Nunu."

"No, you're not. People call me Femi or (a name I don't recall)."

"In the first lesson, you said you didn't have a pet name. You lied." Her face soured, like the first lesson. "It's either Sweetie or Nunu. Which do you like better?"

"Nunu," she said quickly. I'd picked the right moment. She wasn't cross, and the pet name was clever, or I thought it was. She relaxed. She even burped.

"Have you been watching boy cartoons?"

No answer. She didn't look like a boy. She was wearing a tight top. She hadn't done that before. She picked up the comprehension. There were several pages. She found the answer sheet at the end. I reached for it. She wrenched it away. She hadn't done that before, either.

"You shouldn't have stapled the answers." Her first criticism. "It's not professional."

For homework, I asked her to write a book review. I said I wanted her opinion; she shouldn't just retell the story. She had a book about ponies, more pictures than words, based on a TV series. *My Little Pony* again. They're girl ponies, mainly, of school age, who read and visit libraries. They know magic – how else could a pony turn pages? – and they fly. They write, too, but they don't do exams. One is a princess with a long-winded name, like a royal family. Nunu showed me a portrait on her phone, saying the name aloud, adoring each syllable, as if she wanted it, wanted to be the princess. There are boy ponies; you can't ignore them completely, but you don't have to like them. In the program, as in life, most of them are plodders or bullies.

I had got to know her better. But pink ponies? They didn't square with the tight top. I asked about her birthday.

"It's in November. You can give me a present."

"A hug and a kiss."

"That's your opinion."

She never read *The Secret Garden*. For a start, it was an audiobook.

There were no annoying pages. But she didn't listen, either. After a few days, she returned it to the library. I asked why.

"It was boring."

She did the homework, though. It was the only decent one she wrote, but she didn't include her opinion; she just retold the story. Nonetheless, mother was delighted. Nunu had written something, and she had shown an interest in books, if only two, one of which you just listen to, and the other, you look at pictures.

Not everything is magic. I shouldn't have called her Nunu. I checked (too late) in the slang dictionary. Still, I can't give her real name, considering what I'm going to tell you.

Nunu in Wonderland

The following week, before I rang the bell, I peered through the window. Nunu was sitting at the table, reading a book. When I came in, she smiled.

"You're ready," I said. "How did you know I was coming?"

A slight pause.

"I was looking through the window."

She said it a bit shyly, like a girl admitting something. If I knew she'd been looking, I'd think she was keen to see me. Worse, she had tried to hide her keenness by sitting down before I came in. I'd think that, too. *How did you know I was coming?* There could only be one answer. I knew already, or I wouldn't have asked. I merely wanted her to say it. Nunu understood all this then told the truth. There was no point in lying or saying nothing. She wouldn't just look keen; she'd look stupid.

She had a new pet, a white rabbit, which was in its place like Nunu, a different place, that's all. There was a cage beside the table.

"The rabbit's a reward," explained mother, beaming at her daughter. "I'm proud of her. She's doing so well in your lesson."

A plump thing, it had a general cuteness, like little girls when you first see them. The cage was spacious, wide more than tall (when it stood up, its ears stuck through the wire), and there were toys to play with. It was nice enough as cages go, but it lacked something: freedom. If you asked the rabbit, it wouldn't want to be there, like Nunu in the first lesson. I never heard a name. Let's call it Freedom, Freda for short.

I felt sorry for it. There were droppings in the cage. It's not nice living in crap, even your own. In cartoons, rabbits don't crap, but this was a real rabbit. Being real has its perks if you're a rabbit. You don't have to listen or read or write or give opinions. That's a whole pile of crap.

Something else was new. Nunu had a cap on, a sporty one.

"Are you going to model it for me?"

She got up, took five steps across the carpet then returned, wiggling her hips on the way like a model. At least, she tried. Three times, she passed back and forth in front of me. At the end of each pass, she stopped and tugged her cap in my direction. Then she sat down again on the chair beside me. She deserved a break. I started talking.

"A boy gave me a lock of hair." Nunu giggled. "He cut it off and wrapped it in a piece of paper. I've still got it."

"I'll give you a staple."

She had a stapler, small and pretty (like Nunu), the sort of thing girls want.

"It might hurt," I replied.

"I'll *give* it to you, silly."

Her voice had feeling. I looked at her. She shut her eyes, pushed her chin up and puckered her lips. I stared at the little face, the little mouth reaching up to me. She wanted a kiss, a big one, apparently. The moment passed. She opened her eyes and sighed (a groan, really), kissed her fingertips then touched them on my cheek very gently.

The lesson continued. I produced a new sheet, a clean one, if you like.

"Where's the one we were doing?" asked Nunu.

"It was nearly finished. You saw the answers, anyway."

That sheet was fun. Now it had gone, the fun had too. She was disappointed.

"You look like a teenager," I said. "Now you're acting like one."

"I'm bored."

"If a girl I was teaching ever said that again, I'd have to resign."

"I'm bored."

At the end of the hour, mother came in. Like an expert, Nunu lifted Freda and nuzzled her lips in one ear. She was very serious. She was also chewing gum. This time, I couldn't resist.

"I thought you were chewing the rabbit's ear."

"Chewing the rabbit's ear!" mother chuckled.

I know girls who'd give their right leg

A week later, at six o'clock as usual, I arrived at Nunu's. I rang the bell. *I'm on time,* I thought. *Nunu's waiting; she'll be at the table, pretending to read, trying not to look excited.*

I peeped through the window. No sign of Nunu. If she was waiting for me, it wasn't at the table. *She's playing a trick,* I thought. *She'll jump out when I go in.* I rang the bell. The door opened, and I walked in. Still no Nunu. She was upstairs, mother said. Her cousins were staying.

Three children came down: Nunu, another girl and a boy. They were all the same age, but Nunu looked older. Her cousins sat with us as if they were part of the lesson. I regarded them.

"I'll need an extra £5 for each student."

"I've got it," the boy said earnestly, putting his hand in his pocket. He was smart. He'd make a good pupil. Of course, he was joking, He didn't want to sit there, and he didn't have to. In fact, he wasn't allowed. It was Nunu's lesson. He could have some fun, though, unlike Nunu. She sat in silence, eyeing the other children, more like an aunt than a cousin. She was apprehensive. They might embarrass her. When *she* was embarrassing, it didn't matter.

The cousins went upstairs.

"Are you coming next week?" Nunu asked. It was the half-term holiday, a week off school and perhaps the tutor. I didn't answer at once. I watched her as if I wasn't sure what she meant, as if, in her holiday, a girl might want a tutor. Then I said, "Two weeks is such a long time."

"It's a short time for me."

"I know girls who'd give their right leg to sit with me for an hour." Silence. "Deep down, you want me to come."

"Deep down, I don't!"

She sneezed. A cold from school, she explained; PE in the rain, in her PE kit, so her arms and legs were bare, as they were now.

"It was freezing!" she moaned. "We were just standing round."

The lesson finished. Mother came in to pay. I mentioned Nunu's cold. I even described how she got it. Mother stared. She knew about the cold. I didn't need to tell her. I didn't need to know in the first place. I was paid to teach Nunu, to help her learn, and there I was, learning about Nunu. Her cold had nothing to do with the lesson. It was personal. What else had we talked about? Words, like sneezes, come from nothing, but people listen. So did mother. She looked at Nunu, at me, at Nunu again then put it all together, as it seemed to her, and said to Nunu quite cleverly, "You don't wear enough clothes."

Their left leg, too

Every Tuesday, I caught the train to Nunu's. From the station, you turn left then left again. From there, you can almost see her house at the end of the road in a block of terraces. She lives by the railway line in a new neighbourhood, wasteland till recently. It's not far, just a few minutes' walk, but the road peters out. There's a dirt track and not much lighting. The track winds along, the railway on the left and a line of back fences on the right. The houses face away, pointedly, as if they don't like trains. Where the road finishes, and the track begins, you can see the back of Nunu's, but the first time you go, you don't realise, and anyway, you can't get in. There's no door or gate. You need to walk all the way round. I haven't been for a while. They may have fixed the road. Whatever it's like, if you want to get to Nunu's, you have to keep walking.

The first time I went, it was raining. It was dark, too. There were puddles I couldn't see. It depressed me. The streets were so new they weren't on the map. I found her, though, as I had to do before I called her Nunu. After that, she watched for me. Each week, as I walked along, I pictured her at the window, behind the curtain. I was nearly there. She'd see me in a moment. Until last week. I felt miserable, like the first lesson, but it wasn't raining. It was a premonition.

When I walked in, she was reading (or pretending to) as usual, but she didn't look up. She even held the book a different way. It was *Alice in Wonderland* read angrily.

"You're not sick of me already?" I said. "It's a world record!" Silence. "You've been on that page a long time." Her clothes were different too. The tight top was gone. She wore a bulky jumper. "I know girls who'd give their right leg to sit with me for an hour. Their left leg, too."

She choked a giggle, recovered then went on pretending to read. After the giggle, she was even angrier. The rabbit was at it too, chewing furiously. They made a good pair.

Somehow, the lesson started. Nunu had a pen in her mouth. I saw some wetness.

"That's girl slime," I said. "I'd scream if you touched me with that."

She tapped it on my arm.

"Did you fart?" she enquired.

"It was the rabbit." Her pet was beside the table. I could only see its ears, poking through the cage. "I don't know which way she's facing. I can't go on. I need to make sure she's listening."

Nunu stuck her tongue out. At the same time, a thought hopped into my head: *The rabbit's replacing me.*

"I remember our first lesson," I said. "I thought you were mean and horrible." Nunu looked at me. "Then I thought you were sweet. Now you're mean and horrible again."

She'd done her homework, the last half-decent one. It was comprehension. She read out her answers. The first began, 'In my opinion, I think –"

"Wait."

The two phrases, I explained, meant the same thing, like saying it's a very warm, hot day. Nunu sulked; she said her mother had told her what to write. *In my opinion, I think.* It wasn't so bad. It was like two opinions. I was having my revenge for all the times I'd asked and got no opinion at all.

At the end of the lesson, she hurried out. I mentioned the two phrases to mother in case Nunu did.

"She said you told her what to write. If she was five, I wouldn't have bothered. At that age, mummy's always right. But she's not five. She's sitting the 11-plus. I have to tell the truth."

"I didn't tell her to write it."

"You did, you did!"

It was Nunu – shrill, tragic – in the next room.

The cage is open. The rabbit's still inside, twitching its nose. You look away and back. It's not where you thought it was.

I'm going to get you sacked

We had one more lesson. I didn't know it was the last. We did some English, then I handed her a sheet of maths. Ten questions. She got the first one wrong.

"Don't worry," I consoled. "If girls knew everything, I wouldn't have a job." There was a note of irony. She would have heard it. "You don't even know my name." She didn't speak. "It's all right. I'm not proud. You can call me Greg."

"Graham," she corrected kindly. It *was* the last lesson.

"I know teenagers who haven't heard of Pompeii. One boy I teach, in Year 9, didn't know what toffee was." Pause. "If you can't do a question, just go on to the next one."

Nunu smiled and went on answering. Swiftly, her hand slid down the page. She put a dash for each question then, as soon as she'd finished, threw the pen down like a victor's sword.

"I can't do any of them!"

"That was silly."

"I don't care."

"You answered all the questions, so we'll have to correct them. We don't have time now. I was going to do something else next week."

"You won't be here next week. I'm going to get you sacked."

"It's not a good idea. Your mother will just find another tutor."

"I won't have any tutor."

"Yes, you will, someone who's professional and mean and won't let you do what you want – as I do," I added, in case she'd forgotten. "There's always another tutor." Pause. "I'm not resigning. Good luck, though."

She took the pen and zigzagged down a page in her book, the deluxe tome her mother had bought, meaning to inspire her. It inspired her, all right. The whole page was covered in lines, great, jagged things. Nunu had succeeded at last, done her best and got it all right. It was perfect scribble. She had also expressed an opinion. Best of all, it wasn't homework. She did it in front of me.

"The rabbit did that," I said.

Three days later, I got a call from mother. When I didn't answer, she left a message. She asked me to call her back. She didn't explain, but it sounded solemn, like a funeral. In a way, it was. I called back.

"Sorry I missed you."

"Your phone was on. It was ringing."

I sensed a reprimand. I wondered if she was cross. Mothers can be.

"It was on silent."

"I wanted to have discussions." A phrase I hadn't heard. Her voice was odd too. "I'm deciding the best way to move ahead." It wasn't a real discussion. She didn't want my opinion. Like Nunu, she had made up her mind already. But she sacked me gently. Nunu didn't do that. "I think I'll tutor her myself."

It's what mothers say when their child rejects a tutor – me, anyway. It's happened more than once. Nunu's mother didn't know. These were her first discussions. She meant well. When she hired me, she was doing her best for Nunu. When she sacked me gently, she was doing her best for me. I felt sorry for her.

My last memory of Nunu: lesson over, we were at the door; I was outside, looking back. She stood behind her mother, jumping up so I could see her, putting out her tongue and grinning, twitching her nose, with her hands on her head like ears.

Outside, looking back. The other day, when I wasn't thinking about Nunu, I found a piece of paper in my bag. It was a recycled sheet, a photocopy, which I'd put there for the lesson, for Xs and Os or other scribble, so she wouldn't spoil her book and mother wouldn't know. I took the same sheet to several lessons. She never used it. There was no scribble, just a poem on one side. It wasn't Nunu's. She didn't like poems. But the sheet had meaning, the kind of thing that makes a tutor sad. Not this time, not this tutor.

He's a lion

Have you met Ken Livingstone?

Lyan had a rickety front gate. It was also very low. To open it, you had to bend down, and then a hinge squeaked loudly. He would have heard it from the house. Each time I went, I thought to myself, *Why knock? They know I'm here*. But I knocked all the same. On my first visit, the curtain moved. A face; the curtain fell back. Lyan opened the door and said straightaway, without a greeting, "Have you met Ken Livingstone?"

He wasn't joking. When he asked, I didn't understand, but it must have been my clothes. In Lyan's view, I looked like a mayor of London or, at least, someone smart enough to meet him.

"Take your shoes off, Graham."

On my left was a staircase to the upper floor. A mass of footwear lay at the bottom, as if it had washed down. The house was silting up with shoes. I wondered how many people lived there.

Lyan walked into the living room. It was time for our lesson, though he wasn't ready. He was having dinner on the sofa and watching television, the Mecca prayer channel. They were north African. His mother had asked for help with maths and English. She wasn't home, he said, but Auntie was in the kitchen. I sat next to him. When he'd eaten, he put his bowl on the floor then stood up decisively. There was a desk by the sofa. He pointed to a chair.

"I want to go to university, Graham."

He was the right age, eighteen or so. He had the temperament, too. He was very sober. We did a maths example. He read the sum out first then used his fingers, grabbing them in turn with his fist and chanting.

"18 add 6. 18 add 1, 19; add 2, 20; add 3, 21; add 4, 22; add 5, 23; add 6, 24. 18 add 6 is 24!"

Lyan turned to me. He knew it was correct. He leaned back and stared at the wall. For a whole minute. It was a long time in the middle of maths. The shirt flaps parted on his belly. If this happened, and it did quite a lot, you could see his flesh. When he came to, he continued chanting.

"I'm going to succeed in life, Graham. I'm going to succeed! I'm going to succeed in life, Graham. I'm going to succeed! I'm going to succeed in life, Graham. I'm going to succeed!"

A little girl entered with a bowl of food. This was Filsan, Lyan's cousin. She was about seven. Like him, she didn't say hello. Little girls don't have to. She crossed her legs on the carpet, facing the television. There were green bits in the bowl. I had seen them when she came in, but I couldn't tell what they were.

"What have you got in that big bowl?"

"Pizza."

"With brussels sprouts."

"No!"

She said it in a deep voice, deep and warm. Lyan sneezed. A giant sneeze. He didn't cover his nose. He didn't try. The spray glinted, hung for a second in a pretty mist then sank very slowly on my question sheet, my hands and his big, bare belly. When the sneeze had settled, he coughed in my face.

The lesson finished. Auntie gave me the money. Lyan padded after me to the front door. He chanted once more, a single line, softly, "I'm going to succeed in life, Graham. I'm going to succeed!"

Filsan, who had come too, smiled up at me, her eyes shining.

"He's a lion!"

Can I eat Graham?

Auntie asked me to help Filsan with her homework, half an hour a week, after Lyan's lesson. The girl was in Year 2. Next time, when I walked in, she was sitting on the carpet, reading aloud from a book. She kept doing it after I started with Lyan. Auntie came in.

"Is anyone being naughty?"

Silence.

"Are you being naughty?" I asked Lyan. He was bigger than me.

"No," he responded seriously.

"Are you being naughty?" I asked Filsan. She was a lot smaller.

"No!" she responded very seriously. She also shook her head.

"Am I being naughty?"

She grinned. Auntie smiled, said no too then went out. It was clear; in our own way, we were all being naughty.

I'd brought a comprehension for Lyan. It was about camping.

"Have you ever been camping?" I asked.

"Pilgrimage to Mecca."

"Did you enjoy it?"

"Yes. You shouldn't be afraid, should you, Graham? You shouldn't be afraid! You shouldn't be afraid, should you, Graham? You shouldn't be afraid. You shouldn't be afraid, should you, Graham? You shouldn't be afraid!"

"No, Lyan, you shouldn't be afraid."

"Can I use your pen, Graham? Can I use your pen?"

His was fine. Without waiting for an answer, he plucked the pen from my hand.

"Can I eat, Graham?"

I was a little tired.

"Can you eat Graham?" I replied. Filsan turned to me. Her eyes were sparkling. "Haven't you had dinner?" Lyan shook his head. I felt sorry for him. "That's terrible. When did you last eat?"

"Morning. Can I eat now?"

"Go and ask Auntie."

He dropped his head and didn't mention food anymore. We worked for a while, then I asked, "Can I have the light on, please?"

"I don't need it."

Filsan tensed.

"I do," I said. He still didn't move. I almost got up, but I was the teacher, and Filsan was watching with her warm eyes. If I did it myself, I might confuse her.

"Filsan, can I call you Sweetie?" I ask girls that, sweet ones, anyway. They nod gravely, as Filsan did now. Or they say no. "Can you put the light on, please?" She jumped up at once. When she returned to the carpet, I said, "Thanks, Sweetie."

Lyan laughed, the only time I heard him, and we had months of lessons.

"It's not funny!" she cried. Silence. Back to English. I had a spelling question for Lyan.

"Give me a word with a silent letter."

"No."

Sweetie tensed again. She gaped at Lyan then at me. *No.* It was hard to believe. Lyan had no malice. He could say rude things, but so could

I. He was sitting there as placid as ever, as if he knew he was right, while I'd been expecting *knee* or *knock*. Something like that.

"You mean *know*!"

I practically shouted. Sweetie grinned. At last, the hour was up. It was her turn now. She was waiting on the carpet, with a book in her lap, open at the page she'd chosen. In book terms, in sums and reading, she was on a par with Lyan, but she understood more. Imagine it, Lyan and his big, bare belly, sprawled on a tiny chair in a class of seven-year-olds.

There was a spelling list to learn. She had to put each word in a sentence. The first was *animal*.

"I stepped on a hedgehog."

She really did.

"Excellent." The sentence, I meant. "Write it down."

The sentence had to include the word *animal*. I forgot, but so did Sweetie. It's tough in Year 2. She showed me her knee. She'd hurt it.

"Did you cry?" I asked. She nodded. "Do you think hedgehogs cry?"

"No!"

Her deep voice, then she went quiet. Something was different. I thought she'd changed her mind – they *might* cry if they were sad enough – but she stretched her arms out and hugged me. Lyan dropped his head again.

Hedgehog sweet

It was half-term. At Lyan's place, there were more shoes than ever. His cousins were staying, new ones, I mean, apart from Sweetie. All girls. When I came in, they were standing at the top of the stairs. The tutor was here. Girls want to see. They must have felt safe on the landing. I wasn't going up, and they weren't coming down, except for Sweetie. How many girls exactly, I couldn't say. They were close together in bright clothes, the colours mixing, and I didn't like to stare.

"Girls," I muttered. "It's going to be noisy."

It was quiet for the moment. They were shy, or Auntie had hushed them. But in the silence, I felt something else. Disappointment. A lesson goes on and on; they knew very well, and I'd be there for two. It was a long time for girls to be quiet.

Lyan was in the living room, though he wasn't ready. He never was. When I arrived, he'd be eating or playing a game on the computer. Today, he was on the floor in front of the television, but he wasn't watching. He was praying. I moved in behind him. He was on a mat, kneeling. He leaned forward till his head almost touched the floor, got up then kneeled down again. He did it repeatedly, each sequence an

image of the last. He was focused, as you'd expect from someone praying, if not from Lyan. It was Ramadan. He wore a long robe and skull
cap, which I hadn't seen before. His best clothes, surely; all white, and
the cap was special. It had a pattern of neat, little holes. He was im-
maculate; in short, a new Lyan. When he'd finished praying, he rolled
up the mat. I asked, "What have you done this week?"

"I went to Oxford Street."

"Did you buy anything interesting?"

"Boxes."

"Boxes," I echoed and glanced around. He had done well. The
room was full of boxes. They were even on the desk, where we normally sat, stacked to the ceiling. "Boxford Street."

We sat on the sofa instead.

"You need clothes to succeed in life, Graham. You need clothes to
succeed in life. You need clothes to succeed in life, Graham. You need
clothes to succeed in life. You need clothes to succeed in life, Graham.
You need clothes to succeed in life."

"Boxers!" I erupted. Sweetie walked in. She grinned. She was by
herself, like a forward scout. The others were upstairs. She got down
on the carpet, but she wasn't praying; she was watching television, and
she wasn't fasting; she had a Chinese takeaway. The container was on
the floor in front of her. She bent forward, as Lyan did when he was
praying, but she didn't lean as far.

"I'm wearing shorts," she said.

"They're very pretty," I replied. Lyan snorted. There was a menu
next to her. "What's your favourite dish?" She couldn't pronounce
Szechuan, but I couldn't either. "Is there hedgehog sweet?"

"No! You can't eat them!"

"They could eat *you*. You're very sweet."

Again, Lyan snorted but louder. It was *his* lesson, and there I was,
chatting to Sweetie. When all the work was done, and all the chatting,
Auntie paid me but only her portion. This week, Lyan's mother
hadn't left any money. Auntie pondered. She had some shopping to

do; we could go to the cash machine. We set off. I latched the gate behind us. The upstairs window swung open, and girls leaned out
laughing, waving, shouting. For ninety minutes, they'd contained
themselves. The noise had been smothered like embers in a box. Now
the box was open; the flames shot out. Auntie was beside me. The girls
had seen her, but they didn't care. Auntie did. She yelled in Arabic –
prompt, brutal – and the flames went out.

I might drown

The following lesson, Lyan was late home. I taught Sweetie first. The living room was still full of boxes, so we sat in the dining room at a big table. Sweetie was excited.

"I'm having ice cream after."

Her class teacher hadn't set any homework. I gave a comprehension, the town mouse and the country mouse. Two young creatures – all they talked about was food. Lyan came home. When the half hour was up, Sweetie got her ice cream from the fridge. It was a chocolate-covered bar on a stick. She wanted to eat it beside me while I taught Lyan, but his chair was in the way. She couldn't squeeze past, and he wouldn't move. She was about to crawl under the table, holding the ice cream.

"Give it to me," I said. "You might drop it." She was doubtful. "I promise I won't eat it."

"Don't let Lyan have it!"

"I won't. I promise."

She passed it to me then got down on her hands and knees. I studied the treasure I was holding. Lyan chanted.

"You should never lie, Graham. You should never lie. You should never lie, Graham. You should never lie. You should never lie, Graham. You should never lie."

Another voice rose, a little one. It sounded a long way off.

"I can't do it!"

Sweetie backed out from under the table. In my hand, the ice cream was melting.

"Filsan, get a plate," said Lyan. He didn't call her Sweetie. She glanced at the ice cream then at me. I nodded. She was gone a while.

"I'll hold it," Lyan offered.

I nearly passed it to him – I really did – but I remembered.

"I promised Sweetie."

She finally returned.

"I couldn't reach the plates," she explained.

Lyan let her pass. There wasn't much space. She held her hands above her head, clutching the plate. An elbow quivered. She couldn't bend her arm. It was paralysed. Meanwhile, ice cream was running down my fingers.

"Filsan, get a spoon."

Lyan was deadpan. She had got the plate, and it took so long. Now, she had to do it all again. She hesitated, only for a second, yet long enough for the ice cream to slip from its stick, over my knuckles and onto the carpet. I'd seen girls cry, lots of them, but not Sweetie. She had come to sit with me. In a way, the ice cream had too. They just couldn't do it together. It was a lesson in itself, a cruel one: irony. You don't teach that to a seven-year-old. Nor was Lyan happy. He missed out on the treat. Auntie wasn't happy either. The carpet needed cleaning. But when the stain was gone, and everything looked the same, the ice cream still mattered to Sweetie. Sweetie and me. I was the reason she lost it.

When I was leaving, she watched me tie my laces. She had stopped crying, but she was gloomy.

"I'm going swimming tomorrow. I might drown."

"You might. You'll be careful, though, won't you?"

A hug, our second. There wasn't a third. It was the last time I saw her. She didn't drown. I heard her voice a week later. Four words. When I knocked, no one answered. It was pouring with rain. There was no shelter. I knocked once more.

"There it is again!"

A little voice, a long way off. Lyan opened the door. His mother was on the sofa. It surprised me. She was never in. And she seemed angry. No Auntie, no Sweetie, though I'd heard her voice, and no money. Mother said so. She was ill and couldn't make it to the cash machine. If I taught Lyan today, she'd pay me next time.

"I should be all right then."

We did the lesson. Next week, when I walked in, Auntie blocked the passage. Mother was sick, she said. I couldn't do the lesson. Lyan came down the stairs, holding the money for the previous week.

"Mother is at the clinic."

The door to the living room was shut. It had always been open. His mother was on the sofa – I could feel it – her face stiff with anger. Illness made her cross, apparently.

Girls' school

Keep your lips together

At the girls' school, when they talk too much, I do a mime. I zip my lips up with a thumb and forefinger, turn an imaginary key and toss it away with an extravagant flick. Some Year 8s did it back to me once, like a chorus line in a West End musical. When the moment came to fling away the key, a row of hands went up in one flourish, as if they'd practised. At the end of the lesson, as the girls were leaving, one of them stopped in front of me, lips pressed tight. Her friend asked me if I had the key.

Think of all those schoolgirl errors. Think of all mine. I saw a pupil at the bus stop on the way to school. Tina was in Year 10. When the bus came, she got on before me. I sat next to her (there were no other seats) and looked down at where she was sitting.

"I usually put my bag there," I said and propped it on her lap. Her face at that instant – it's one of those things you remember. She had a scarf around her neck, not covering her hair. She always wore it, even on a warm day. I asked her why. She said it stopped her head falling off. I said if I saw her head on the ground, I'd take it home and put it on my mantelpiece. Tina thought for a bit. She must have seen it in her mind, her head on my mantelpiece, like a trophy.

"That's a pretty weird thing to say."

"It's pretty weird to say your head'll fall off."

For most things, there's a price to pay. I must have known this when I sat next to Tina and put my bag on her lap, but I did it anyway.

The next time I saw her, we were in class. She was chatting loudly when the other girls were trying to work. Someone called me over and, in a soft voice, complained.

"Tina," I announced, "you're making too much noise. I've had a complaint from one of your colleagues."

There were fifteen desks clustered in groups of three. In a girls' school, the groups compete like teams on a netball court. Tina knew where the complaint had come from. She either heard the girl or guessed who it was. She swivelled round and looked at the right desk, smiling ironically.

When I'm not speaking, I move around. I rarely sit down. The teacher's desk can feel like a trap, but Tina's back was pointing that way. It seemed like a good place to be. To get there, I had to walk past her. I was very quick (I flitted by), but she looked up straightaway.

"I get goose bumps when you walk behind me."

"That's interesting," I replied, "but there's nothing I can do. You should contact a qualified healthcare professional." Then I asked the class, "Is there a school nurse?"

"Yes, shall I go and get her?" someone said. It was the girl who had complained.

"On second thoughts."

Tina got even noisier. It was time for a talk.

"Just because I see you on the bus," I said, "it doesn't mean you can behave badly in class."

Zaina, by the window, turned her head towards me. To Tina, I went on, "You look so sweet and innocent when you're waiting for the bus."

"That's different."

She put her books in her bag, strode across the room and sat on the floor in front of the door, facing it, with her legs crossed. She was quiet until the bell rang, then slipped out before the others. A few seconds passed. I realised some girls were still there. It was Zaina with two of her friends. She had stayed by her desk till I looked up, then started walking. She stopped in front of me and said, "I love you so much!"

You can't always tell when someone loves you. It can be a quite unlikely person. And when you find out, there may not be a lot you can do. I didn't know what to say. It deserved something, though, this declaration – a word, at least; an arrow on the heart line, somewhere between "I love you too" and "Don't be ridiculous."

"You love me so much?" I repeated with a rising tone like a question. I felt relieved; I had almost laughed – in surprise, not cruelty. You don't mock the heart.

She was at the door now. She was nearly gone. The question mark didn't feel enough. It was cowardly. I knew it, Zaina knew it, and her friends did too. I needed to say something else. But no words came. How could someone take so long to speak? The silence said it all; it echoed what was in my mind. Nothing. In the end, I managed this.

"I'll remember that forever."

Zaina turned her head a final time. Heads aren't so heavy, normally, when a lesson's over. She stared at me briefly then walked out. As soon as I said it, I knew it was wrong. It was impersonal, worse than no reply, and it put her in the past. But that wasn't all. *I'll remember that forever.* A feeling mightn't last so long. A girl can change her mind. She mightn't want you to remember.

I taught you that

September, the new school term. I was covering Year 11. The maths teacher was off already. She'd set some work, multiple choice questions. I merely had to sit there, but that's hard for me. The girls were coming in. One of them had a red coat. She sat in front of me. I didn't know her, and I don't remember her name. She stood out, though. Everybody else was blue.

"That's a nice coat," I said.

"Thank you."

"Is it red for danger?" She giggled. "Embarrassment?" She giggled a bit more.

Then Zaina walked in with her friends. When she saw me, she stopped dead, no longer so sure about doing maths. I said her name. It's not what teachers usually do when a girl walks in, unless there's a reason – she's misbehaving or has been away, sick perhaps. Zaina was sick now. Something was disturbing her. Either she still loved me, regretted telling me, saw I'd not forgotten or (D), all of the above. I know. In maths, there's only one right answer.

Hundreds of girls go to that school. They say things all the time. A whole summer had trickled by, yet I recalled what one girl said. Whether she still loved me or not, Zaina must have felt unlucky. She sat down at last. Everyone was chatting. The teaching assistant looked annoyed.

"If you make too much noise," I said, "the teacher next door will hear. I'll be sacked." The girl in the red coat giggled again. "Be careful, or I'll give you a window of opportunity."

"What's that?" she asked.

"It's what I call detention. If I give you a detention, your parents'll complain. 'Who does he think he is? He's just a supply teacher. He can't give you a detention.' But if I give you a window of opportunity, it's another matter."

Red Coat giggled again. The assistant got tired of it and told her not to.

"It's partly my fault, miss. I might be encouraging her, without meaning to, of course."

"That's right!" said Red Coat hotly, as if she'd been absolved.

"Now I know what the red stands for. Anger."

She giggled again. A girl came in with a message for the class. She must have been a prefect or something. She stood at the front of the room as if she was used to it, and addressed the girls like a teacher. They all listened closely. When she'd gone, I told them, "That's not fair. You listen to her but not to me!"

"I need water," Red Coat gasped. She was giggling non-stop. "Can I go to the toilet?"

"I don't recommend it. (Her name) and toilets don't mix."

She giggled even louder, so I let her go. When she came back, she was calm. After a minute or two, she looked up from her work and said seriously, "Do you like Tina?"

"Tuna?"

She shrieked.

"Why do you keep talking to him?" Zaina said. She was a quiet girl. That lesson, it was all I heard her say.

Tina was in a different set for maths. I saw her later at the bus stop.

"The last time I had you," I said, "you were very bad."

"I wasn't."

"You were."

"I wasn't."

"You were."

"I wasn't."

Pause.

"You're being bad now." She smiled. "You sat on the floor."

"I was feeling dizzy."

Pause.

"Tina, have I ever taught you anything?"

She thought for a moment, smiled again and gave her head a little shake. It made her pigtails wiggle. Then the bus pulled up. She was in front of me, about to get on.

"Wait," I said. "If I go first, I can't follow you. You can avoid me. At the same time, you'll look polite, waiting for your elder and wiser."

"That's true," she reflected.

"I taught you that."

Do you really love me?

I like February. It's a short month. The month of love. This year, for Valentine's Day, a scratch card was on sale, £1 each, nine red hearts, match three. Two win nothing.

Lunchtime at the girls' school. When the bell rang, I headed for the gate. I hadn't been sent home. It was a half-day booking. Some girls were by the fence, which was steel wire, ten feet high.

"You're on the right side, girls," I said. "It's dangerous out there."

The teacher on duty opened the gate, and I stepped out. Something made me glance back into the yard. I saw Famina in the distance with Melissa, two Year 9s. They saw me too and ran over. The teacher reopened the gate, and I went back in. Famina gave me a high-five. When she saw it, Melissa complained.

"I want to do that!"

"Excellent high fives," I said after they were done. A pause. My small talk is not so good. It's even worse when teachers are listening. I could only say, "Are you wearing lipstick, Famina?"

She didn't answer. I often asked her this. Sometimes, I added things, other questions, but I never got a straight reply.

"Are you allowed to?" I said, thinking the answer would be *no*.

"It's sexy!" was all she said that lunchtime, by the steel fence. Was I the only teacher who noticed her lips? She had a blue scarf around her head, covering her hair completely. Her face was like a flower. It's a cliché, but there's no better word.

We'd been friends for a while, Famina and me, and best friends after that. In the middle of a lesson, French or history, she popped her head up and asked, "Best friends?" as if she knew the answer already.

"For life," I said.

"What?"

"For life."

"For life, for life," she echoed solemnly.

The next time I saw her, it was Double Art. A famous lesson now. In the weeks that followed, around the school, when Famina walked by, her classmates would point her out to me.

"There's that girl!"

The Year 9s are filing in.

"Hello, Sheldon."

"Mr Cooper to you," I say.

"Oh, that's so sweet!"

"Some girls called out 'Hello, Sheldon' at the traffic lights. I was running for a bus."

"What did you do?"

"I waved."

"So sweet!"

They settle down. Girls like drawing.

"I love you!"

It's Famina. She's standing by my desk, on the right. I hadn't seen her. We look at each other. Then she returns to her stool.

The room is so quiet, quiet and still, like a photograph. Lessons aren't ever like this, not mine, anyway. But Double Art never ends. Famina pops up again. This time, I see her from the start. She leaves her stool, circles the room and stops on my right, abruptly, as if she's on a string.

"I love you!"

We look at each other. She returns to her stool. While she's drawing, I pop up in front of her.

"Do you really love me? You don't know me."

She thinks then says, "Like a teacher!"

She's sitting with her friends. I ask if they're from Bangladesh. They don't answer. A moment later, Famina is up again, dancing around, giving each girl a hug.

"Famina's very affectionate," I say to the row in front of me.

"She might hug you," someone says.

"She might."

The lesson is about to end. In my teacher voice, I say, "Start tidying up now."

"I love you too!" replies Famina.

What about me?

I was on the bus to school. My stop was a few yards ahead, but there's traffic near the station, and at that time, in the early morning, it's very bad. The bus stopped moving altogether. I saw Famina on the footpath opposite, alone, walking slowly, a schoolgirl on her way to school. She was by the betting shop, the take-away; she was almost at the corner, but she walked very slowly. If she'd gone any slower, she would have stopped, like the bus. She'd walked a hundred mornings like this, another hundred and hundreds more, to the same place, at the same speed, as if she didn't want to get there. Her eyes were straight ahead. She didn't see me. I couldn't bang on the window. Adults aren't supposed to. I just watched her go.

The bus edged forward. Now, it was quicker than Famina. I caught up with her in the school grounds, at the staff entrance. Steps climb to a great, wooden door. At the top, as I held the handle, I called out.

"Famina!"

She stopped and looked up like a girl waking. Then she smiled.

"You remember my name."

"I remember everybody."

She smiled again, a little, unbelieving smile.

The last time I saw Famina, it was maths. I walked in. The door was at the back of the room, so the girls faced the other way, towards the teacher, who was waiting for me. I couldn't see their faces. One girl, the closest to the door, heard me come in. She turned around and whispered, "Have we got you?"

It was Famina. I nodded and stayed where I was. The teacher was lecturing the girls, something about the perils of failure. It was desperate. Famina gazed at me. The girl next to her turned around too. Teachers at the front notice that kind of thing, blue scarves where faces should be. Miss suffered it for a short while until her patience ran out.

"Face the front, girls. You'll have the whole lesson to look at him."

She finished her lecture and walked off. Maths. There are too many numbers. Finally, the lesson was over. Everyone left, except the girls at Famina's table. They weren't budging; they had business to settle. A cross silence, then the girl next to Famina asked me, "Who's your best friend?"

Girls are good at this. Whatever I said would be wrong, but I had to answer. If I didn't, if for any reason I didn't say Famina, Famina would be annoyed. But if I said Famina, someone else would be hurt. That was the intention, at least, when the girl asked her question in her casual way.

I didn't say Famina. I pointed at her. And it was hardly pointing. I only raised a finger. It was still too much.

"What about me?" cried Melissa. Her voice was truly pained.

I don't ask where girls are from anymore. Melissa had a scarf on her hair, like the other girls, but her face and hands were white. And she was naughty. She was on behaviour report – forever, it seemed – and carried a yellow card around. She'd leave it on the teacher's desk at the start of the lesson and pick it up at the end. I had to put a comment in the box, just a word or two. She was never bad for me, though she didn't do much work and she did like to sit on the floor. Each time, I wrote that she'd been excellent, even if she wasn't. Girls check what you write. Melissa was no different. The week before, I put *Excellent* once too often. We both knew she hadn't been. She nearly said something. Her lips opened. Then they closed. Who wants the truth? The rest of the class had gone. We were taking too long. Some friends came back to find her. One asked, "What are you two doing?"

And Melissa was the one on report. She had tested me once, if I knew her name. Famina had too, more than once. A girl's name needs to be remembered. I passed those little tests, but others, like the best-friend, I failed. Afterwards, Melissa stayed as usual to get her report. This time, a friend was with her, the girl who'd asked the question. Melissa had for once been excellent, really excellent, and I wounded her by lifting a finger. I thought she was going to cry.

"Can I have my report?"

"It's on the table."

I could have passed it to her. She was on my left; the table was on my right. I made her walk in front of me. It seemed cruel. But when she drew level, I said, "You're my best friend too. I just couldn't say so in front of Famina."

"Have you been cheatin' on us?" said the other girl, mimicking the accent from a cowboy film.

"It looks like it," I said, and they ran off giggling.

A tank of crocodiles

Tables

Kirin is my newest student. When I write about people, I normally take them from the past then dust them off for you, but I'm still tutoring Kirin. I go to his house. On Saturday, if you came by, you'd see him next to me, a young man with a cute smile, sparkling in his own silver dust.

In the dining room, there's a massive, wooden table and six chairs to match, all dark brown. When I walk in, Kirin is always ready in the same place. I sit at the near end. He's on my left around the corner. The other chairs are in the same place too. No one touches them. That's how it feels. I've taught on a lot of surfaces. This one is shining clean. When I sit down, I don't need to flick crumbs away or call for a cloth. No one eats at that table. There are no dinners. In Mummy's dining room, the most formal thing is the lesson.

There's a pile of books in front of him. The first time I went, I saw the books before I saw the boy. If he's seated, they're taller than he is. His chin barely pokes above the table. Kirin is an only child. Sitting on that chair, he looks like one.

Every son is a genius. It may not show straightaway. He needs to concentrate, try harder. That's where Mummy comes in. All Kirin's books are new. There are, in fact, two piles, one of textbooks for maths and English, and one of dictionaries. That's right, a pile of dictionaries, heavy, adult things. Like Kirin, they're in the same place every week. Perhaps Mummy leaves them there. You wouldn't want to move them. Just looking at them, you feel the weight – and the expectation. How to shift the learning into the little head? The books, like the table, are against him. That's where Tutor comes in.

"Those dictionaries may be a little hard," I said to her quietly.

"But I help him with it."

She's doing all she can. You can't say she isn't. She knows what she wants from me, too. Before each lesson, she decides what I should teach and leaves it out for me. It makes another pile.

Like Mummy, Kirin is always ready with an answer, although – like her again – it may not be the right one. There's a word they both like. *But.*

"Keep your foot still," I said.

"But my shoe came off."

"It came off because you moved your foot."

I answered back. I don't do that to Mummy.

I've been tutoring Kirin for a few weeks. When Mummy is in the dining room, he's perfect; when she's in the kitchen, he's OK; but sometimes she isn't there at all. Once, when I arrived, he was screaming. I could hear him from the front garden. I knocked. Silence. More silence, then the childminder opened the door. Inside, everything looked the same. Kirin was in his place as usual, bobbing on the lake of polished wood. The books were in front of him in their usual piles, still and silent, as if they were waiting too.

On his left is a pencil case, a huge one like a suitcase, full of equipment, with several ordinary pencil cases, each full of stuff as well, whatever a boy might need to prove his intellect. When I got to know him, I joked about it. I said it was a pencil case in a pencil case in a pencil case. He didn't smile the first time I said it. He smiled the second time. I didn't smile either the first time he fooled around.

My father is Chinese

Kirin's family is from Bangladesh. He's small for his age, a little, male version of his mother. Like all children, he looks up a lot. Mummy noticed and put things on the wall for him to look at, charts and tables full of information. It was clever. When homework is finished, and most children look up from their books, Kirin looks up too, but he goes on learning.

During our first lesson, one of these charts caught my eye. It was on the wall next to me.

"That's my old timetable," he said.

It was like a classroom timetable but for seven days and more detailed, with all his activities in half hour slots. I looked for it the next time I went. It wasn't there. *She doesn't want me to see it,* I thought. *She forgot to take it down last week.*

"The new one's in the kitchen," Kirin said. We were doing maths. Afterwards, I told Mummy he didn't know his times tables.

"There's a chart in his bedroom," she said. It was up to him to learn it. I expect there's something in every room, a chart or table on the wall, for him to do his best, and to show she's done hers.

She came in once while we were working, and stood behind us. He had maths from school, equivalent fractions. In Year 2. Not surprisingly, there was a question he didn't understand. Mummy chuckled. It wasn't a pleasant chuckle; it was Mummy's, a sarcastic noise. When he still didn't understand, she chuckled again. Kirin swivelled round and looked at her, pain on his face, then he turned back and stared at the wall. But there's no chart for laughter.

"He knows all that," she said. "He doesn't concentrate."

When I was speaking to her, Kirin interrupted. I was halfway through a sentence. I thought she'd say, *Be quiet. Your teacher's talking*, but she turned to him and answered as if I wasn't there. When she left, he moved his legs around beneath the table. He went on doing it. I told him to stop. He put his feet on the chair opposite and pushed.

"Don't do that," I said. He did it again immediately. We were near the end of a long lesson. "Don't do that again, ever, or I'll tell your mother."

I spoke softly. It was the tone that counted. He looked across at me, his eyes wondering, but he didn't push the chair anymore.

We heard the front door. Someone had come in.

"That's my father," Kirin said, adding, as if with regret, "He's Chinese."

The dining room door was open. Daddy was still there, at the doorway, talking on his phone. He didn't sound Chinese. I had my back to him. I wanted to turn around, investigate, but that's what a child would have done. I was the teacher. I just looked more closely at Kirin. I couldn't help it. *That's a Bengali face*, I thought, but I didn't tell him.

"He's a builder," Kirin persisted with the same, sad tone, as if he had a list of things, all disappointments, which he'd locked away but was now revealing, one by one. Parents are touchy about their children, yet children are touchy about them. Think of the playground. *Your mother married a Chinaman! You get your clothes from Oxfam! Your father is a builder!*

Daddy was still at the door. He wasn't coming into the dining room. I couldn't resist. I turned around. He had his back to me, so his face was hidden. He wore a suit, though.

Kirin's father is a Chinese builder, or Kirin is sick of learning.

Fox crimes

"What's that red thing on your face?"

"I don't know," I said. Kirin has an eye for imperfection. "Hopefully, it'll go away."

The summer holidays. He still had homework from school. There was a non-fiction booklet on foxes, bats and owls. Someone had stapled the pages together, but they were upside down and out of order.

"Mrs – did that," said Kirin. "She's the teaching assistant."

I got him to underline the words he didn't know. There were lots.

"Crepuscular?" I read aloud.

"Don't you know what that means?"

Afterwards, I showed the comprehension to Mummy and said it was too hard for Year 2.

"That's what he has to do," she replied coldly. "He's going into Year 3."

"Crepuscular? How many adults know what that means?"

Silence. I was sick of Kirin's questions and Mummy's answers; the cheek, the coldness. And the silences. Like mother, like son, they were rude. Worse, she seemed cross, as if she didn't want me. She was trying to pressure me – I'd have to work hard to please Mummy – or she didn't like paying when the lessons mightn't make any difference. I put up with it. I wanted the money. But I was losing patience. *I'm going to sack you*, I thought. I just haven't done it yet.

There's always another story. In Year 3, he had this for comprehension. A farmer kept a fox in a cage, a handsome brown fox. The animal was unhappy and howled at the moon. The farmer thought it was yearning for its freedom, so he opened the cage, but the fox didn't move. It went on howling at the moon. Then the farmer understood. It wanted a wife. It was howling at the fox in the moon. The farmer reached up into the night sky and lifted down the fox in the moon. Her coat was bright silver. As soon as her feet touched the earth, she shook the silver colour from her sides. She shook and shook until her coat was brown, like her husband's. There was baby-making. This story was written a while ago.

When the cubs were born, there was silver on the tips of their fur. I asked Kirin why. Kirin. The name means poet in Bengali.

"Like your hair," he replied.

I enjoyed the part where the moon fox shook the silver from her fur. I said it was like a wet dog shaking off water. I thought it would impress Kirin.

"A fox moves like a cat," he retorted. He had seen them in his back yard.

"A fox poked its nose through my window," I said. "It was hungry. They come at night and look for food in the rubbish bins. They'd steal a baby if there was one. Or a child."

Foxes have their own timetable. Kirin stared.

"Your hair's orange," I said.

Every so often, when Kirin is working well, I let him play with one of his toy cars. I say, "You've got thirty seconds," and pretend to time him. He runs the little wheels along the table and across the book in front of him, controlling each arc like a racing driver. Last Saturday, I picked up one of his favourite cars. It was small and disappeared in my hand.

"What would you do if I kept it? Forever."

He looked at me, half-smiling. I put the car down. He has a plastic ruler, the flexible kind. I play with that, too, like a floppy sword.

"I know how to break it," I said.

"You can't."

"I can. How do you think I'd do it?"

Kirin thought a moment and suggested things, but I shook my head.

"Put it in the freezer," I said. "Leave it till it's frozen hard, then take it out and snap it in two." I held my fingers up and snapped an imaginary ruler. "Don't do it, though. Mummy wouldn't be pleased."

We read one more story, about a vain emperor. I went through *vain* and *vein*, showing the blue lines in my wrist. Kirin placed his arm on the table. He had veins too.

When the lesson was over, I got up as I always did, but this time he said, "I don't want you to go!"

Do it quickly and slowly

Kirin wanted to play in the lesson.

"I wish we could play," I said, "but we can't. Mummy's paying."

In a private lesson, if a child misbehaves, there's not much you can do. You can tell the parents, but however strict they are, they're not the headteacher. And you can't keep a naughty boy in, not in his own home. If you did, you wouldn't get paid extra. One day, I tried, "Watch out, I'll stay another hour."

"I want you to stay for four or five hours!"

There was something grown-up about it. The imprecision. He wasn't exaggerating.

For literacy, Kirin doesn't have his class teacher. He has a specialist in English. It's nice to be taught by an expert, however old you are. Kirin got a comma wrong in his homework. When I told him, he replied, "Our literacy teacher said that commas mean *and*."

A fable, *The Fox and the Sparrow*, was for comprehension. Mrs –, the teaching assistant, had reduced four pages to one, to save paper, I suppose. It was admirable, but the print was too small. I asked him to read it aloud.

"Do it quickly and slowly," I said. He read for a moment then looked up.

"How can I read it quickly and slowly?"

"Just checking you were listening."

He continued reading. My mind wandered off.

"I wasn't listening," I said. "Please repeat the last bit."

My confession interested Kirin. He pointed out that it was he who normally didn't listen. I agreed. I now owed him. Whenever I make a mistake, and it happens quite often, I give him a 'life.' Given the size of this mistake, I awarded two and a half. He grinned. He needed all the lives he could get.

In the fable, a fox sees some grapes on a wall and tries to reach them. The more he tries and fails, the more aggressive he becomes. In the end, he gives up and says he never wanted them. A bird lands lightly on the wall, next to the grapes, and eats them in front of him. In the comprehension, a question asked, Why *lightly*? I didn't know the answer. But this was Year 3. There had to be one. Was the bird being careful not to knock the grapes off the wall and lose them to the fox, or was she just making fun of him – *You clumsy fool, look how easy it is!* – or both or something else? After I'd gone through all this, I still wasn't sure.

"Let's face it," I said, "have you ever seen a bird land heavily? Unless it's been shot." I glanced at Kirin. "You can't write that, though."

His eyes glinted.

For maths, the expanded column method. We were getting bored. I thought I'd improvise.

"If Farmer Brown" (pretending to read from his book) "had 137 sheep in the field, 214 in the yard and 306 in the bathroom, how many were there in the fridge?"

It's a risk being silly. Kirin can either wake up or stop trying completely. Now, he kept making mistakes and rubbing them out. The slightest error, and he'd rub out the whole thing before I could stop him. We weren't going to finish. He made one mistake too many. I took his page and corrected it myself. Straightaway, there were tears in his eyes.

"You snatched my work!"

"I didn't" – the swell of tears was growing – "mean to."

It was too late. A big drop ran down his cheek.

"I still had a life!"

A naughtymatic

"I have to write a letter," Kirin said.

"Did your teacher tell you how to write a letter?"

"No."

I turned to Mummy.

"How can he do it, then?"

"That's how they teach these days. They don't go through every-thing."

"Good teachers do."

When I said it, she was walking out, and I spoke quietly. I don't think she heard.

The letter would be addressed to an astronaut, a real one, a woman. It was breaking down barriers in gender, if not in letter writing. There were other barriers.

"You could ask her if it's nice in space."

"*Nice* is a banned word."

The literacy lady again. She had banned *nice* and *big* and *little*. And *happy* – that's a good one. (*Good* was banned too.) She meant well. She wanted to improve the children's writing. For the whole of

Year 3, she'd been banning words, and now she was banning them in space.

"OK," I said. "Ask about the space jellyfish."

We talked about floating in space, if a jellyfish would move the same way as it did in water, and how you might feel if you had to float forever.

"I can see you in a space suit," I said, "your little face at the window, but I can't hear a word you're saying."

Kirin fell silent and began writing. When he'd finished, he put his pencil down.

"That's a nice, big letter," I said.

Time for comprehension. A beggar knocked on an old woman's door. Did she have some water for nail soup? He had the nail already. He showed it to her. He only needed water. She couldn't refuse such a small request, so she boiled some water, and he added the nail. He let it cook for a while then tried a spoonful. It could do with some season-ing, he said. Well, she could spare a little seasoning. She added salt. It went on cooking. He tasted it again. Some vegetables wouldn't hurt. A little meat. Tasting each time. In the end, a delicious bowl of soup was ready. The beggar shared it with her.

Kirin had to write about the old lady. We agreed that she was stupid. We also agreed that he couldn't write that in his book. His teacher mightn't like it. *Dumb, foolish* and *idiotic* didn't sound good either. In the end, he just wrote that she wasn't very clever, and played with a couple of toy cars. That wasn't very clever either. Mummy had banned them from the lesson. We discussed whether he could trick her the way the beggar had tricked the old lady. Kirin thought not. Then he talked about his cars.

"This one's an automatic."

"A naughtymatic," I said. He chuckled. "You're not the only bad boy in the world."

"Me not bad."

"Me not stupid."

I told him about a trick I'd played at school on a girl called Precious. It was Year 6, ICT. I was standing in front of the class. I asked her what the opposite of *shut down* was. She thought for a moment.

"Log on?"

She knew it wasn't right. I pushed my hand down in the air beside me.

"If this is shut down," then I lifted it again, "this is –"

"Shut up!" Precious cried.

"Tut, tut, tut." I shook my head. "Precious told me to shut up. I'm telling miss."

Kirin chuckled. Then he asked seriously, "Did you tell miss?"

I shook my head at him, too. You can't always tell on a child. Kirin was still thinking.

"What did Precious do?"

"She went, 'Oh, sir!' in a deep voice. But she knew I was joking."

After the lesson, the one with Precious, the children left for lunch. In the corridor, I saw one of the boys with a teacher. He was walking beside her, taking three steps to the teacher's two and looking up purposefully.

"What's the opposite of shut down?"

When I'm twenty-five

Last Saturday, Mummy let Kirin bring a toy car downstairs. I can't remember which. He would have done it anyway, in secret, but this time he was allowed. He sat at the table, grinning at the toy then started to play with it. She snatched it off him, saying he could put it there, but he couldn't play.

"It's prohibited."

He burst into tears. He calmed down and opened his book. I've got him to write in pen – it's easier for me to read – though he still uses a pencil at school. He doesn't have a pen licence. His handwriting isn't very good. On the page where he'd done my homework, a splash had smudged the ink and dried. I stared at it.

"Is that a teardrop?" He nodded. I was horrified. "What happened?"

"The homework was too hard."

I thought, *A lot of crying goes on in this house.* Yet this was my fault. It was my homework.

"It won't happen again."

"What's that on your finger?"

There was a plaster.

"I cut it. Not on purpose. I'm easily hurt."

"How did you do it?"

"With scissors."

Kirin was sceptical. He wanted to know how a grown man could cut himself with a pair of scissors. He didn't say it. I could tell.

"I was using one of the blades like a knife, and it slipped. I said to myself, 'How could a man your age do such a stupid thing? What a fool I am!"

While I spoke, Kirin observed me. I don't know if he believed me, but by the end, he was happier.

"Have you done anything stupid lately?" I whispered. "I won't tell."

"I threw a piece of cheese at a fox, with a nail in it." Kirin spoke softly. "When he ate it, the nail was pushing at his cheek. I could see the lump."

"You shouldn't give food to animals you don't know." Pause. "If you hadn't mentioned the nail, I would have believed you. It's a good story, though."

For his school homework, he had to read a passage and answer questions. It was the old tale about the wolf and pigs but a funny version for older, more sophisticated children.

"You don't eat pork, do you?" I asked. Just warming up.

"It's *haram*."

"Kirin!" Mummy called from the kitchen, adding something sharp in Bengali.

He rubbed his eyes and said he was tired. He had started doing that whenever he had to read.

"I should give you a spanking," I said in a very low voice. "When you're twenty-five, will you still be doing that, rubbing your eyes? I won't know what to do with you." He suddenly looked sad. "What's the matter?" He didn't answer. "What is it?"

"You won't be tutoring me then."

"I could be. You might do English at university. Your mother might ring me and say she needs an outstanding tutor."

He still looked sad – worse, actually. Then I understood.

"You think I'll be dead when you're twenty-five?" He nodded. "I'm not that old!" But he needed cheering up again. "People die all the time. I could die on the way home, on the bus."

"How can you die on the bus?"

"You can slip or get thrown out."

I'd seen it happen, both things, though no one died, and it didn't convince Kirin. But it made him smile.

Busting

In the dining room, fixed to the wall, there's a giant bookshelf shaped like a steam engine. Kirin loves it. He ignores the books. In fact, they're Mummy's – law, finance, psychology. They'll be his one day. He'll chug off to any profession. Meanwhile, trains are fun, and learning can be, though Mummy doesn't think so. When she picked that bookshelf, she missed the irony.

Fun or not, we need a break. Every lesson, Kirin asks to go to the toilet. Every time, I say no.

"I'm busting!"

He presses his thighs together and screws up his face. I let him go. Who knows? He might need to. Once, I added, "Don't break your leg on the stairs. I'd have to go home early."

He went out. There was a catastrophic noise, a series of loud thumps, like a boy breaking his leg on the stairs. He appeared in the doorway with a cunning grin. Then he ran upstairs.

I thought I could smell something. He hadn't done it, had he? I peered at the empty seat, leaned down and sniffed. I really did. Children wet themselves; they vomit. They do in my lessons, anyway. But it didn't seem right to wet yourself one moment and break your leg the next. No one could be so unlucky, not even Kirin.

When he got back, he announced, "I'm the most intelligent child in my class."

"It's not very intelligent to go to the toilet when you don't need to."

He had homework from school. The expanded column method. An old friend. It was no match for us. For English, there were antonyms. They were no match either. For *fun*, we got *unfun*. And synonyms for *small* – we came up with *micro*-banana. Then similes. There was a bowl of fruit on the table. We discovered that my brain was *like a fruit salad*. Next, rhymes for *mumble*. We alternated. He said *rumble*. I said *humble*. *Crumble, stumble, tumble*. My turn again. I paused then said *bumble*. He giggled. I knew he would.

We had to put the words in a sentence, not one sentence for all of them, though we did that, too. His teacher wanted 'wow words.' We let her have them. Kirin was fond of *flabbergasted*. We checked the spelling in the dictionary, the biggest one, before creating, "Kirin may be miniscule, but he's flabbergobsmackeredlyblasted intelligent."

It was hard to be appropriate in every sentence, not violent or off-colour or in some way disturbing, for his teacher, at least. I tried my best. So did Kirin. If something I said sounded wrong, he'd go, "Too violent!"

"The rumble in my stomach had no earthly explanation."

"Too violent!"

"The humble shark apologised for eating the lady."

"Too violent!"

"The family car tumbled into the sea."

"Sharks swam in through the windows."

"Too violent!" I said. "I stumbled on a baby's booty washed up on the shore."

"Too violent!!"

Each time he said it, his voice got louder.

"Kirin!" Mummy barked. She was in the kitchen, eavesdropping.

I told him his teacher would know that someone was helping with his homework; no one his age could write sentences like that.

"If she asks, tell the truth. Otherwise, you'll look silly."

He didn't speak, but he understood. No one wants to look silly. It still happens, of course.

Schoolwork done, it was time for my activities.

"Write the date," I said. The fifth of September came out 19.15.15. I said, "This is pointless."

He looked upset.

"It's as if you think I'm useless."

"No. If I thought you were useless, I'd say, 'You're useless.' But I don't think you are, so I didn't say it. I meant if you can't get the date right, there's no point in going on." Pause. "Stop trying to make me feel sorry for you. If anyone needs feeling sorry for, it's me. I've got a boy who refuses to write the date."

We don't do the date anymore.

"Has he been behaving?" Mummy asked when she came in at the end.

"Oh, yes."

"He left the room."

"He needed a comfort break."

She almost smiled. I was learning how to deal with Mummy.

Money well spent

Kirin told me to say the letter x five times. I did as he wanted, with modest pauses in between. He understood but tried again. He's only seven.

"Say it quickly!"

"I used to be a boy, you know."

He started singing in a baby voice.

"Kirin!" Mummy called. We went back to work. He asked in a low voice, "Are you gay?"

It was, I should point out, 'apropos of nothing,' as people used to say when I was seven. In his homework, as in our lesson, there is no sexual content. It doesn't feature greatly in Year 3, not in the syllabus, anyway. But I had to say something.

"Have you been talking to the bad boys at school?"

"They're just boys."

"You don't talk to girls, do you?" But he'd lowered his voice, so I added kindly, "Not at your age."

For comprehension, there was an extract from a play. Some children were watching a magic show. A rude boy was trying to spoil things, making comments which he thought were clever. The magician would surely take revenge. (What he might do was the last question.) We began our answers. The first question was about the setting. The first question is meant to be easy, for the children, let alone the teacher, but I wasn't sure. My spells weren't working. I said to Kirin, "You're good at questions. What's the setting for the play?"

He wasn't sure either. I had a few ideas.

"In the text, a floor is mentioned, so they must be in a building, which is all we can tell for certain. There are balloons in the illustration, and the word *party* is in question two, so it's probably a children's party. Still, the balloons could be part of the magic show, and the whole point of doing comprehension is to find answers in the text. You shouldn't have to look at the next question or the illustration. In other words, it's a stupid question. One more thing. If the characters are gay, it's fine."

I was speaking softly too. To finish off, I raised my voice.

"Put all that in your own words,"

He began to write. With his free hand, he covered his work, the way a child does in a test. It didn't take him long. I read what he'd written.

"It's a stupid question."

At the end of the lesson, Mummy came in as usual. She wasn't happy. To me, she declared, "He didn't behave well today;" to Kirin, "I heard everything. Everything."

He grinned.

"He's a lot better than he used to be," I said. I wasn't just defending Kirin. I was defending myself. If she knew he'd been misbehaving, she would also know that I'd done nothing about it. But she agreed with what I said.

"The school said he's improving. He's in the top group for English now, the same as maths."

I remembered something he'd told me about his homework. His teacher had asked where all the crazy, fabulous sentences came from.

"What did you say?" I'd replied.

"I said I've got a tutor."

"What did she say?"

"She was pleased."

I repeated this to Mummy – he hadn't told her – adding, "His teacher's happy because she'll take the credit for his improvement. The headteacher will love her. Everybody's happy."

"Everybody's happy," echoed Mummy. "It's money well spent."

I realised that she was saying thank you, that this was the closest I would get to hearing those two words from Mummy. It took a moment for all the realising, then I just said "Thank you."

The Lost Lending Library

There was something exciting at Kirin's school. The Lost Lending Library. If you didn't know what it really was, it might have looked like an old London bus, a double-decker. It turned up in the yard on Wednesday morning, just like that, and nobody knew where it came from, not even the teachers. That's what the headteacher said in morning assembly. Every class, she stated, could go inside. There were, however, one or two things the children should remember. To begin with, when they arrived, the door would be open, wide open, and they'd see a man reading a book. He mightn't notice them at first, so they'd have to cough politely. The head also spoke about the chairs. Each one was made out of books, but it was all right; the children were allowed to sit on them.

When it was their turn, Kirin's teacher, Miss So-and-so, brought the class down. They'd had to wait a very long time. Let's hope it's still there! Maybe it got lost somewhere else. But it was in the yard, and sure enough, the door was open, wide open, and they could see a man reading a book, sitting on a seat made of dictionaries, and he didn't notice them, just as the headteacher said.

"Remember what you have to do," Miss So-and-so prompted.

Someone coughed, another child followed, then everybody did. Nothing happened. The man didn't hear.

"Cough louder," miss said. But it was no good. He still didn't notice. "This time, let's do one big ahem, all together, no shouting, though."

It worked. The man looked around at the crowd of little faces as if he was waking up, and said in a startled voice, "Have you been there long? Come in, come in!"

There was one more room, he explained, further in, full of books to read. He showed them a bookcase that was really a door with no key or handle. Instead, you put a book through a slot, and the door opened by itself. The man let someone do it. They all went in.

"Inside," Kirin said, "there were millions of books, and all the chairs were made of books too."

"Millions?" I queried. "Did you count them? Did you use the expanded column method?"

Kirin chuckled. And was the library really lost? There was no name on it, Kirin said. The sign, I admitted, could have fallen off as it bumped across London, searching for its home; but lost or not, a library had a name, and every book in every library had the name stamped inside the front cover. He was surrounded by books, *millions* of them. Did he not open one? Kirin didn't answer.

"Why didn't the man hear you? He wasn't deaf, was he?" Kirin shook his head guardedly. "He was just pretending not to hear. Why?" Kirin didn't know. "He was showing you how magical books can be. When you read them, you lose track of the world around you." Kirin wasn't chuckling anymore. "And when you put the book in the slot, and the shelves opened like a door, what did that mean?"

We'd been doing metaphor, but I didn't wait for an answer.

"Books open up a world of adventure."

Back in the real world, Kirin had some homework to do, a list of questions and a sentence to finish: 'Since I visited the Lost Lending Library, I...' I told him to say something his teacher would like, "For example, 'I've decided to read as many books as possible.'"

Kirin thought a moment then started writing. Though he frequently annoys me, when he gets down to writing, it's worth it just to watch. He's so serious, so composed, I forgive him everything. He rarely writes much, but this time I could tell he'd done his best. He had really concentrated. When he stopped work, I took his paper and read aloud, "Since I visited the Lost Lending Library, I thought they are the most boring places in the world."

I'm a big deaf one

Kirin was wearing a new T-shirt. It had *I'm a big deal #1* on the front. I studied it then said, as if I was reading aloud, "I'm a big deaf one." He chuckled. I added, "Have a comfort break."

"Why do you need a comfort break?"

It was Mummy. She was in the hall. The lesson had just started. She walked in suspiciously.

"He needs some water," I replied.

"Are you eating chocolate?" she asked.

"He's got some biscuits," I replied. "He was hungry."

When I mentioned the comfort break, I didn't think Mummy could hear, but she has sharp ears. I used the term ironically. Perhaps she heard that, too. After she came in, Kirin had not spoken. I realised I was answering for him. It was something else that Mummy might notice.

"Make sure you listen!" she said. She went out, he got his drink, and we relaxed.

With Mummy, it's all questions or commands. Though she banned toys, he's still smuggling them in. A while ago, we thought up a way to talk about them which, if she was listening, she wouldn't understand. Instead of *car*, we say *three-letter word*. For *ball*, we say *three-and-half* as *four-letter word* won't do.

"Can I have that three-letter word?" I say in a loud voice when I've had enough of his Batmobile, and nobody gets into trouble.

There was an English exercise. He had to guess words with missing letters. Each time, three consonants were given, in the right order. It was difficult – for me, anyway. One of them I couldn't do at all. The consonants were *m, p* and *t*.

"Armpit!" cried Kirin and produced a toy car. I couldn't say no.

At the end of the lesson, Kirin's face was shining. He told Mummy he got *armpit* before I did, adding, "He said it's his favourite word!"

It was true. I had. Mummy smirked. She's been doing that lately, a strange shade of mirth on her jaw.

"I may have exaggerated," I said.

She smirked again. Then she confided something, which was strange too, coming from Mummy. One of Kirin's cousins, a girl, was better than him in English, while he was better at Maths. Mummy couldn't understand. That's what she said, but I think she could. She just didn't like it. He had to be number one in everything.

Intellectual naughtiness

Mummy says that Kirin doesn't listen; he doesn't concentrate. She's told us more than once. We need reminding. Perhaps we don't listen.

"He's still improving, though, in English."

His teacher had told her. I looked at her. She was being positive. It always surprised me. She seemed surprised too. How could he improve when we wasted all that time, when we chatted about things that had nothing to do with the lesson? But this was what he needed. It was the reason he improved. She couldn't understand, but what we did worked, so she let it happen. She had something else to say.

"He wasn't happy with his teacher at school. She used to shout at him. He didn't want to go to school at all. He wouldn't get up in the morning. I was desperate. That's when I rang your agency."

I thought, *I've saved her son's education*. She must be delighted. She just can't say so. Nice and impersonal – that's Mummy. She started talking about the 11-plus. Now he'd agreed to go to school, this boy in Year 3, she was planning out his whole education.

"The 11-plus doesn't follow the school syllabus," I said. "It's much harder."

It's also, as the name suggests, for eleven-year-olds. Kirin is only eight. I told her the books to buy, for ages 8-9. She said she'd order them on the internet. Next week, when I came in, a parcel of books was on the table. She opened it in front of me.

"I don't know if they're the right ones," she said indifferently.

They weren't the right ones. They were for ages 10-11. It was written clearly on the cover. I wondered if she'd done it on purpose or simply not concentrated. Either way, Mummy hadn't listened. I wanted to tell her; I wanted to very badly, but I didn't. And no one shouted at her.

The power of books. Mummy worked it out a long time ago. The more books Kirin had, and the harder they were, the more intelligent he would be. She bought a series of paperbacks with pastel-shaded covers. He was very proud of them, the covers, at least. When he showed me the books, he was really showing me the colours. He claimed he was reading them and had finished the yellow one already. The book looked unopened. I think it was just his favourite colour. I picked it up.

"You say you've read it. What's the seventh word on page ten?"

"That's not fair!"

He began fiddling and asked the time.

"You can't wait to get rid of me?"

"I want you to go, and I don't."

Mummy had also bought some mental tests designed for year 6. We're working through them. Each test has twenty questions. Kirin gets the first fifteen right then starts to make mistakes. He puts his head on the table and rubs his eyes.

"You weren't really listening," I said after one question.

"I was. I just misheard."

"Most teachers call that not listening." He reached for a book. "That's odd," I said. "When boys fiddle in my lesson, it's usually a car or a ball. You fiddled with a book. Your naughtiness is intellectual."

He was doing ancient Egypt at school. Mummy bought two encyclopaedias and some more reference books. He had reached for one of these, about King Tut, the nine-year-old pharaoh. Being a boy, Tut had tutors; being a king, he had twelve, the wisest ones, old men with long, white beards and robes. Also being king, he could throw them to the crocodiles whenever he liked (there was a tank beside the temple), so he often had fewer than twelve.

"Just think of it," I said, "a tank of crocodiles in your back garden." His eyes strayed to the window. "One more tutor gone."

"How long have we got now?"

I was sick of the question.

"Only fifteen minutes," I said. "Yay!" adding a couple of fist pumps with my right arm. His face clouded, but it takes more than that to make him cry.

You know the piles of books on the table. When I started, there were two, but it's three or four now. I used to wonder if they were there all week in the same place, waiting for me and Kirin. They're so heavy, who would move them? Well, Kirin does. Each Saturday, he has to carry them down from his room, one pile after the other. He does it before the lesson, when I'm not there, but he was late once, and I saw him. He said he carries them back up as well. He's so slow, so careful. It's like a ritual. You can understand Mummy. They're his books; they need to be with him, in his room with his other possessions or in the lesson. At the same time, carrying the books himself will make him more responsible; he'll have more respect for them and the knowledge they contain. In short, he'll be a better student. Besides, if *he* does it, she doesn't have to. To me, watching it all – the piles, the steep stairs, the little boy – it was like torture. It was just another insult from Mummy, as you give a man a shovel and make him dig his own grave.

You're not perfect

Last Saturday, when I got to Kirin's, the front door was opened by his childminder. It's the term he uses. It's a bit clinical, especially from a child. He doesn't say *nanny*, much less her name. I suppose he's just repeating what the adults say, but he lowers his voice too, even if she's outside, as though he'd rather not refer to her at all, and his tone is cooler.

I agree; the woman is annoying. I christened her Crazy-lady. When Mummy's home, she's hardly visible, but as soon as Mummy leaves, she takes charge. She's always poking around like a little Mummy, saying bossy things, so we can't relax. I think Mummy told her to. Still, when she opens the front door, it means one thing that's best for everybody: Mummy isn't home.

"Do beetles have blood?" Kirin asked. At first, I thought he didn't know, but he was testing me. I said I wasn't sure.

"They've got black blood," he informed me. It hadn't come up in science. One lunchtime, he'd been playing with a friend. The two boys had found some large stones. They tried to hit a window on the first floor, but their arms weren't strong enough. (He didn't say that.) When they missed the window, they found a beetle and smashed that instead. It wasn't quite so hard. (He didn't say that, either.) I summed up thus far.

"So, you just happened to have a rock in your hand and thought, 'Oh, I wonder what a broken window looks like.'" Kirin grinned. "You couldn't break the window, so you thought, 'Oh, I wonder what colour blood beetles have.'" He grinned again. I hadn't finished. "Throughout the history of human existence, men have used science as an excuse for cruelty."

His school homework was to make an information leaflet. He said he had to use bullet points.

"Isn't that a bit violent?" I asked. "At school, you aren't allowed toy guns, but you have bullet points. Mention it to your teacher on Monday."

Kirin grinned again. His bullets were blobs, anyway.

"Let's call them cockroach points. You can mention that, too."

He grinned his biggest grin and said in a loud voice, "Cockroach points!"

I popped a sweet in my mouth. It was lemon flavour.

"For my throat," I said. I offered one to Kirin. He sucked it manfully for a few seconds, spat it in his palm then went upstairs without a word. I didn't do it on purpose. Children like sweets.

"Kirin!" called the childminder from the kitchen, like Mummy, less rudely, though. "What are you doing?"

When he sat down again, I screwed up my sweet wrapper and threw it at him, aiming for his mouth. I missed. I held my hands up.

"It wasn't me. It was the poltergeist." I thought he wouldn't know about those. But he did, from some computer game. "Let's face it," I said. "Most of what you know comes from a machine. Spell *poltergeist*." He got it wrong, of course. "*I* before *e*, except after *c*."

"There's no *c* in *poltergeist*!"

"Just testing."

At last, the lesson was over. The childminder came in just like Mummy.

"He was very good today," I said, as I say to Mummy.

"I could hear you being naughty," she said, the way Mummy does.

"I said *very good*, not perfect. Even I'm not perfect. You may be, though."

I wouldn't say that to Mummy. Kirin was standing in front of her. He turned his little face up and chanted, "You're not perfect! You're not perfect!"

He wouldn't say that to Mummy either. We were being cheeky to the childminder.

Sixty minutes of your life

Once again, Mummy wasn't home. When I arrived, Kirin was hiding under the table. He kept me waiting for a bit (he knows about suspense) then jumped out as if he was going to bite me. I think he has shark DNA. He can't stop talking about them. He told me how a dozen sharks came down through his bedroom ceiling wearing jet packs. He's very fond of hammerheads.

"Isn't broom head more appropriate," I said, "or vacuum-cleaner-fitting head? Show me your teeth." He's growing adult ones. "You look more like a shark than they do."

He asked about Douglas, a boy I used to tutor. They're the same age. Like Kirin, Douglas hid when I arrived, but he wasn't playing. He screamed when I rang the doorbell, crawled behind the sofa and wouldn't come out.

"Did you like him?"

"No. I like you better. He did hug me once when I was going."

"So, he liked you."

"He liked me when I was going." I glanced around. The lesson was half over. "You can have a comfort break."

"I don't need one."

"I need a rest, so have one now."

He left the room. Just then, Mummy got home and saw him in the hall.

"What are you doing?"

"He told me to go to the toilet."

He was hesitant. At times, your own words surprise you. I'd been naughty, and Kirin understood. If I could be naughty, so could he When he returned, he played nonstop. There was always something in his hand – a car, a ball, a jigsaw piece. In the end, I got cross. Kirin looked down.

"Sometimes, I don't like it when you come."

"You go on too long. I don't like being cross. If I liked being cross, I would have been cross an hour ago. Mummy is paying a lot of money for this lesson, and we're not doing any work. One day, I won't come anymore. Nothing lasts forever."

Our eyes met. It was too late. I had said it. Kirin thought a moment.

"Something lasts forever."

"Do question three." A silence, then I asked forlornly, "What lasts forever?"

"Space."

"I meant time. But you're right. The stars are so far away, the distance is measured in years – how long it takes their light to reach us. You know how fast light is."

"You see the lightning before you hear the thunder."

He had chatted, but I knew what he was thinking. *Nothing lasts forever*. We did some more questions. When the lesson was done, his mother came in.

"I could hear you being naughty."

She meant Kirin.

"Near the end," I said. "He was letting off steam." I turned to Kirin. "You did get up and run around the room." He grinned. I went on to Mummy, "He's come a long way."

"He said he wants to do an extra hour with you."

We were doing two already. I turned to him again.

"That's sixty minutes of your life."

He went solemn then walked across and whispered in Mummy's ear. She didn't answer. Instead, she spoke to me.

"Is he improving?"

"Yes. He wrote some excellent sentences today."

Kirin ran for his book, found a page of similes and read them out. After each one, he looked up and grinned.

"The grass was as soft as green cotton wool."

Mummy smirked.

"The lightning struck like dragon's fire."

She stopped smirking, though she still didn't speak. She's not short of words. She thinks before she says them. Things like *Well done*, she avoids. Sometimes, she won't speak at all. Now, she just said, "You can do three hours."

You've had lots of practice in your long life

Last Saturday, when I got there, Kirin wasn't hiding beneath the table. It's what he usually does when Mummy isn't home. He was on his chair instead, holding a pencil. There were printed sheets in front of him, a sample maths paper. The 11-plus. I know the school. It has one of the hardest exams.

"My mother said I have to do at least four pages."

"OK. Let's have a look."

He might have managed question one, even question two, but there were over twenty on the first four pages. There was no point in starting.

"I can see it's too difficult. I've had lots of practice in my long life."

I told him I'd explain to Mummy when she got home; he wouldn't get into trouble. We then discussed ways to hoodwink her, like how to hide a toy car if she came in unexpectedly.

"See what you can do. You have thirty seconds. You wouldn't have three if I was Mummy."

He put the car on the table in front of him and piled his books and papers across it. He tried to make the pile seem natural, but it just looked a mess. I said it wasn't a good idea; Mummy didn't like mess; she'd tell him to clean it up, and she'd wait there and watch while he did it. He'd already started tidying. He knew Mummy better than I did.

I suggested keeping the toy behind his giant pencil case and slipping it inside when she came in. There'd be enough room for a Belgian minibus and the small fist which enclosed it. He smiled.

"What if she caught me with my hand inside?"

"It's *your* pencil case. Suitcase," I corrected. Mummy knew very well; she herself had bought it for him, the biggest and most expensive she could find. But she couldn't see through the flap, so she wouldn't see the toy. If she saw his hand inside, he mustn't pull it out too quickly. He'd look guilty.

"Just say, 'Where's that red pen?' and peek beneath the flap. I'll say, 'Don't worry. I don't need it now. You haven't made any mistakes.'"

Mummy would poke around for a minute, on the coffee table, at the bookshelf, then slip out in silence.

"Children lie badly," I concluded. "Some adults do too. I'm a very good liar."

"You've had lots of practice in your long life."

Mummy still wasn't home. It was pay day. She pays four weeks in advance. It saves her the bother, she said, of bringing cash every week. If she's going out, she leaves the money in the bookcase, near my chair. Kirin calls it his cash machine. Today, the machine was empty. I hadn't seen her for a few weeks. I thought she might have forgotten, so I decided to text her. Kirin stood at my shoulder and waited for me to type.

"Don't stand there. You make me nervous. When I talk about money, I sound grovelling or rude. I'll show you later." I texted for a while then stopped and pretended to read what I'd done. "Kirin is being very naughty." Then I looked up. He was watching me with his half smile. "Only kidding!"

Mummy replied immediately. She hadn't forgotten; she'd be home soon. It was true, at least the part about being home soon. When she came in, she repeated, "I hadn't forgotten!"

It wasn't shrill, but she needed to stop saying it. I mentioned the sample paper. I told her it was too hard. I didn't mention her command to do four pages. She didn't either.

"I just wanted to give you an idea," she explained, "of what the school required."

That's typical Mummy

Kirin, Year 3, said Mummy gave him Year 8 maths.

"I believe it," I replied. She hadn't told me. I wouldn't understand all that, the special algebra that flows between them.

It was Eid. Kirin showed me his presents. There's always plenty of those. In religion, as in math, Mummy is unsparing. This year, he got a cell phone and a watch.

"I don't need to ask you the time anymore," he yawned. "I've got two things to show me."

In case he doesn't get it the first time, I thought. It wasn't fair on Mummy. She probably didn't mean it that way. He also had new pyjamas, but they made him hot. She didn't mean that, either. He hadn't slept well. He said he'd told her, but she hadn't believed him.

He'd had a haircut, too. I thought, *That's typical Mummy. She gives with one hand and takes with the other.* I'm a bit anti-Mummy at the moment.

"Wouldn't you like long, golden hair?" I asked. My most unctuous voice.

"No."

"I don't believe you."

There was homework from school. He had to do a comprehension about King Arthur and the sword in the stone. The first question ran, 'What time of year is it, and how do you know?' I thought it was too easy. Worse, it was boring. They could have asked something else, a more engaging question. *How did he feel when the sword came out? Like a king?* I didn't wait for Kirin. I answered for him.

"It says it was freezing, and it's not freezing in summer, you idiot."

It just came out, like a prompt blade. Kirin bolted. He got as far as the corridor, where the childminder caught him and sent him back.

"What happened?" I asked. He was hurt, disbelieving.

"You called me an idiot."

"No, I didn't. I was talking about the person who wrote the question. It's too easy. You're too clever. I never call my pupils idiots even if they are. Only an idiot would think I called him an idiot."

He regarded me. He has a sense of humour. He's smart, too, smarter than I was at his age. And he gets over things quickly. He doesn't sulk like me. I asked him to read the rest of the passage aloud. He reached the part where Arthur does his bit.

"The sword came out," Kirin read, "like a knife through butter."

"I knew it!" I cried. "I thought of that, 'like a knife through butter.'"

"But you didn't say it."

I regarded him.

"For a child, you're very sceptical." I pointed to the dictionaries. "Actually, it should have said butter at room temperature. Chilled wouldn't work."

"Or melted."

"You mean they should have said it, or it wouldn't work."

It wasn't revenge. I wasn't sure what he meant. When he didn't answer, I went on.

"You're right, I think. If the butter melted, it wouldn't work either. The knife would be on it, not inside it, and you could just pick it up. But why didn't they say 'like a knife through butter at room temperature?'"

He said he wasn't sure.

"It's ugly; it spoils the rhythm, and you don't need to say it. People know what you mean. That's ugly as well, when you explain too much, like your old tutor." Kirin's mouth opened, but I got in first again. "I know. I'm ugly too."

The Home and School Diary

It's September. Kirin has made it to Year 4. Mummy told him to show me his new planner. She said it in her stern voice. The planner was in his bedroom. He had to go and get it whether he wanted to or not. Her stern voice, her only voice, really. Perhaps they baby-talk when I'm not around, and tickle each other. I could ask him.

There's always a homework diary, a planner. Every school has one. The name will vary. Kirin's school has gone a step further. The cover says *Home and School Diary*. Mummy likes it, of course. It implies commitment twenty-four hours a day.

When he reappeared, she told him to read out the Expectations. She reminded him to behave.

"Do as well as you can," meaning *Do even better*, then she left the room.

The Expectations. Rehearsing them would highlight their importance and help to fix them in his brain. There was a list inside the cover. Mummy likes lists, as you know. She makes them herself then sticks them on the wall. She loves bullet points, adores imperatives. Here was a real list, official-looking, with all the right things, if rather positive (numbingly, in fact – it's a London primary school), more 'thou shalt' than 'shalt not,' unlike Mummy, but then, like Mummy, short of clues on how to deal with failure.

On the facing page, there was an illustration, with the same title in bubble letters and exclamation marks, set against a warm, yellow sun. It was a Year 6 poster. It wasn't bad, if predictable. The whole class had done one, Kirin said, at the end of last year, and the teacher picked the best (or his pet pupil's). A girl had signed it. By the look of it – the time it must have taken – she had signed up to the ethos, too, or else she was just fond of her teacher.

"Did you know her?" I asked. No answer. She was older than Kirin, and he doesn't speak to girls. She didn't sound like him either. I wondered about her, the girl who pleased her teacher and said what he wanted to hear. When she drew the poster, she was leaving, going to secondary school, and now she was gone. She could smile at her old school, at the platitudes, but kindly. She never had to listen to Mummy.

"Read it," I said, like Mummy, without the coldness. More silence.

When she told him to read, then left the room, it was classic Mummy. She was busy; she couldn't stay, and she didn't need to. She knew what the planner said, every word. She had picked through it like a scholar. And when she left, it showed her confidence – in herself more than Kirin. Mummy had spoken. She expected him to read it, so he would, no matter where she was, whether he wanted to or not. If he seemed reluctant, I'd remind him. In short, Mummy had met the first Expectation, the most important one: *Believe in yourself* (or look as if you do). She had more than met it. She embodied it like a living poster.

"Read it. Mummy told you to."

He looked away. I thought, *We've rubbed his nose in it enough*, and read it for him, with a hint of irony. He would have noticed. The list itself begged for sarcasm. *Expectation* wasn't right. It was exhortation in a printed form; the sort of thing Mummy admires, despite the warmth and brightness: a piece of paper, a list of empty words.

What a fool

Crazy-lady, Kirin's childminder, has finished. She resigned, or Mummy sacked her. When I press the bell, a new lady comes to the door. I asked him if he liked her.

"No. She's too old."

"Old people are best."

I call her Ancient-lady. I don't dislike her, not yet. You never know. She mightn't interfere or spy on us like Mummy or Crazy-lady when Mummy wasn't there. I gave him a few tips on innocence or not looking guilty; how to sit still, for instance, and not call out, so ladies wouldn't be suspicious. As for the Ancient one, I'd assert myself before she settled in and felt more important than me, as she would very soon, if she didn't already.

The sofa is next to our table, so it's great for spying. Ancient-Lady saw it. The first time she sat there, I asked her not to. She didn't seem to mind. She got up, went out and hasn't used it since.

"I like her," I said. "You might too one day. Did you like Crazy-lady at the start?"

"No."

"Did you like me?"

I remember the first lesson; how cold he was, and Mummy. He asked for the toilet three times – in one hour. I told Mummy afterwards. She was annoyed. With me.

"You can't stop someone going to the toilet!"

Good old Mummy. She defends him when she shouldn't and attacks him when she doesn't need to. There are parents like that. They scold their children tirelessly but get upset when someone else tries to. She expects him to sit with me for three hours. She'd want a break, wouldn't she, for herself? For her son, nothing. It's all "Concentrate!" He's still playful and wants to trick her. When he sneaks into the kitchen, I remind him not to steal too many sweets. She might notice. She might be counting. You know Mummy.

His father is suspicious too. He's only come in once in two years, but even then, he was negative. He stood over Kirin and said in a cross voice, "Have you done your homework?"

That's all he said. Are they showing me how to act in the lesson, or are they the ones acting? *We don't spoil him.* Or – and this is most likely – are they just unpleasant? They do see his earning potential. The more he studies, the more he'll earn. It's obvious. Right now, he avoids work. He said he hurt his finger. I told Mummy.

"He may recover when I go," I joked.

He asked for the doctor. She smirked. *What a fool!* When she judges him, she uses adult standards, but when she tells him what to do, she expects the obedience of a child. She's not so stern with herself. One lesson, she changed a light bulb above the sofa. It wasn't going well.

"Shit!" she said, softly, but I heard. Kirin did too.

"Pardon my French," he smiled. He's only eight. I thought, *He's better behaved than she is.* What if *he* said "Shit!"?

We didn't need the light. She could have done it later. She distracts him like this without realising or without caring. Then, she rebukes him when he gets distracted.

Ancient-lady didn't last long. There's a new lady, who's a lot younger. We had to choose a name, something with an A-sound to go with *lady* and a mocking edge. Kirin was stuck, so I picked for him. At first, I wouldn't tell. It was rude, I said. Naturally, he begged me.

"Anal-lady," I revealed at last. "It's a science word."

I needed to explain. The name was perfect – the assonance, the elision, the meaning – but it wasn't child-friendly. He knew it was wrong. I confessed, "I don't think Mummy would like it."

"She wouldn't like *Crazy-lady*."

The webcams

Anal-lady hates me. She'd hate me even more if she knew what I called her. Like all the ladies – Crazy, Ancient, Mummy herself – she's Bengali, but they weren't all angry. Anal-lady is. Just knowing I'm there upsets her. The first time we met, at the front door, she was sullen, like a teenager. Perhaps she is. When I said hello, she didn't answer. It's not as though I'd said something rude – 'Not another one! How long will <u>you</u> last?' – and I didn't look cross. *We've got a new Mummy,* I thought. She's never spoken to me, that day or any, and I haven't spoken to her again, except on one occasion. She was in the kitchen, watching television. It was too loud; it was distracting Kirin. That's what I said. I told her to switch it off. She did, but it was like the front door when she let me in for the lesson. She didn't want to, and her face showed it. She had no choice, of course. It was her job. If she refused, I could tell Mummy she'd distracted us. She wouldn't have a job any longer. But anger doesn't stop in the face, not with most people. If she wasn't plotting against me already, she is now. She can tell her own things to Mummy.

Mummy is getting more suspicious. She isn't home much. When she is, she sits in the kitchen, listening, like a predator waiting to pounce. You know what she's like. I think we're meant to fear her. Once, when Kirin left his chair, she barked instantly, "Does he often do that?"

"Not really," I said. It was true, though I would have said it anyhow. She didn't believe me. She didn't say so, and I couldn't see her, but I could tell. She was in the kitchen, thinking, in silence, the kind you can hear, full of meanness, like Anal-lady. The next week, I didn't see her at all. She had left in the morning, Kirin said, and was coming back on Sunday. She's done it twice. She doesn't tell him where she goes. She doesn't have to. The first time, I saw a webcam on the floor, plugged in the wall.

"It's something to do with her office," Kirin said.

The second time, I saw the webcam again, along with two others, pointing at the table and each exit. They were switched on, with the light showing.

"It's so Mummy knows what I'm doing," he admitted. He might as well. I'd work it out. He was sad. "She can see me on her phone."

Maybe she never watches; she set it up to scare him. Either way, I didn't like it. The absences, the secrecy, the spying – does she work for MI5? She can do what she wants. One day, Kirin will too. She's offended us so often, but still, with the webcams, she surprised me. It out-Mummied Mummy.

I prodded a camera with my toe so it faced away. It occurred to me, as my shoe poked forward, that she might be watching. Kirin turned a camera to the wall. He had followed my example like a good pupil. I forgot to tell him, if she asked, to say I did it. She might sack me, but she might anyway.

Conspirators, we went on learning. Sadly, though. At school, he was doing imagery. His teacher said a metaphor was a weak simile. I said it wasn't.

"Even if it was, does that mean anything to an eight-year-old?"

He thought for a second then smiled ironically and shook his head. We'd done metaphors.

"Can you think of an example?" I asked. He grinned and repeated one of mine, for sunset. (I say *mine*.)

"The orange ball sank into the ocean."

"And left not a ripple behind."

I won't forget you

I've had my final lesson with Kirin. Mummy hasn't told me. It's only Tuesday. She cancels on a Thursday. She sends a text that starts *Hi Graham*, like a friend, but doesn't put her name at the end. This time – the last – she doesn't have to tell me. I've worked it out for myself.

Two weeks ago, she wasn't home. She'd forgotten to leave the payment. When the lesson was over, she still hadn't arrived. She texted the childminder to say she was coming. She didn't say when. And she didn't text me. I waited for ten minutes then phoned her. She was sorry; could I wait? She didn't say how long. I was late for my next lesson.

"If you'd told me earlier…," I said and left.

The next week, she wasn't in either. The money was in an envelope in the bookshelf, Kirin's cash machine. It's what she normally did if she knew she wouldn't see me. This time, however, when I picked up the envelope, it didn't feel right. It was too thin. She always paid four weeks. I checked inside. There was only enough money for two, up to and including the present.

"Is Mummy stopping our lesson?" I asked. A pause.

"I don't think I'm meant to tell you this. She said she's cancelling the tuition. She said I wasn't doing any work."

"Would you have let me go without telling me?" No answer. It wasn't a fair question for a child. "Did you ask her to stop the lesson?" This was even worse. It was stupid. It didn't deserve an answer.

"No."

"At least we can say goodbye."

"You'll have less money."

It was my own fault. If I'd waited that day when she was late, she would have paid four weeks. She wouldn't have cancelled. I'd held my tongue for more than two years then, for two seconds, let go. *If you'd told me earlier....* I said it quietly, without irritation, but I corrected her. It's worth the sack with Mummy. She was right. He wasn't doing enough work, but he never was nor ever would be in her opinion. She was blaming him for her own mistakes.

"He must be sad," a parent said when I mentioned our three-hour lesson. Kirin mentioned it too a few weeks ago. He asked me if we could do an hour less. I didn't answer. Mummy might have cancelled the lot. That's what I told myself. I was right, probably, but it was the money talking. I was no better than her.

Kirin is often sad. I once said, as a joke, that we'd be having tuition when he was twenty-five. He nearly cried. He thought I'd be dead then. He has just turned nine. I didn't even make his tenth birthday.

"Did you get lots of presents?" No reply. I tried again. "We had some fun. Remember our crazy sentences?"

No reply. There weren't many answers that day.

"I wish Mummy would let you come, not as a tutor." Silence. "I'll miss you."

"I'll miss you too."

"She might forget to cancel or change her mind. I might convince her."

I shook my head. The money on the shelf had spoken. The money always had. But I shook too firmly. He was nine. It brought tears to his eyes.

"Can I have a comfort break?"

He needed one. I needed one myself. I'd wondered, off and on, how I'd feel when the lessons ended. I was finding out now.

Sometimes, words don't work. We did a page of non-verbal questions. I'm not so good at those. I made a mistake.

"I couldn't see the line," I said truthfully. "My eyes."

It's not all true. *Kirin*, for example. *Poet* in Bengali. It's not his real name. Would Mummy call him that? I looked at the wall. There were photos in expensive frames: a boy, twelve months or so, dressed up, with a grin I knew. Three big photos, one beneath the other, all more or less the same. She was overdoing it before he could even talk.

For years, they'd grinned like that, the boy in the photographs, the boy in the lesson. The final day was here. Only the photos were grinning. *Nothing lasts forever.* I had said it once when I was angry, a long time ago. The words came back, as words tend to, in a cruel way, when you're not expecting. There was another question. There usually is. Three pairs of words; he had to choose the closest in meaning: *come/go, depart/leave, last/ever.* He ticked the wrong box – you know which – then put his pencil down, got his phone out (like him, it was full of games) and made a hybrid monster.

The childminder was moving in the kitchen. Time was up. For once, I hadn't checked the clock. She was happy. I sensed it. She knew, everybody knew, that this was my final lesson. She hadn't lurked or distracted. She spent the whole lesson upstairs. Three hours. She never had before. Her job was to spy, but she didn't need to any longer, not on me. Nor would I spy on her. She had won. Now, she wanted me gone. Kirin – I'll still call him that – stood in front of me. I hugged him and whispered so she couldn't hear, "I won't forget you."

He left the room. I walked to the front door then turned my head and looked down the hall, as I often had, one more time, to see what he was up to. He was facing the wall, in the shadows at the end. The last image. I thought, *This will haunt me*. It was haunting me already, before I touched the door.

The sideways heart

Céline

"What did Céline give her pet snail for Christmas?"

The Year 4s were passing through a joke phase, and I thought I'd help out, beyond the lesson plan. Céline tipped her head at me and made a funny face. She had her own charm. She stressed the first syllable of her name. A French girl can do it. The children had picked it up. I took a bit longer.

For my riddle, there were some hopeful answers, but I shook my head. After a certain time, like a vaudeville routine, the whole class chanted, "We don't know, Mr Spaid. What did Céline give her pet snail for Christmas?"

Céline. They got the intonation even when they chanted. They weren't so good at riddles. As for the snail one, there must have been an answer. I don't remember. Céline didn't speak, but her eyes sparkled.

The windows were open. A smell was floating in. Some children were sniffing the air.

"That's the Chinese restaurant," I explained. "It's just over there." I pointed. "They do snails."

"Yuk!" someone said. It was true about the snails. I'd seen the menu.

"What are you having for lunch?" I responded.

"Chicken with salad," someone said.

"Are you sure?"

The riddles got sillier. We could do one more, I said. Céline raised her hand.

"Why did Mr Spaid go to the toilet?"

As she spoke, she looked at me sweetly. The toilet. Mr Spaid. It was a tricky one. The children were stuck or preferred not to answer.

"We don't know, Céline." Céline with the golden curls. "Why did Mr Spaid go to the toilet?"

"To have a poo!"

It was lunchtime. The children filed out. I was sitting on the soft chair at the edge of the carpet. As Céline passed, she stepped over and put her arms around me.

Every day at half past three, the children were collected by their parents. We waited in the yard. Céline's father came. She'd be standing next to me. She didn't run about like the others. She kept an eye on the gate. When her father walked in, she made a sad face. One day, she said, "I wish he didn't come so soon."

He was never the first in, but he wasn't the last, either. There were still plenty of children about. He looked around sympathetically and said things like, "They are running you a merry race, monsieur."

Once, he complained about Céline.

"I speak to her in French, and she answers in English!"

In summer, she wore a frock like the other girls, but she also had leggings that came down over her knees. She always wore them, even if it was hot. Her mother was Algerian. We never met. One home time, I prompted Céline about her.

"Your daddy likes me. Do you think your mummy would like me too?"

She thought for a few seconds then answered carefully, "I told her about you."

After school, I caught the bus. It stops opposite the snail restaurant. Bus shelters aren't very big; the seats fill up quickly. A moment ago, there were places, but you won't find one now. Céline was standing with her father. I raised my hand. When she saw me, she called out my name and ran to me as if she knew why, past the shelter and the row of people, as fast as she could, so fast I thought she'd tumble into me. She pulled up, though, a yard away and smiled coyly, at me and at herself. She had almost hugged me, there, in front of everyone.

I nearly called you miss

In one classroom, a girl called me dad. In another, a girl called me miss. Both times, everyone laughed.

"Miss is short for mister," I explained. A boy eyed me suspiciously. "No, it's not!"

An independent mind. The children had to do a written task. I was standing at the front with one of the teaching assistants. If they're women, and they usually are, I call them miss. I looked down at the child beside me. She wasn't writing. I opened my mouth to speak, something encouraging, but stopped and said, "I nearly called you miss!"

It was the first thing I said to Varahna. She looked up in delight, and her heart was mine.

The assistant told her to concentrate.

"Varahna!" she said several times in a warning tone, and each time the little girl grinned at me as if sharing a private joke. It was a good reason not to concentrate.

On the whiteboard, there was a list of expectations in the teacher's best writing. Three expectations, the most important, I expect, in her view; not many for a list of this sort, but the board was small to start with, and miss had to use it for teaching.

- Be resiliant
- Contribute in class when the need arrises
- Show independance

In spelling, too. Next, we had a test. You guessed it: spelling. There were ten words. At the end, Varahna put her hand up. She was grinning again.

"What was number five?"

I wanted to repeat it, but if I did, I'd have to do the same for everyone. We'd never finish. I said I couldn't tell her. I explained why. She still grinned. During break, I corrected the test. Varahna got every word wrong and practically every letter. I'm not exaggerating. It was the worst spelling test I've ever seen; so bad, it was touching. When she asked about number five, she must have known that every word was wrong. *Be resiliant.* That's Varahna.

I make mistakes too. Once, I called her Varhana, another Bangladeshi name.

"Not Varhana, Va<u>rah</u>na!" she replied, as if she was telling me for the hundredth time, scolding almost, like a teacher, but her eyes were laughing.

The last lesson of the day. A class can be naughty. I was getting cross.

"I might not come again!"

There was a cry of pain, a soft one. *When the need arrises.* Céline. I wasn't looking at her, but I recognised her voice. Some cries are like words. I explained (I do this a lot, even for a teacher), addressing the whole class, but the words were for Céline. I said I'd always come if I was called, though a lot had to happen before that: their teacher had to be away; the school had to call the agency I worked for, and there were lots of agencies; then the agency had to call me, and agencies had lots of teachers. When I finished, I glanced at Céline. She wasn't feeling any better.

At home time, the assistant took the children downstairs, all except Céline and Varahna. They stayed behind when they shouldn't have, and sat together in the front row. *Show independance.* Varahna put her arms out then Céline, and the hugs were done.

"I'll miss you," I said as they walked away.

A few weeks later, I returned to the same school for a different class. At lunchtime, a group of Year 4s appeared at the door.

"What's my name?" one asked.

"Céline."

"Oh, my God!" She pointed to a child who was hanging back, then asked me, "What's her name?"

"Does it start with V?"

Céline turned to the other child and whispered, "I told you!"

I love you too

Varahna's school is in south-east London, across the river, a few minutes from Tower Bridge. I took her class on a walking trip. It wasn't my idea. No lesson plan; we were simply told to go. There must have been something to teach – all that history, all that river – but I couldn't think of it. When we got there, we stepped on the bridge, stared down at the flowing water then walked back again. It was a waste of time, except for Varahna, who walked next to me and put her arm in mine.

Walking. You do a lot of it in school. Schools slow things down. For a child, the year never ends. Varahna's school is Victorian. Signs say Girls' Entrance, Boys' Entrance, but no one bothers now. The signs are carved in stone, fixed in time, like the school itself, a well-meaning ogre, clumsy and hard to be with. Wherever you are, stone is in the way. The stairs are narrow. There are big footprints painted on them: yellow on the left for going up, blue for going down. They're on each step, meant for walking feet. All you have to do is follow.

I didn't go back for several months. When I did, I was late. The children were in the yard, lined up, waiting. Varahna's class again. I came down to get them. Céline saw me first through the open doorway. Her eyes lit, and her mouth opened, but I did nothing, so she was silent. Then the others saw me. Everybody cheered. They knew someone was coming, but they didn't know who. Varahna was at the front of the line, in the doorway, facing out. She still hadn't seen me.

"Hello, sweetie," I said. She turned around, said my name and hugged me. The children filed in; another girl hugged me; a couple of boys shook my hand. As Céline approached, she kept her head low and tried to sneak past, as a girl does when she thinks she's forgotten. I hugged her, too; a giant one, fit for the footprints on the stairs. She waited at the side.

"I missed you!" I said, like an apology. She waited some more, then she walked on. Varahna stayed till everyone had gone. When she spoke, she was looking at the wall. She was only nine.

"I love you."

"I love you too."

In class, I wrote the date on the board. 10.10.10. Some children giggled.

"And next year, will it be 11.11.11?"

"Ye-e-s," they answered.

"Then 12.12.12?"

"Ye-e-e-s!" they all chimed.

"Then 13.13.13?"

"Ye-e-e-e-s!"

"Oh, children!" cried the teaching assistant. *The year never ends.*

Varahna preferred games to lessons, running to walking. The next time I saw her, we were in a corridor, at different ends. She was outside the staffroom. She shouted my name. The door was open, and there were teachers inside. They couldn't see her, but they must have heard. Varahna didn't care. She ran the length of the corridor into my arms, without slowing. She's started doing this. She runs across the playground too. As long as there is space between us, she runs – the bigger the space, the faster she runs – except three times that I remember. The first time, we were in assembly. She didn't look at me. If she did, she'd have to run, and you can't do that in assembly. I wondered how long she'd last till she couldn't not look any more. The whole assembly. As she walked out, she smiled, but she still didn't run. The second and third times were connected. It was lunch. She was in the hall, talking to the deputy-head. When she saw me, she took a step forward then stopped. In the yard, minutes later, when she saw me again, she didn't run either. She was self-conscious. I thought, *She's growing up*. But she hugged me as she always did, then turned around with her back against me so I could hold her.

"Where's Céline?" I asked.

"She went to another school."

Varahna was holding something, a few strips of blue cellophane. They were tiny. Most of them blew away. She gave the last one to me. It's on my desk, as bright as ever, in a little dish along with some paper clips and a lock of hair.

You are, you are

The Year 6 teacher was ill, and I was filling in. I didn't know the class. The first lesson was English, a comprehension. We read through the text together. It was all predictable, all a bit dull, like a normal lesson. Then we came across *cadaverous*, tripped on it, rather, like a dead body. It's not a normal Year 6 word. I woke up. I told the children what a cadaver was.

"It's a metaphor here. Your teacher goes to a party and has too much to drink. In the morning, when she wakes up, she looks in the mirror. What do you think she sees?"

"A dead body," someone said. The children had woken up too.

"Then she calls in sick, and I come."

I smiled wryly. For a minute or so, we discussed the metaphor, how their teacher could resemble a corpse. There was a pause.

"You're the best teacher we've ever had."

A boy said it, a couple of desks away. I turned to him.

"Really?"

"You are, you are!" said a girl with wide eyes in the row behind him. The lesson continued. Some children were misbehaving. The boy was one of them.

"If I was the best teacher you'd ever had, you wouldn't misbehave, would you?"

He smiled wryly. I don't remember his name, but the girl with wide eyes was Mahjida. Her family was from Afghanistan. I teased her when I knew her better. When I said her name, I emphasised the Mah. I stretched it out. "Hello, M-a-hjida" or "Yes, M-a-hjida." I said her name when I didn't need to, just to play with it.

"Why do you say M-a-hjida?" someone asked.

"I like it. I think she likes it too."

Mahjida. The name means *glorious*. Whenever we met, she gave me a hug. She didn't run like Varahna. She was two years older. She stepped up demurely and put her arms around me. Once, she did it in the line for assembly. I was standing near the hall entrance. As she walked past, she hugged me in front of everybody.

She had several cousins, all girls. The ones I knew were younger than her, in other classes. Their names all began with Ma, like Mahtab and Masooma – *moonlight* and *sinless*. They all wore headscarves to conceal their hair, and they all had trousers, even when they went swimming.

"It's our religion," the youngest explained.

Mahjida had one more cousin, Marzia, in Year 5. Marzia was different. For a start, as you can see, her name had an *r* in it, and the meaning wasn't so positive. Marzia was *satisfactory*. There was another difference.

One day, I mentioned Mahjida to her.

"Oh, Mahji-i-da!" she groaned. "She thinks you're the best teacher ever!"

"Mahjida loves me. Masooma loves me. Mahtab loves me." Pause. "You love me."

"No, I don't!"

"Yes, you do. You just don't know it." A longer pause. "I saw your hair in Year 4."

"Fine!"

They should have called her Marwa. That means *stone*.

The sideways heart

Varahna the piranha. I didn't call her that, though someone did, not a child, either; a member of staff. It was in the yard. The lady hugged her and gave her a kiss. You aren't meant to, are you – call children names and kiss them? Not in primary school. Not in any school. Varahna didn't mind. She stood for a moment, giddy from the hug or the kiss, then grinned. She was a sweet girl.

One lunchtime, Varahna the piranha came to visit. I was alone in Year 5, eating a sandwich. She was alone too. I hadn't seen her for a while. We remembered things.

"You taught us about a rat."

I did. It was a bilby, actually, but it looked like a rat. We called it Bob the bilby. It wasn't in the lesson plan. I was pleased she remembered. As we chatted, Varahna drew pictures on the whiteboard with the teacher's black pen. A Year 5 girl came in to get something. She'd been in once already.

"Varahna, are you still here? Stop bugging sir!"

Then she went out. After a few minutes, Varahna pulled off her headscarf, shook her hair and told me to feel it. She didn't put the scarf on again. When she left, she was holding it in her hand. I got to the door first and placed my arm across it.

"Password!"

She hesitated then ducked under – she wasn't very tall – and scurried off giggling. As the children were lining up after lunch, some Year 5 girls ran over. They were breathless.

"Varahna said, 'I want to kiss Mr Spaid and marry him and live with him and have babies with him.'" I smiled and said she was sweet. The girls looked surprised. "Do you want me to be angry with her?" They were still doubtful, so I added, "It was a bit inappropriate."

In the classroom, someone saw a drawing on the board, in black pen, in the bottom, right-hand corner. Varahna had rubbed off what she'd done, except for one little heart. She told me to leave it there. The corner was the safest place, at the bottom as she couldn't reach the top. The heart was on its side, and the pointy bottom faced right, as if it was lying down.

"Varahna did that," a boy said.

"How do you know?"

"She does hearts like that."

It wasn't her first. It got rubbed off, but I didn't do it. You take care of your little hearts.

On Monday, at the girls' school, I had Year 7. A girl removed her headscarf, like Varahna, but she didn't speak; she just put it on the desk beside her. Another girl glared at her.

"Why did you take your scarf off?"

In the afternoon, I had Year 10. Summer term. Videos are good, especially after lunch. We watched *Of Mice and Men*. They had read the story. Now the books were shut and stacked neatly on the teacher's desk. It was dark inside the room and warm. Heavy curtains kept out the sun but swelled with a gust of air. We came to the part when Lennie kills Curley's wife. She tells him to touch her hair. He's about to touch it; you know he's going to. A couple of the girls called out instinctively, as one, "Don't do it!"

"It's too late, girls," I intoned. "There's nothing you can do. Destiny will take its course."

The class exploded. Then he kills her, and the bird flaps violently inside the barn.

I didn't find any sympathy among the girls, not for Curley's wife. She was a man-eater, a slut who had it coming.

"You girls are hard-hearted."

"Do you feel sorry for her?" someone asked, surprised.

"I feel sorry for everyone."

I'll remember that lesson – and the lunch hour, the sideways heart. I'll remember Varahna the piranha.

Me, me, me, me, me

The kids were stuck to the floor

You hear him before you see him. His voice comes down the corridor. It's by the office now, searching for space to fill.

"Me, me, me, me, me."

It's getting louder. He's passing the hall. When schools lock their gates, they lock the noise in, too. They lock in the sound of the music teacher.

"Me, me, me, me, me."

He's in the corridor. His voice is so loud, too loud for a human voice, for a human corridor.

"Me, me, me, me, me."

There's always music somewhere in a school. In primary, the music teacher goes from class to class. He usually rolls by – *It's not our turn!* – but once a week, he stops at the door. The music teacher's here.

"When father papered the parlour..."

The same, booming voice, but you still don't see him.

"... you couldn't see pa for paste."

Then he sails into the room like Pavarotti in a village hall.

"Mother was stuck to the ceiling; the kids were stuck to the floor."

The first time I heard him, it was thrilling.

"You never saw such a bloomin' family so stuck up before!"

The children were entranced, or I thought they were. They couldn't leave, could they, even if they wanted? It was like the voice of God, the singing voice. No fun at all. It subdued the class. Very soon, it subdued me. There was no space to move, to misbehave, so no one did. You just waited for it to finish. He only sang the chorus, but when that was done, he didn't go back to his normal, speaking voice. I don't know what his normal voice was. The instructions he gave were half-sung too, like recitative, and had the same rhythm as the song.

"All stand up in your places, and hold your hands in the air."

These days, they do a lot of clapping. It helps children understand rhythm. The big man's class understood. They had the fiercest clap I've ever seen.

When the lesson ends, Luciano reprises the parlour song. He picks up his stuff and surges out the way he surged in.

"Me, me, me, me, me."

He's in the corridor.

"Me, me, me, me, me."

A one-man opera.

"Me, me, me, me, me."

The big man's favourite word.

Don't itch yourself

In one school, the music teacher asked me to sing. Whenever that happens, I give excuses, but this time I didn't. The song she wanted had a bouncy tune. When I finished, she told the children, "Give Mr Spaid our clap."

They placed their right hands on their hearts and patted quietly. Then she turned to me.

"What was that, a rap?"

In another school, the music teacher thought I was shy. Some children were fooling around, and I didn't stop them. He glanced at me a couple of times then said, "Feel free to intervene."

I was there to assist. For him, that meant discipline. For me, that was his job. He was the teacher.

"You want me to interrupt your lesson?" I replied. At the end, he ran from the room, actually ran, like a child, to tell on me.

I don't get on with music teachers. It started when I was a boy in Year 5. We had to do a voice test, notes in a scale. *No, no, no, no, no.* Looking back, this was, for me, the perfect word. But I was only ten. I didn't get the irony. One by one, my classmates sang. They sauntered up the scale like monkeys up a ladder. I remember a boy with plump lips. He cleared his throat, filled his chest then played out a string of flawless sounds. He got A++. I got A-. It was the lowest grade. I had, in fact, failed. Why upset the parents with a D?

The teacher was a slender young man with small eyes and a pointy nose. His surname rhymed with *lash*. He lined us up and made us sing. Sometimes, he stood in front, sometimes behind, always with a cane – whip or baton, as required. We did *The Vagabond*, a poem set to music by Vaughn Williams. In case you don't know, it celebrates the joys of homelessness. *Give to me the life I love...* It couldn't have been more distant from our own subject world. *Wealth I seek not...* More irony. Meanwhile, sir was hovering. *Let the blow fall soon or late.* The music and the words annoyed me. When I'm annoyed, I itch, or I did when I was ten. I reached down and scratched my leg; the kind of thing sir was waiting for. He told me to keep still.

"I was just itching myself."

"Well, don't just *itch* yourself!"

When he said *itch*, he stressed the word and – for extra stress – flicked the cane down sharply on my calves. A red line appeared on the skin. It got brighter as I watched. I didn't like the song any better. I don't like it now.

I know. It's tough when you're a music teacher. You only see each class for an hour a week. How do you stick the kids to the floor? You try anything.

There's a boys' school I used to work in. 97.9% Bengali. Probably more now. It's a while ago. The music teacher was Canadian, a slender young man with small eyes and a pointy nose. He didn't have a cane, but one day, when I arrived for Year 8, he was holding a video cassette. *Swan Lake.* He looked pleased.

"My wife's a ballet dancer," he said, as if explaining the cassette. I didn't reply. He was pleased all the same. The boys would see something new, and a video isn't hard to play.

After ten minutes, he stopped the tape. The boys were behaving.

They didn't usually. Sir looked delighted. They must enjoy the ballet. Was everybody following the story? One boy said that the film had no words. The beauty of great ballet, sir replied, was that you understood without the need for words. Then he turned to me.

"Mr Spaid will tell you what's been happening."

"I'm afraid I've no idea."

I have my red lines. He peered at me and pondered for a second then pressed *Play*. The swans resumed their flapping. The boys went on behaving. Their eyes never left the screen. In that part of London, girls don't show their hair, let alone their tights.

A boy with no tie

Per tela, per hostis

I studied Latin right through secondary school. That was in Australia. The longer I studied it, the fewer pupils there were. By the final year, I was the only one. The man who taught me came from England, like the name of the college and its architecture. Freaky was an old-style Classics master. His name was hyphenated. He put *MA (Oxon)* after it, which made it look even longer. The word before the hyphen rhymed with *freak*, so we called him Freaky, with affection but with accuracy. He stood out from the other staff. He must have taught Greek in the past. It would have helped my writing, my poetry of ridicule. He rhymed with *Greek*, too.

I knew Freaky for five years. At the start, he didn't notice me. When he did, he was disappointed. I was too quiet. You'd think that, with the help of puberty, I could make a noise. But I couldn't. As a classicist, Freaky valued public speaking. Public noise came first. He advised me to go somewhere deserted and shout at the top of my voice. Let it out! I had a mentor now. It was *Karate Kid II* in Roman numerals. What did he care if I didn't make a noise? I think, when he looked at me, he saw himself when he was younger. A shiny, little

Freaky. I had his bent shoulders, the same dopey eyes, without the bushy thing beneath the nose. But there was hope for me. I could still avoid his life-in-diffidence. When I looked at him, I saw a baby in a crib, silent, sleepy, with a miniature jacket and moustache. Let it out! Somewhere deserted. He could have followed his own advice. He wasn't the most assertive Latinist.

There are advantages in being the only pupil. It was like a private lesson, and I always came top. I had a rival just once, at the State Latin-speaking Competition. Don't laugh. There was one other entrant, a pupil from a different school, who for some reason was not as good as me. I excel at pointless things. *Move on*, you're saying, but let's stop a moment and grapple with my excellence at speaking. Freaky entered me – in the contest, I mean – to help me be assertive. He didn't think I'd win. How could someone who hardly spoke win a prize for speaking? As for the speaking, it wasn't conversation. We recited verse. I culled a few lines from Virgil's *Aeneid*, book two, the sack of Troy. Aeneas escapes with his father, who is too old to walk, so he carries him on his shoulders. The old man on his back – I empathised.

A teacher told me that Freaky was generous, that he was giving up his time for a single student. I was meant to feel grateful. For a few hours of Latin. For five, long years, I had picked through that faultless skeleton. What's more, Freaky's disappointment annoyed me. His lessons were nothing to shout about. I took revenge and wrote my own verse, the obscene type. I fleshed out the skeleton then showed it to my friends. My favourite is *Freaky want a tweaky*. It involved bananas. I won't quote it here. Freaky could have said it all in Latin. He might have liked it too. The ancients were pretty rude. They had no word for banana. They had no bananas. If they had, it would have gone like this: banana, bananae, first declension, feminine. Not the one I had in mind.

Freaky: Decline *banana*.

Me: Just say no.

Freaky Holmes

Being an only pupil, like an only child, means you'll be spoilt. You get away with things. In Latin, I got away with cheating. I know. I was only cheating myself – well, me and Freaky.

The old chap left the room a lot, even during tests. As soon as he shuffled out, I got a dictionary and looked up the words I didn't know. I needn't have bothered. I was, *ipso facto*, coming first. I cheated for the sake of it, because I could. After one of these tests, I told another boy about the dictionary. He swivelled his lips in pleasure and said, like a compliment, "Spaid, you're basically dishonest."

Outwitting sir was not merely fun; it was expected. I didn't guess it then, but Freaky was outwitting me. He had his own deceptions, like anybody, and walking out of class was one of them. He never told me why he left. He didn't have to. I'd think it was teacher business, something important. He just wanted out. In his view, the lessons were a favour. Besides, he didn't think I'd misbehave. What could one boy do? A timid one at that. In Freaky's class, neither of us openly rebelled, so we didn't realise. In short, we underrated each other.

On certain mornings, we had assembly in the hall. The whole

school was there. Almost whole. I missed it. I arrived late deliberately. I set my alarm so I had no chance of waking up in time. My tie in my pocket, I strolled into school like a visitor. It felt good in the empty grounds. The spaces looked better without people. The best part was knowing they were there, ranked in the hall. A thousand boys had acquiesced, and I wasn't one of them.

I had never been caught. I was getting careless. Once, when Freaky's lesson was after assembly, I strolled up to class to wait for him. When he padded in, he looked surprised. The masters left the hall before the boys. He had come straight up. How could I have got there before him?

His surprise was, well, surprising. There was never much emotion on his face. I peered at him more closely. The moustache, I knew. It was identical each day and didn't seem to grow. It was hair-in-portrait, fixed every morning like a medal; trim, dry thatch where birds wouldn't nest. It was, in fact, a replica of Arthur Conan Doyle's in the photograph from 1907.

We trusted each other, me and Freaky, when we shouldn't have. The time he found me in his room, a red flag waved. I must have skipped assembly. There was no other explanation. He stared at me. I had never seen him so alert. Somewhere in his face, along with the surprise, I saw the first doubt. Perhaps I wasn't so timid after all.

He asked me if I'd gone to assembly. I said yes, but you couldn't fool Freaky. He persisted. He asked me what the Head had talked about. There was a new theme each day. I paused before I answered, as if regretting what I had to say.

"I don't listen all that closely."

Freaky relaxed and mumbled in his old, sheepish way, "I don't either."

The history of rooms

At the end of the year, we had exams in the hall, except for Latin. I was, of course, the only candidate. They couldn't waste the hall, so they put me in a classroom instead. I had economics there. I was learning about money. Ironic, isn't it?

That room brought out the worst in me. It was on the first floor. Once, in economics, the teacher went down to speak to someone. They were standing on the pathway below. To fill in time, I spat through the window, judiciously, but a moment later, the teacher reappeared.

"Who spat out of the window?" He was very angry. Silence. "Who spat out of the window?"

I lifted a forefinger. When he saw it was me, he shook his head. I mouthed the word *sorry*. There was no punishment.

Another afternoon, the boys were all working. Sir had set an exercise then sat back in his chair. At times like this, when he followed his own thoughts, you could feel him ebb away like water over sand. A bird stopped singing, started and stopped again. The windows were open, and the sun was shining. It was one of those days which people say are perfect, when even a room at school seems the right place to be. A workman on the path raised his voice. I said quietly, "Fucking working class."

Sir went "Ah!" like warning a puppy. Again, no punishment, and he thought I meant it. Even though I didn't, he should have punished me. It might have been a cure. I had irony, the schoolboy kind. I still do.

One morning after break, he confided, "When teachers criticise you in the staffroom, I always defend you."

He was being nice, but I pictured them in their armchairs, all the old boys, sipping tea and backbiting Spaid.

Rooms have history. Pedestrian economics. You don't hear people ask, *What's the point of learning this?*

At last, in my Latin exam, the world caught up with me in the shape of a cleaning lady. There was no invigilator. I understood about the hall, but this was insulting. It wasn't about trust. They simply hadn't bothered. I didn't bring a dictionary. I hadn't bothered either. I thought it would be confiscated. In every exam I'd ever done, there had been an invigilator. Now, the teacher's desk had never looked so empty. It was like being tricked. After months of fertile cheating when it didn't matter, I was stranded in the desert in my final exam with nothing but a pen. *That's* irony. Freaky had dictionaries, a whole cupboard of them. For once, I wished I was there. The day was over, except for my exam. He didn't need his room. There was no Latin club. He didn't coach a team in ancient history.

Then you walked in with a mop and bucket like an actor from a casting agency. You had an apron and a scarf in your hair. You had muscles, too. In terms of rubbish, you invigilated. You examined every corner of the room and held all the answers in your hand. You also distracted me. I only answered half the paper. It served me right. You punished me, when no one else did, for the wrong things I'd done. You were some cleaning lady.

A year later, when I'd left school, I bumped into the economics teacher. He smiled warmly and began to speak, but I looked straight through him. The man who defended me, who forgave. Add it to my jobs-to-do, the list of wrong things. You didn't see his face.

The best freakin' teacher in the world

In my first year of secondary school, at lunchtime on the grass, I saw two dogs copulating. The one on top had his tongue hanging out (hanging out as well, that is). I told another boy, then we ran inside to find the science teacher. We weren't telling on the dogs. Sir had just been teaching us the facts of life, and we thought he should know. We were thirteen.

He told us the dogs' behaviour was normal, but talking about it obviously wasn't. The smile dropped off his face, the half-smile that was always on his lips, his own fact of life, which meant, *I know more than you*. He was embarrassed. It didn't occur to me, but he wasn't the best teacher in the world.

On the shortlist this year – that's right, The Best Teacher in the World – there was another science master, the UK winner. He sang and danced during lessons. As for my old master, the only shortlist he could make would be in centimetres. I mean his height. He was bald, too. His head was as smooth as an electric bulb, though I never touched it, and came with a laboratory shine. The room he taught in was set up for experiments, like a real laboratory where discoveries are made. The other boys adored it. Standing at the bench, my partner slipped away to a place I couldn't follow and didn't want to, a world of Bunsen flames, test tubes and powders.

At the end of one term, the science master came to Latin, a folder in his arm. He stood in the doorway and looked knowingly around. *No randy dogs up here.* Freaky, gentle Freaky, was behind his desk, where he mostly was, the rows of pink cheeks ranged against him. To be honest, when he sat there, it wasn't a desk at all; it was a rampart. In Freaky's room, which was always dusty, even after sweeping, and full of ancient words, experiments would fail.

Baldy had his smile, the half-crack in the breakfast egg. You sensed he was making phrases in his head, quips that would explain the smile but were too clever to waste on us. He'd brought our test results. He opened his mark book in both hands, the way a priest holds the Bible, and read out the scores. He wasn't the best teacher in the world, but I wasn't the best pupil. There was a boy who used to come bottom in science, then he got expelled and left his place for me.

When Baldy finished reading, he closed his mark book and addressed the class, but he was gazing at me.

"Spaid has no interest in science."

He asked Freaky how I did in Latin.

"Oh, he's not too bad."

"He's going to be a lawyer, not a doctor."

Baldy smiled warmly. A lawyer, not a doctor. We know how things turned out. He was being kind. How could a boy not like science? How could a teacher not wait for his own lesson? He interrupted Latin and the modern world's most deferential master. It makes your tongue hang out. He didn't butt in on geography. I was good at that, too. *He's going to sail the world.* He didn't trespass on PE, and I've spent a lifetime running.

Doing violence to the fruit

Going to bed

I arrived in Rhodes, looking for a room. It was midnight. In the old town, alleys spread out like stone tunnels. There'd been some rain, but it had stopped and was trying to soak in. A poet might have said, on such a night, in a place like this, the stones were damp with history. But there were no poets around.

I heard the noise before I saw the people making it.

Show me the way to go home.
I'm tired and I want to go to bed.
I had a little drink about an hour ago,
And it's gone right to my head.

You know how the Brits are when they go abroad. The ladies take their tops off in bars, and the gents piss on war memorials. They like to sing, too. There was a bar full of twenty-year-olds. A few of them had spilled into the alley. That's a cliché, I know, but they were drunk and holding pints of beer. The boys had circled a girl, the most attractive, I suppose, in their view. They were leaning over her, singing loudly, the same verse again and again. The girl stood still and quiet in the ring of faces. She wasn't drinking, but her cheeks glowed.

At the second line, they sang even louder. They shouted, "I want to go to bed!" and pushed their heads down until they nearly touched her. Then they weren't so sure. They needed a new line which focused on the bed and didn't just rhyme with it. But nothing like that came.

I walked into another alley and couldn't see them anymore. I could hear them, though. I knew what they were doing at the second line, the boys pushing their faces into hers. I knew when I could no longer hear them. I know now after thirty years.

Dead Dave

There were two Daves. I remember the Dead one. A wag had found the right adjective, something that was cruel but funny, as cruel things often are, and summed him up, alliterating, with a metaphor. It wouldn't have worked with Sidney or Jack. It distinguished him, too, from the other Dave, who must have been more lively. Still, no one said it to his face. He was big.

In Salonica, expat parties were always the same. You tolerated them until the boys started throwing beer at one another. My memories of Dead Dave come from a single night, and I was drinking too, so I could be wrong, but I don't think I am.

The party that night was like *Weekend at Bernie's*. Did you see the film? The Italian name is better, *Weekend con il morto*. Dead Dave was fascinating the way a corpse is. If you could, you'd have the body removed. Meanwhile, you can't forget it's there. Your eyes keep travelling back, although you don't speak to it. No one spoke to Dead Dave. People must have given up trying. As far as I could see, he didn't talk or even move much. He did lift his glass, of course, and he put his other arm around a Greek girl, ignoring the English ones, who weren't so pretty, but only when she came close enough – quite often, actually – because, like Bernie, he never left his chair.

The Greek girl (her name escapes me) wore tight, black leather and rode a motorbike. She had a boyish figure and a big, powerful bike. An English girl told me that she couldn't pick it up if it fell over, implying that she wasn't just weak but stupid, too. I saw her once with the bike when it had toppled over. She was waiting for someone to pick it up. It looked as if it didn't belong to her.

I asked her for some lessons in Greek conversation. We fixed an hourly rate and arranged to meet at her place on Sunday morning. When I turned up for the first lesson (there weren't any more), I had to knock several times. At last, the door opened. She was in a bathrobe, sleepy-eyed. We sat down, and the lesson started. It wasn't real conversation. I had a textbook with dialogues, question and answer, that I wanted to memorize. With the book on her lap, she would read a question, and I recited the answer. We went on for a couple of minutes, then I heard another voice. I looked over. The bedroom door was ajar. She had slept in but not by herself. Whoever was in her bed, it wasn't Dead Dave. A Greek boy was repeating my lines, mocking them, laughing softly. Dead Dave didn't laugh like that. Dead Dave didn't laugh. There were plenty of boys. Prised away from one, she simply found another. I had to pay to talk. The boys made love for free.

The lesson continued. At first, the mocking noises made her frown. Then she smiled as if she remembered something. The boy was cheeky; the boy was cute. I pictured him in bed. He wasn't as dull and he wasn't as heavy as Dead Dave was. She could push him off, at least, to answer the door. Try doing that to your Dead Dave or your dead motorbike. Dead Dave. It was probably an English girl who first called him that.

She had a shelf of books, as a tutor might, but these weren't for teaching, not me, anyway. They were graphic novels, the erotic sort. She opened one and showed me some illustrations. The characters were naked, with inflated breasts or giant penises.

"I like them," she laughed.

I pictured her in bed. It wasn't hard. The bathrobe, a light thing, tickled the very tops of her thighs. She had nothing else on. In leather, she was agile. In the robe, she was tender. I looked for signs. Her hair was messed, but so was mine. It doesn't mean a Greek boy has been lying on top of you. They were sleeping when I knocked. You can't make love forever. You can't keep the world at bay for very long at all.

Graeme with an *e*

I need to clear up one thing straightaway. On the next few pages, I make a lot of references to a person called Graeme. I am not talking about myself. Graeme with an *e* was someone I knew in Greece. He was, in fact, a lot like me. For a start, he was annoying. He thought he was clever (he was) and didn't miss an opportunity to prove it. He shot laconic sentences at people as if he was trying to trip them. When I said I was teaching English, he replied, "You can explain the past aorist."

His questions were even more exacting. Our conversation turned to underpants. I don't remember why. There may have been an incident concerning trousers. I may have said something like, "Just as well you had your underpants on," or "At least you were wearing underpants!" Something reassuring that took the use of underpants for granted.

"Do you wear underpants?" he retorted with more heat than you expect when you're discussing underwear; the right tone, perhaps, if I'd told him I punched babies or ate mice. Worse, when he said it, he jerked his face toward me in a devastating way.

I didn't answer his question. It might have provoked him.

Graeme, thank God, was not like me in everything. He cut his nostril hair. I know what you're thinking. How did I find out? It wasn't like the underpants. It didn't come up in the conversation. And most people would do it in private if they did it at all. Well, Graeme did it while he was sitting next to me. Only once. Once was enough. I can see it now, like a video that keeps playing. He had a pair of nail scissors in his right hand, concealed behind his thigh. He waited for me to look aside, raised the scissors, snipped quickly and hid them again. I could have missed it, but I didn't. One snip per nostril. That's all it took. He couldn't wait till I'd gone. Did he think I wouldn't notice? He didn't really care. *Screw you. My nostrils need trimming.*

Unlike me, Graeme didn't worry about dirt. He asked me around for a meal. In the vegetable stew, there were several chunks of soil, each about as big as a one drachma coin. Small as coins go, but not for the dirt you have to eat. It was good Greek earth, carved from a desiccated field. He must have seen it, stuck to potatoes or on the stalk of a whole champignon. There were loose bits, too; lumps of earth so hard that they didn't fall apart in the cooking, unless he tossed them in at the end, like a pinch of salt, to perfect the dish.

I wash vegetables before I cook them. I fuss around the cold tap. I hold mushrooms under running water, when other people wipe them with a cloth, like dusting ornaments. I tell myself that a plant which is shaped like an open umbrella can deal well enough with a short rinse. But I didn't say this to Graeme. It was like the underpants. I didn't want to provoke him. And it was like the nostril hair. He didn't really care. I just ate it. The soil, I mean. I couldn't leave it on the plate. He would have seen it. He would have fired another question at me from that hostile face.

Do you wash potatoes?

Graeme and Cinzia

For the expat, there were always more eating places than sexual partners. If you left out the ones that were too noisy or full of smoke, or stank of retsina, there weren't so many places. There weren't so many partners, either.

When it came to swapping soul mates, Graeme with an *e* was as ready as anyone. I didn't realise for a while. He was edgy, though, from the beginning. I said I might go and work in Pakistan. His face lit. He only wanted to get rid of me, but at the time, I thought he was interested. I added brightly, "You could do it too."

"No, I couldn't."

"Yes, you could."

"I'm telling you I couldn't."

I thought he missed his wife, who was in Australia. He told me she was coming over soon. I tried another genial comment, one that couldn't fail.

"That's good news."

"Is it?"

His wife's name was Cinzia. That's Italian, but she wasn't. She pronounced it *chintzier*, without the long *ee*. We had a meal when she arrived. She told me how they'd met. She was studying.

"He was the coolest tutor at uni." She giggled at Graeme. "You had a ponytail!"

It was a loving giggle. I conjured the ponytail. So did Graeme. He bent his face away from her, like an aside in Shakespeare, and twisted it brutally. It was the last time I saw them together.

Someone organised a day trip to Litóchoron, the village at the bottom of Mt Olympus. Climbers pass through before they set off for the peak. We weren't going up today, just having a pleasant walk around the village. Or trying to. I kept sniggering.

"I wish you wouldn't laugh like that," someone said.

"I'm laughing at Cinzia."

"I know."

"Did you see her earrings?" someone asked.

"They're not earrings," I said. "They're portable televisions."

Graeme hadn't come. For his wife, it was another pointless trip, a mountain that she wasn't going to climb.

One afternoon, I dropped around to see him. I didn't quite make it. There was a café at his bus stop. When I got off, I saw him with a girl who wasn't Cinzia, sitting at an outside table, not a good place if you'd rather not be seen. Maybe he didn't care or had nothing to hide. Still, in the half second before he saw me, I felt something needed hiding. I wasn't sure what. He wasn't being romantic, but his body had more purpose than when Cinzia was around. The instant he noticed me, whatever it was disappeared. He wasn't expecting visitors, not Graham with an *h*, at any rate. I could tell from his face.

The three of us had a conversation, a sad, disturbing thing. At moments like this, you pick something neutral to talk about, like cats or travel. You can't go wrong there. I mentioned my trip to Vergina, where they found Philip of Macedon's tomb, but I said it the wrong way. The girl laughed.

"I like that, excavating vagina." When no one else laughed, she apologised. Silence. She tried again. She turned to Graeme, as I used to,
with encouragement. "You said you were going to Pakistan."

Graham and Cinzia

In Salonica, bus 23 serves the Old Town. It's one of my favourite buses. It starts near the waterfront then winds up the hill. The road is very steep. The bus feels sluggish, as if it doesn't want to go, especially when it's crowded. On top of the hill, at the arch, the 23 reverses. It's just too big to get through. It lets passengers off and on before turning back along the wall. You take a bus for a reason. There's somewhere you'd like to be. One day, Cinzia came up to see me. She didn't tell me she was coming. Perhaps she didn't know until she came. She got off the bus, walked through the arch, as you did if you were coming to see me, and knocked on my door. She was by herself. I thought it was revenge on Graeme, the husband who didn't love her and went with other girls. *I'll show him!* Whatever was in her mind, I wasn't pleased to see her.

Cinzia was twenty-something, like the bus; fair-haired, light-skinned and attractive. In the Greek sun, her arms and legs were caramel, a deeper layer each time I saw her. She was boyish in spirit and in build. She reminded me of a classmate at school, a boy I knew for eight years, but who looked like her most when he was twelve. She was stronger, though. When she stepped into the house, she hugged me from behind and lifted me. My feet were off the floor. She held me like a bunch of pillows, though you don't squeeze pillows like that, not so long and hard.

"People might think it strange," she said, "me being here alone with you." Cinzia hadn't touched me before. It was straight to the embrace. "Why are you so *skin*ny?"

She emphasised *skin*. Was she lifting other men, hugging around?

I had a second-hand fridge. In the Old Town, objects, like people, got passed around. I bought it from someone who was leaving, squat and yellowish. The fridge, I mean. It was very old, with the trademark *Spring* on the front – an appliance so decrepit, made to keep things cold. It even hummed coldly. Now and then, it snored. Cinzia and I stood next to it, or she did. I was in the air. She was showing him. Saying things, too.

"I *hated* you when I first met you!"

I almost said, "I really liked *you*."

Of Cinzia's visit, the hug is all I remember, except for this. As she was leaving, she hesitated. Her hand was on the doorknob, her face hidden.

"I don't know where Graeme is."

She didn't wait for an answer. There wasn't any. I felt sorry for her then, when she was going. She had shown him, wherever he was.

I didn't see her again. A year or so later, I bumped into Graeme in Singapore in the airport transit lounge. We were changing planes. You can live in the same house and not meet. I asked about Cinzia. He said she'd remarried. She had his books and was refusing to give them back. Still showing him.

She lifted me so easily. The fridge was snoring. I could have slept with her.

Byzantine arch, Old Town, Salonica

Αγάπη μου

A pair of English girls arrived in Salonica. Jade and Joy. In the party language of the day, they were *lots of fun*, Jade in particular. She had a boyfriend in England. He was a long way away. She must have felt vulnerable. She complained that the local boys kept asking for a "connection." A girl's euphemism, but she stressed the second syllable ironically.

We tended to insult each other. Jade, however, had her confidential moods. She asked me about the first time I'd "had it." I thought her tone was still slightly mocking, so I didn't reply. To prompt me, she said, "My first time was with Jeremy."

There was almost someone else. She had given Joy the slip and come up by herself to see me. She told me this story. She'd been stuck without transport, somewhere in Greece, and a man on a scooter gave her a lift. He was middle-aged. Before their destination, he turned off the road into scrubland and asked her for sex. She burst into tears, which surprised him.

"What's the matter? I'm clean."

More euphemism. We're a polite lot, humans. Innocent abroad, if not at home, she hadn't understood what he meant. I told her.

"Oh, probably," she said.

Later, I repeated the story to Joy, sarcastically, in front of her.

"It's the last time I'll tell you anything," she said.

Joy was more intelligent than Jade, though Jade was no fool. Joy was better at repartee. If I couldn't think of an answer, I'd just be rude. One day, we went to a taverna with a nice American girl. There *are* nice girls. Joy said something caustic, and I replied, "Be quiet, number two."

The American wasn't used to this.

"Number two?" she inquired. "And is Jade number one?" She wasn't smiling. "Does that make me number three?"

If only life were so simple.

"You're never serious!" Jade berated me. "Why don't you say something in Greek?"

"Αγάπη μου!" *My love*. She shrieked with laughter. The American gave an excuse and left.

Jade discovered that she'd lost her ring. She was frantic. She searched under the table, in her pockets, in her bag. When she couldn't find it, she went to see if she had dropped it in the bathroom.

"It's a very important ring," Joy explained. "Jeremy gave it to her."

I saw it on the floor, picked it up and held it out when Jade returned. She seized it off me.

"I could kiss you!"

She was looking at the ring. I asked Joy if she needed the bathroom.

"I'm not washing my hands in there! Do you know how many germs there are on a bar of soap?"

She described an experiment she'd done at university. It was a lengthy experiment. When her voice stopped, and there had been enough silence, I said to Jade, "I'm waiting for my kiss."

After twelve months, they flew back to England. I gave them each a toy koala. Jade grabbed hers and hugged it. As we said goodbye, she kissed her fingertips and touched them on my cheek.

Their flight left from Athens. They took the train to meet it – the final con*nec*tion, if you like – but the engine broke down on the way. They had to get a taxi. Hours were wasted, and they nearly missed the flight.

"It was awful," Jade said when I saw her in England in the summer, "and just typical. We suffered right to the very end!"

I asked about Koala. She lost it in the panic on the train. She lost Jeremy, too, a few months later. He dumped her. I wonder if she kept the ring.

Death in Salonica

It turned cold. One day, it was minus five. I saw Jade at the university – we were doing a Greek course – and called out to her. I must have looked as if I had news, and she was keen to show it didn't matter.

"Guess what?"

"I know, I know. Your washing froze."

She informed me that, in England, washing didn't freeze because it wasn't put outside in the first place.

Πολύ κρύο. *Very cold.* It began to snow. My bathroom was in the backyard, with no glass in the window. Snowflakes hit me when I had a shower. The girls laughed when I told them. It was so cold my pipes froze. I told them that, too, then clutched my chest and repeated with alarm, "My pipes are frozen!"

They laughed again. Jade informed me that, in England, pipes didn't freeze because they weren't put outside in the first place.

When I got home, my neighbour, Adonis, was standing in front of his house. His wife was in the background, beating a blanket.

"Πολύ κρύο!" I called. I'd said it to him before. I said it to all my neighbours. It was easy to pronounce, and I didn't know much Greek.

I hadn't been there long. Later, Adonis came over to my window, a coat in one arm. He said it was his son's. The boy had died, but he didn't say that. Someone else had told me. Greeks do military service, usually in their late teens. A year or two on the Turkish border. Sometimes, they don't come back. Here was the boy's coat. I wonder who thought of it first, Adonis or his wife. *It's just sitting in the cupboard. Why don't we give it to him?* I was touched. They hardly knew me, yet they wanted to help. Perhaps it helped them, too. When I wore it, they could see the boy again, on the corner or walking through the arch. I took the coat. I was very grateful, but I never wore it.

An English girl came to cut my hair. She was actually a hairdresser. I sat down. She lay a cloth around my shoulders and started cutting. She spoke a little, as hairdressers do. I needed to take more care with my sideboards, she said, and other things to do with hair. Then she talked about herself.

"I'm seein' a Greek boy."

It was warmer now. The windows were open. Adonis appeared. He laughed when he spotted us, the girl behind me, snipping my hair. He rested his forearms on the sill, hands inside the room, and settled down to watch. I didn't understand all he said, but his tone was clear. He was making fun of me. A couple of men stopped to see what was happening. They joked along with Adonis.

"Greeks!" the girl muttered. She only came once.

Jade and Joy had gone to Delphi and were expecting me later. I arrived a day after them, stood on the road outside the hotel and shouted their names. I can still see Jade's face, the laughter on it. when she leaned through a window and saw my hair.

We walked up to the ancient site. At the temple, you turn and gaze down. The plain is green with olives. There are no other colours. I said it looked like a dark cloth spread among the hills. Silence. It was a bit pretentious. But the girls said nothing. I thought my simile had winged it, though it didn't get far. On the bus next day, to pass the time, they mocked the poor thing, repeating it with pitiless variation.

There were other passengers. One of them was smiling. The girls had always teased me, and it was always cruel, but with an audience, it was thrilling. I let them go on. When it was enough, I said, "If you knew how close I was to tears, you wouldn't continue."

In Salonica, that first winter, it really was very cold. Adonis thought I was suffering, but I wasn't. He was.

Just like Jade

Another time, the three of us went to Mt Pelion. We stayed a couple of nights in Makrinitsa in a triple room. The first morning, while Jade was in the shower, I said to Joy, "How's my favourite English girl today?"

"I don't know," she replied. "I haven't spoken to Jade yet."

We went down for breakfast. There was an old English lady in the dining room.

"It's going to rain," I said.

"Oh, don't be so pessimistic!" she chirped.

"I was just looking at the clouds."

The old lady had come to find a beetle, the Dogbane Leaf, which doesn't live in Britain. It has a shiny, rainbow-coloured shell.

"They only feed on certain plants, so I find those first."

"Like the tribesmen in the Serengeti," I observed. "They can tell from a pile of dung which animal has passed and when."

"How big is beetle dung?" Joy complained. I peered at her. "They can even tell how much something weighs."

The old lady had been to Pelion before. One day, she found a plump beetle, placed it in her jar and screwed the lid on.

"It was raining. I was on a steep slope, trying to –"

"You slipped and dropped the jar, which rolled down the slope and vanished."

Silence.

"Well done, Graham," said Joy. "You spoiled her story."

Joy had used my name. Joy was cross. Her enthusiasm for the old lady irritated me. It was also beginning to rain. As if I'd remembered something, I asked Miss Marple, "Have those beetles got horns?"

"The Dogbane? No."

"I trod on a bug last night."

"Did it have horns?" she inquired. I nodded. "It might have been a stag beetle. They're endangered."

"Don't listen to him," said Joy. "He didn't tread on anything." Then, glaring at me, "You know very well what a stag beetle looks like."

The TV was on. No sound, just images flicking on the screen. It was a travel documentary. Each place was so calm and far away. The Golden Temple, the Ganges at dawn, houseboats on Dal Lake.

"I've been there!" I cried then mumbled, "Sorry."

Jade said she understood. My apology, Jade's understanding – all this was new, if the view wasn't. I had photographed the same place from the same angle: the path to the centre of the lake; the trees spaced along it, too airy for real trees, fixed to a line of shade on the water, hardly a real path, with the mountains rising behind.

The old lady said the water would be cold; it was cold in Turkey, too. She had gone with her late husband.

"We nearly froze."

I nodded sympathetically.

"I read an article on penile frostbite."

"You did not!" Joy protested.

"But I've been to Istanbul, on the coach overnight. I was late for the coach back and had to run. It was pitch dark. A workman was laying cement on the footpath, but I didn't see him. He'd finished a whole strip –"

"You ran right along it!" Joy laughed.

"You spoiled my story."

Who lays cement in the dark? I sat there on the coach and looked down, a grey mess on my shoes and trousers. I saw the workman, too, in my head, calling out and waving his trowel. I had kept running.

Jade wasn't so fond of Miss Marple. You could feel it. She was being silent, but you know Jade. She couldn't stay silent for long. She asked the old girl if the bug was endangered, the rainbow-coloured one. It was common in North America, she replied, but not in Europe.

"Keep an eye out for it. The larva has a brown head and white body."

"Just like Jade," I said.

You're the clever one

You could fill a Greek taxi – those little yellow ones – with the girls I met in Salonica then bumped into on the Acropolis. You could do it, but you wouldn't want to. Too many girls in too small a space.

Gelda was Dutch. Jade said she couldn't stop talking about me. We met in Salonica then – you guessed it – bumped into each other on the Acropolis. In case you don't know, that's the large rock in Athens with a temple on it (the Parthenon). It can be romantic, and I had to attract someone sooner or later. Gelda's enthusiasm intrigued Jade and Joy, who weren't infatuated with me. They wanted to know everything, all the details about me and Gelda, but there was nothing between us in Athens or anywhere else. I wouldn't have told them, anyway. When they tired of this, we discussed the Parthenon.

"It's one of my five favourite buildings," I said. For Jade and Joy, this was something rare. I was being serious.

"What are the others?" Jade asked.

"King's College Chapel in Cambridge, the Blue Mosque in Istanbul, the Duomo in Florence and the Taj Mahal."

Jade went quiet. She didn't have to tell me, but she hadn't been to most of those places. What about the buildings I didn't choose, the other piles of human genius which I'd looked at, mulled over and then discarded? She hadn't been to those, either.

It was a deep conversation, deep and satisfying. It proved I could bother Jade without even trying. It also depressed Joy about the Parthenon.

"I can't see what's so good about it," she lamented. "I must be missing something."

"Yes," I said.

"It's a matter of taste," said Jade.

"Good taste and bad taste," I said then turned to Joy, "You're meant to be the clever one."

"I resent that!" she snapped.

"Relax. I'm just comparing you to Jade."

Depressed joy. That's an oxymoron.

I answered an advert for a private tutor. It was a Greek woman asking for English conversation. She had chosen the topic, Graham Greene, who was popular in Greece at the time but an author I'd never read. I was on my way to our first lesson (there wasn't a second) when I saw the two girls. I told them where I was going.

"Is your shave good enough for her?" Jade remarked. More lecture than question. Like the Acropolis, in a certain light, Jade was a pale stone.

One day, I saw Gelda at the university and didn't say hello. She looked hurt. I had talked to her before, at least twice, in two different cities. She must have wondered why I was ignoring her now. She was attractive. When she spoke English, something cute happened which only foreign girls can do. Her accent was so slight you could miss it. If you didn't know she was Dutch, you'd think she had a cold. I decided to notice her next time.

A few days later, at the university, I saw her again. She was walking up the stairs in front of me. Unfortunately, Jade and Joy were there. They were due a laugh.

"Do you want to have dinner?" I asked Gelda, cute with English words.

"No."

All in the framework

I was down in Athens again. Jade had gone separately with a friend from England. They were bound to visit the Parthenon. In front of the temple, I picked a good rock – the Acropolis is not short of these – and sat down to wait. It was midafternoon. The Greek sun was blinding. There's no other word. I'm not sure how long I would have waited. In less than five minutes, they came along. You won't believe me, but it's true.

It was all in the framework. I haven't told you about my framework. I arranged things (events, conversations) to end as I wished. At least, that's what I told Jade and Joy.

"It's all in the framework," I said. It infuriated them, Jade particularly.

The path she was on led to my stone. When she saw me, she didn't react. I'd seen her first. It was too late to escape. She just kept walking. Greece had always vexed her – the people, the climate, the lot – and she was generally cautious. She was extra-cautious now. She halted several steps away. Her companion must have known about Jeremy, the boyfriend in England. Jade didn't want to talk to me in front of her. But the coolness didn't last long.

"What a lovely coincidence," she said.

"Not really. I've only been here an hour, and I've already seen two people I know."

"I think you've been sitting there too long," she said, eyeing my trousers. "Your pants are so tight they're going to split."

"One girl had a bum like a cauliflower."

The friend woke up. From a distance, before they saw me, they had both appeared lifeless. Maybe it was the heat. Maybe it was Greece. Maybe they were sick of each other. Jade was excellent at ennui, especially on trips, when she moved like a duchess on the Grand Tour.

"It's in the framework, I suppose." She turned to her friend. "He has a *framework*. Everything that happens is what he intended. It's all in his stupid framework."

I don't recall the friend's name. She made a schoolgirl pun on *feta'd* cheese. She wasn't as thin as Jade. They both had big, floppy hats, and their arms and legs were pink. That's all I can tell you. Shall I make it up? The wrong words can spoil a simple thing: a rock and two girls picked out by the sun. Behind the Parthenon, to the left as I was facing, sat Lycabettus hill, a grey cone with a skirt of trees. Another sacred place. I climbed it once. It's a good spot to view the Acropolis. People tell you, *Don't stop at the café; it's too expensive*. But – and they tell you this, too – there's nowhere else to go. I could see the path now, around the middle, a streak at that distance, like a thin smile. When you glance back and see where you've been, a path can look sardonic. It won't remember you.

For the first time and probably the last, all three were in a row: Lycabettus, the Parthenon and Jade. I know, she's sacred too.

The quips had roused her, and I thought I'd done enough, but the line I was hoping for – "Would you like to come back to the hotel?" – never made it into words. I imagine this: they get to their room; Jade pokes the shutters open, turns and sighs.

"I'm just too tired to cope with Graham."

It wasn't in the framework.

The devil on the door

You can apologise in Salonica for being rude in Athens. Jade did, anyway.

"I'm very sorry we didn't invite you back to the hotel."

I like the *we*. The friend she'd been with, a girl of equal froth, had flown out from England to see her. Jade could be cruel wherever she was, but in Salonica, it was just Jade and Joy. In terms of English girls who came to Greece and trifled with Graham, they were the first. New ones turned up each year, usually in pairs. Their names usually started with the same letter. When the two Js had gone, I mentioned them to the next pair, the two Cs: Candy and Cassie. Cassie said, "Who the hell are Jade and Joy?"

It was a good question. The names sat neatly on the tongue, and one syllable was easier than two, but Jade and Joy were not a perfect match. To begin with, they weren't friends in England. They'd been paired together to 'teach' English at the university in exchange for Greek lessons. Jade was an aristocrat, and Joy wasn't. I think they annoyed each other, but dealing with me, who annoyed them even more, they were united.

Jade and Joy lived at the *estia*, a multistorey, modern dormitory inside the campus. Their rooms were like hollow tins and echoed if you tapped them. The first time I went, they invited me. They took me down to see the toilets, a row of cubicles with wooden doors to shoulder height, one of which had *devil* written on it in thick, black letters. Jade or Joy – I've forgotten – gave me a camera and showed me how it worked, then they both got into that cubicle and shut the door. In the photograph, two heads are sticking up, very young and slightly mad, behind the door marked *devil*. I hope I still have it. I don't know where it is now.

The last time I went to see them, I dropped in. It was a mistake. Jade came out with her Walkman on, pressing the earphones to her head, dancing around with her elbows in the air. Joy came next, sedately, and together they drove me back to the foyer.

"Do you like George Michael?" Jade spun past, not waiting for an answer. She suddenly stopped and stared at me. "What happened to your hair? You're always so careful with it." She lurched off then suddenly stopped again. "I like men with fair hair." She looked me in the eye sarcastically. "Jeremy has fair hair."

I don't remember what Joy said. She was rarely as cruel as Jade, but now they were in league. They punished me for being there.

"Are you gay?" asked Jade. "You can tell me."

I wasn't in the stocks. I walked off.

You can apologise in the Old Town for being rude at the *estia*. After I left, they came up to see me. I wasn't in, so they left a note, which I threw away. I wish I had it now. It was like this.

We are very, very sorry for being so awful to you. Of all the people who are awful to you, we are the sorriest. Please forgive us. Tragically yours, Jade and Joy.

Friends for dinner

In general, Joy was friendlier than Jade, to me and to the locals.

The three of us were waiting for a Greek class. Joy said, "There's one of my students!"

A young man was approaching. She said hello with a tone of real interest and warmth, like a friend, not a teacher. He walked straight past her as if she wasn't there. She was desolate.

Jade wasn't so positive. She asked me once why I kept annoying her.

"I just do it because I like you."

"I know."

With Jade and Joy, I apologised twice. Here is the second occasion. They'd been around for dinner. It was warm. They both wore summer clothes. Jade took a bit more care. She was almost pretty. She had 'freshened up' before she came. She had freshened up for me. It was almost flattering. For Jade, of course, it was a normal part of going out to dinner. In Greece, as in England, she arrived home by midafternoon, relaxed a little and then got ready. You could tell that she had looked in a mirror.

I had two chairs, so we sat on the floor. The windows were open. There was movement in the street, a mixture of air and shadow, and one or two people. The Old Town was cooling off. We hadn't been sitting there long, when Joy got up for something, and Jade said confidentially, "Graham, have you been drinking?"

"Yes," I answered. I was sombre, too sombre for someone who had merely been drinking.

"Why?"

"I don't know."

Not know anything, and you couldn't be more sombre. Joy came back.

"Graham's being the nervous host," she chuckled. With Jade and Joy, I had never been awkward.

"Say *shark* for me," said Jade, waiting to laugh. My accent was Australian. I hesitated. A moment later, when I said the word, she was no longer listening.

"Australian tennis players are *so hunky*." She had a picture in her head – tight pants and muscles – and no one could take it away.

Joy made her Jade-is-so-pathetic face. I don't know what kind of man aroused her, but I know what kind didn't: the ones Jade liked and me.

A fly was on her cheek. She brushed it off and said, "The flies are early up here."

"I'll catch it if you like. You can take it with you when you go."

The first fly of summer, like the last rose.

A girl appeared at the window. Her house was at the end of the street. She was Scottish and nineteen (she told me several times) with a soft frame and long, red hair. She looked sweet and spoke buoyantly. When she saw Jade and Joy, her eyes shone. If you find someone where you're not expecting, it can feel like the answer to something. They hadn't met before. They introduced themselves. Smiles, polite words. Silence. As soon as she'd gone, Joy scolded me.

"That was mean. She obviously wanted to come in."

"You don't know her" – *My boyfriend says my Greek is perfect... I won prizes every year at school... Everyone tells me how good I am* – "She's unbearable."

"So are you," said Joy, "but we're still here."

I could see some bare ankles. I grabbed one of Jade's and said something crude.

"Get off!" she barked and pulled her leg away.

They'd brought a cake, so we ate it. At last, they were going. Jade turned to me. When you've been to dinner, there's one more thing to do. You say, in a pleasant tone, without sarcasm, "Thank you very much for having us."

I saw Jade the next day.

"You were horrible," she said. I agreed. Then the apology. They were leaving Greece, and I was anxious. They mightn't let me visit them in England. I needn't have worried. The whole country disappointed them. They were so keen to leave they were crossing each day off the calendar. It was a nasty dinner, but when the insults were over, and the two girls were back in their rooms, another Greek day had been erased. That was all that mattered.

Old Town, Salonica

Egnaysha Street

Jade's brother arrived from England for a visit. He looked younger than her, and she talked to him like an older sister. I forget his name, his age – if I ever knew it – and everything he said, but he'd just had a birthday. We went out to celebrate. We chose a taverna on Egnatía (that's *Egna-tier*). The Romans called it Via Egnatía, and it went to Constantinople. It's still the main road. A summer evening, and our tables were outside on the pavement. Birthdays were mentioned. Jade turned to me.

"How old are you, Graham?"

I didn't reply. I resisted personal questions, Jade's in particular. They made me suspicious. She knew enough about me to guess I was older, if I didn't look it. Her tone was sarcastic. She wanted a laugh. I wasn't telling.

"That's unusual," said Joy, "a guy who's coy about his age."

They were going to laugh anyway.

"I'm twenty-nine," I said. Laughter. "If you're lucky, you'll be twenty-nine one day."

"But you'll be thirty-six," Jade returned. For once, I had no reply. I considered the idea, me at thirty-six, and watched the traffic as it passed by a few steps away. I say *pass*. It was doing its best to speed, in the Greek fashion, but there were too many cars. They kept stopping, revving and honking. I noticed an old lady on the pavement opposite, waiting to cross. She had shopping bags in each hand and peered tensely, repeatedly, to her right and left. Then she stooped low, like the start of a race, and sprinted with her head down, blindly, across the road. Somehow, she made it, avoiding the peril on either side, like a meal with Jade and Joy. I pointed her out.

"How has she lived so long?"

There was a policeman in the middle of the road, blowing a whistle, not at the old lady, not at one car or another; at every car, at the world. He blew madly, non-stop. The drivers didn't listen, but they didn't hit him. He was a short man, not much taller than the cars. Perhaps that's why he blew so frantically. I pointed him out, too.

"Never give a Greek a whistle."

"You're always criticizing," Jade said.

"I adore you" – then, with the same breath, in Greek, to a waiter – "A little water, please."

Brother turned to me. I'd impressed him. Jade was drinking gin. She mostly did when she was out. Back then, it was probably imported. She would have liked that. Gin, in her eyes, was a taste of England, elegant and traditional; a primrose in the wasteland of Greece. After a few sips, she sat back and exclaimed in her patrician voice, like a trumpet roll, though with irony, "Here we are on E*gnay*sha Street!"

She mispronounced the name on purpose, acquiring it for England – and the road – like a colony.

"I shortened my trousers," I said. I don't know why I said it. Inspiration. I raised a foot, the one next to Jade, and propped the heel on my chair. She leant across and sat her armpit on my knee (she had sipped her way through a whole glass of gin) then took the hem in her fingertips, lifting it slightly.

"You did a good job," she said, startled, as her brother had been.

Her finger brushed my skin. A moment passed. Slowly, she withdrew her hand and eased back onto her chair. Jade had never touched my leg or any part of me and had no wish to. She didn't say it. Her body did. She recoiled.

Someone called for the bill. I wouldn't split it evenly.

"You eat meat. It costs more."

"Cheapskate," said Joy.

"You criticized me."

"What a pseud!"

"Why should I pay for you?"

"A Greek would pay it all!"

It was true. The girls had won again. We stood up to go.

"Now you've met my brother," said Jade.

"He's just how I thought he'd be."

Pause. I needed a reprimand, a firm one, but when she spoke, she murmured, almost with a smile.

"It's very rude of you to say so."

The Simpering Sindhi

Before Jade and Joy returned to England, we had one more meal. We invited a student from our Greek class, a young Pakistani woman. It wasn't my idea. I didn't like her. I don't think Jade did, either. The invitation would have been from Joy. When I didn't like someone, she normally did. and vice versa, though that didn't happen much. Joy, as her name suggests, was positive, and in those days, among the expats, there weren't too many people I admired. Now, we disagreed about R. As usual, Joy was enthusiastic. She told her that she was the first Pakistani she'd met. She grinned like a child in a sort of wonderment. The first Pakistani she'd met! Think of all the millions there are – in Pakistan, admittedly.

Regarding R, Joy saw the country while I saw the person. I thought R smiled too much, that she wasn't sincere and the opinions she expressed weren't her own. Someone referred to General Zia, the dictator of the day.

"He's a very re*lig*ious man," R said. She was being diplomatic, I suppose, but it annoyed me. I asked if he wasn't just using religion as a tool to control the masses. She didn't reply. Joy was furious. But she often was. It didn't matter. They all invited me to visit in the summer. They didn't all mean it. Jade and Joy kept me waiting for their addresses. I asked Joy about it when she was alone. I must have sounded hurt. She explained it was Jade's idea, a plot to tease me. They planned to tell me at the last moment before they left for England. In the end, I got their addresses, formal invitations in fancy script on A4 paper with a decorated border. Jade presented hers in a scroll, triumphantly. At the bottom, like the fine print in a contract, it said that I should use the tradesmen's entrance. R, on the other hand, gave me her address straightaway, at the dinner. She was very effusive. I visited her first.

R lived in Islamabad in a large compound with high walls. The only way you could see in was through the gate, a gigantic iron one with bars like a prison. A man appeared in the yard and spoke from a distance. He said he was R's husband. She hadn't told me about a husband. Nor had he heard about me. Worse, he frowned; he wasn't pleased to see me. She wasn't home, either, so he said. Then he walked away. It was getting dark. A neighbour turned up, a man I'd never seen before, like R's husband, though he didn't frown. He fed me and gave me a place to sleep. He was very generous. True, I hadn't come for his wife.

I had more luck with Joy. To begin with, I warned her I was coming; she was home when I arrived, and there was no husband at the front gate. I met the whole family. There was even a bouncy dog. We sat at the dining room table, which was odd as we weren't eating. When Joy's sister came in. I got up instinctively.

"You don't have to stand up for my sister!"

"I'd stand up for the dog."

"Did you hear that?" said her father quietly. I told them about my visit to R and the husband who wouldn't let me in. Joy laughed merrily – at the story, of course, but also in revenge for all the insults I'd given.

"Did you get my letter?" I asked. She nodded. I'd sent copies to her and Jade, begging to be forgiven, apologising for everything. I exaggerated and made it over-formal. Joy said, "It's dead good!"

"If you wrote it," said father in his quiet way.

No Hawking

Before Jeremy dumped her, Jade arranged a picnic. I was coming to England. If I wanted to see her, I'd have to see him as well. In Cambridge. It wasn't where she lived, but she didn't want me sniffing around the family home. I can understand that, but why should I sniff around Cambridge? Jeremy had studied there. She was showing off. But a Jade picnic was not as simple as that. For her, Cambridge was the antithesis of Greece – civilised, superior; in a word, British – the kind of place she felt she belonged. Here was the real Jade, or the Jade she wanted to be. She was showing this, too. Perhaps, like Jeremy, it was just an illusion.

We sat on the grass by the river. Jade's sister and a third girl, a friend, made up the party. Their faces always pointed at Jeremy. They laughed when he spoke, like applause, even when he wasn't joking. If I said something funny, they were silent. Jade must have warned them about me. There was a picnic hamper and a tablecloth. Everything was right, except the wine. Jade had asked me to buy it. She said there'd be five people, but I only bought one bottle. Wine's expensive. She told me in front of the others that I should have got more. I'd made enough blunders in Greece, champagne ones. The faux pas used to pop all day. It amused her then, but now, with Jeremy, she expected me to cork it.

The embarrassment began before the picnic. On a nice road, I cleared my throat then spat on the footpath. I'd been living in Greece and, before that, India. In parts of London, spitting is against the law. But this spit was ages ago, and Cambridge isn't London. In that polite town, a law against spitting would be as helpful as a law against feeding statues. When I spat, there was a young man on the footpath ahead of me. He was probably a student. I didn't hit him, but he heard, swivelled his head sharply and looked disgusted.

At the picnic, I knew not to spit. Nonetheless, by the river Cam, on that perfect summer day, I brought up the subject of the Indian papers, their quality and how useful they were. It was never going to please the picnickers. I knew that, too, but I still did it. Jade was back from Greece. The friend asked her how she had kept up with the news, the British news, of course. It was important in itself, but Greece only mattered because of Jade. No one was curious about India because no one was curious about me. The last thing they needed was this anecdote.

I lived near Madras. There was an English girl who subscribed to the *Guardian Weekly*. Her copies were flown in from the UK. After she read them, she handed them on to me. I was delighted. News was hard to find, toilet paper even harder. It was a luxury, like chocolate, so you did without. I tried the local paper, but it fell apart. The *Weekly*, on the other hand, was durable. Designed for delivery by air, it was thin and light; it was also silky smooth – in short, ideal for my purpose. It arrived each week without fail. For economy, I tore each page into eight pieces. The pages were small to start with. A gentleman would have made four.

At the picnic, I didn't go into all this. The story, in its raw form, was a wee bit strong. What can be termed 'the Cambridge version' was briefer and more sophisticated. It got to the rub more quickly. In fact, not much happened before the punchline, when I criticised the paper. That's right, I panned the Weekly.

"The print came off."

Hawking

Jade had another admirer, an Englishman a few years older. We never met. When she first mentioned him, she giggled. They used to joke around. She teased him about his age. He teased her about her figure, called her his lamp post. She was very thin. But you know men. It was probably what attracted him to her. Anyway, he had loved her faithfully for several years with no reward. Things weren't about to change. Sad, clearly, but we can laugh a little regarding lamp posts and girls. Was there nothing more romantic to call her? Perhaps she wouldn't let him. She didn't tell me what she called him. Fido or something. His lamp post, her poodle.

Forget the lamp post. Jade was as thin as a punting pole. After the picnic, we hired a couple of punts, one for Jade, Jeremy and me, one for the other girls. I was a novice. Jeremy took the pole and showed me what to do. For a while, he propelled us very skilfully along a channel of the Cam. What could be more English, more refined? Then Jade piped up, "Give it to me!"

She clutched the pole like a bird of prey. I remember her arms, bare to the neck, just tendons and bone. She strained her whole body, focused on the pole. To push it, she had to lean towards me. Gravity did the rest. When her head came down, her blouse did too – the Cambridge physicists were spot on there – before I had a chance to blink.

Lily pads, floating on the surface of the stream; they sailed serenely by.

The water was narrow here. Trees touched overhead. After a few minutes, Jade gave up. Without a word, she handed me the pole and lay back next to Jeremy. I punted for hours, the novice and the two lovers. They lay very still with their eyes closed. They looked asleep, but now and then, like someone in a dream, Jeremy would say, "You're doing well."

The stream forgot his voice. Bird calls and splashes, that was all I heard – along with the twang on Jade's radio.

When our time was up, Jeremy roused himself and tossed in his final compliment; the same one, in the past tense now. I did well.

Kay

Kay was like a pill that seized your insides. She was older than the rest of us. She'd been around, a citizen of the world, she said, in her Kay voice, like an actress. She told us an anecdote. On one flight, the pilot announced, "We're now landing in New Zealand. Put your clocks back thirty years."

Over the next few weeks, she told the anecdote twice more, each time with the same, marvelling laugh. I don't know if she listened to herself.

Kay was English. We met at the university in Salonica, on the housewives' course, as someone put it – Joy, most likely. It was Greek conversation, how to travel, shop, entertain; all the things that Kay did best. You felt the real learning went on elsewhere. The only housewife was Kay.

Citizen of the world, she did all her travelling on her husband's back. That was Ulrich, a jovial German who worked for an airline (in the office, not the cockpit) and got shifted from country to country. Whenever they moved, she learnt the new language. She had hours to fill.

"Kay's quite a linguist," Ulrich said. "When we lived in Kathmandu, she spoke Nepali with the local children."

At the start of our course, we had a class trip to the ethnological museum, an elegant, old building with a tiled roof and shutters – the kind you see in the islands, a whole row along the waterfront – but crowded now by grey apartment blocks, as though someone had left it there and never come back.

Another warm day, but in the museum, it was cool and dark. One room was set up as an old-style kitchen. More housewife stuff. Everything looked heavy and hard to use. A guide explained in Greek. Kay kept nodding as if she understood, but she couldn't have. She hadn't been in Greece very long. She didn't just nod. She also asked questions in Greek. At least, she tried. The guide didn't follow; he replied in English, but Kay wagged her finger, like charades, and pushed her lips out elastically.

"Ocky, ocky!" she declared, agitated as she couldn't express herself. Οχι. *No.* It's a popular word in Greece. She couldn't do the guttural middle sound, but she wouldn't have, anyway. She wasn't going to clear her throat in public. I may be exaggerating, but so was Kay.

In the end, she stopped trying. She pushed her lips out a final time, gently now, like sucking through a straw, and fell silent. The tour moved on. Joy said, "I find Kay quite alarming."

Jade never criticised Kay, not in front of me. They were, in fact, quite similar. They were both patricians; both declaimed, but Jade was younger, less exaggerated, and her words had an edge. I liked that. Kay wasn't good with irony. I think Jade admired her; she saw an image of herself, the way she'd like to be when she was forty, a woman of the world, with opinions – and a man paying. Like most girls, Jade approved of freedom (what looked like freedom) and spontaneity, or she thought she did. With a glass of gin beside her, she approved even more.

A few weeks ago, I found Jade's photo on the internet. She's older now than Kay was then. Put your clock back thirty years. I don't know what Jade remembers.

Panórama

Kay lived in a big house in Panórama, outside Salonica, among the hills and the chestnut trees and the rich people. Once, she invited us to dinner, Jade, Joy and me, with some others from the course. She was most comfortable when she'd been rehearsing, and she'd hosted a lot of dinners. She took control or tried to.

When all the guests were there, we sat down at the table. A moment later, Jade got up and straightened her chair.

"Are you leaving?" I said.

She laughed like a child. Kay glanced over, interested, and was about to speak but saw that no one else was laughing. Jade asked for gin and Coke; Joy, for Coke. I was drinking wine. I forget what I ate, but a bowl of roasted chestnuts was in front of me. I won't forget those.

Kay was speaking to Manur, a young man from India. Did he know any relaxation techniques? It was one of her dinner moves, like a party game, the kind of thing she excelled at. India meant oriental wisdom. Manur should have some, even as a student. Manur agreed. He stood behind Maia, our class teacher, brought his hands up and pressed her temples with his fingertips. He did it seriously. He was a

Gandhi man. It wasn't the Olympics or a spelling bee, but when he fingered Maia's head, he did it for his country. She was just as solemn. Everybody was, waiting to see what would happen.

"Manur's touching Maia," I said. Jade turned to me and smiled. Not her sarcastic smile or the giggling one. A new, conspiring smile, as far as lips can go when you're out to dinner.

"You've got lovely hair," Kay said to Maia. She was right. Maia had blonde curls. Jade reached for the chestnuts like popcorn at the cinema. She picked the largest she could find and revolved it in her fingertips suspiciously.

"Take your hand off my nuts," I said.

She didn't answer. At least, not in words. She just peeled the nut with special care, like a surgeon, then placed it in her mouth, probing with her teeth and tongue. She took her time to eat it. At last, when she'd finished, she said, "Is that a wig in your hair? I've always wanted to know."

In those days, I had a lot of hair. She pulled a clump above my eyes then sat back in triumph, though it didn't came off. Had she thought what to do if it had?

A few months later, when Jade and Joy were gone, Kay invited me to dinner. There was another guest I didn't know, and good old Ulrich. I was bored without the girls and probably showed it. I didn't feel like talking. Afterwards, as I was leaving, Kay handed me a book of recipes. International cuisine. I was pleased. Despite my silence, she was still being friendly; she must have forgiven me. The book itself had been well-used, with dog-eared pages and cooking stains. It looked precious. There'd be another dinner – at least one more – so I could give it back. The very subject of the book, food preparation, also pointed to dinner. Everything fitted. So I thought. Kay was acting till the end. It was just an old paperback she didn't want. She had no intention of inviting me again. Cookery for citizens of the world. Cook for yourself in future.

Maia Silly

That's what Joy called our teacher, whose Greek surname sounded like *silly*. Joy wasn't being funny. She meant it. She didn't like her. I did. Maia was entertaining. One day, her mouth filled with blood. I didn't see any, but that was the excuse she mumbled as she left the room, a palm cupped under her chin. She returned a few moments later and went on as if nothing had happened. She said she was thirty-nine and had a father complex, which led her to marry a much older man. She also liked to mime, oddly for a language teacher. Once, she had no choice. When the lesson started, she wrote on the board that her throat was bad and her doctor had forbidden her to speak. Again, tricky for a language teacher, though it got our attention. She was good at that. She sang, too, when her throat let her and she wasn't bleeding. The first time, Kay nodded thoughtfully and said she had a pretty voice. These are the things I remember. They surprised me – the confessions, in particular. Perhaps they're why Joy called her silly.

When the course began, I knew no Greek at all. In Australia, I'd applied for a scholarship to learn it at the university in Salonica. After a few months, I received a letter. It was in Greek. I took it down to Tony,

the Greek greengrocer, and asked him to translate. He couldn't understand much himself, the formal style, though he nodded and said, "I
think you got it." In Salonica, I told Kay, assuming she'd laugh, but she
stood staring.

Jade and Joy had done some lessons already, in the summer, before
I arrived.

"There were thunderstorms every day," Jade said. The foreigners
were grouped in an old building, the classical sort, to please them, I expect. Most were paying. It was like a palace. I imagined the two girls in
a grand room with a high ceiling, working quietly to a backdrop of
thunder. Now, in our class, they seemed more intelligent than me;
they learned more quickly. It was irritating, but it came in handy.
When we planned a speaking task, Joy wrote my lines for me.

"What are you doing. Graham?"

"I'm drinking ouzo."

I couldn't even say that.

"What did you eat for lunch?"

"Bread, cheese, olives."

This amused Maia. Her eyes widened, then she said, "I like the
smell of hot bread."

"Hot bread, hot bread!" Kay echoed, nodding earnestly. The
Americans were more earnest still. They made up half the class, learning Greek, one of them said, so they could read the New Testament in
the original. Then there was Kitty, a blonde Fin in her early 20s. She
was like a Barbie doll, and teacher's pet or one of them.

"The sun shines out of her backside," Joy said, attacking Maia. After class, of course. It would have sounded strange in Greek.

We had an end-of-year exam. In our last lesson, Maia read out the
results. When she got to me, she shook her head sadly.

"Graham, you didn't do well,"

An American girl, one I must have offended, turned to me and
shook her head like Maia but with sarcasm. She was delighted. In fact,
I came second. Maia was teasing me, the sort of thing you do to a pet

student. The girl muttered that I'd "aced" the exam, like a line from a Girls' Annual, though with bitterness. I must have offended her very badly.

"You don't speak," Maia reproached me. At the end, she pressed everyone's hand, but when she got to me, she held on longer, and a tear formed in her eye.

Maia Silly. Of all the memories, the tear and the bloody mouth are clearest, and the farewell dinner. It was at a restaurant. The whole class went. Maia danced on the table, her arms out like Zorba. The Greek experience. She was teaching even then.

The day after, when I saw Jade, she mentioned the dinner. I said Maia had danced well. Jade smiled sceptically but with a glow of pleasure.

"You said she looked like a stranded dolphin!"

Waiting for the revolution

In Salonica, I didn't have a lot of male friends. There was Manur. You know him. He went to Kay's party and fingered the Greek teacher's head. Like my other acquaintances, the male ones, at least, he annoyed me. I annoyed them, too, of course, although we kept quiet about it on the whole.

Manur came as a postgraduate. Like me, he'd won a scholarship. Like Jade and Joy, he lived in the *estía* or student hostel, but he couldn't move in immediately. He rented a basement in town. I went to see him. He told me how he'd felt at the beginning.

"I cracked. It was freezing cold. I just cracked."

When he said *cracked*, his head trembled slightly, at what he'd suffered, I suppose, as if the memory of it could still make him shiver.

While I was there, a workman came to fix something. Manur and I had arrived recently, and we didn't understand much Greek. When the workman spoke, I stayed silent, but Manur nodded and agreed. He said 'Yes, yes' a lot in Greek. It was the first thing about him which annoyed me. After a time, the workman stopped and regarded the two of us. He rebuked me for understanding less. It was the second annoying thing. For once, Manur said nothing. That annoyed me too.

In a group of people, Manur was unassuming. He had a little smile and his brown eyes blinked. I didn't like it. I thought he was doing it consciously. Did he want us to underestimate him? Whatever the reason, he did it very well, the ingénue abroad, a male one. Jade did this herself, and he fooled *her*. She called him 'the little Indian' when he wasn't listening. There was no affection.

When we were alone, he changed. He showcased his skills, his powers of observation, in particular. Once, we arranged to meet in the centre of town, on Aristotélous Square. He got there first. While he was waiting, he watched a young couple. He told me what he'd learnt – how the girl had arrived before the boy, what she did, how they greeted each other, how intimate they were – all with his little smile, like an expert on human nature.

Manur had a sense of wonder. A bus passed on Egnatía. He said the number on the front was different from the one on the back. He probably saw it by chance. It's not something you'd check. I remember his tone – incredulous, laughing at the folly of human kind, the Greek kind, in this instance. At the same time, concerning the general folly, he set himself apart. That sharp eye of his – he didn't train it on himself. It was something else I didn't like.

We walked down to the harbour. There was a ship in the distance, and I pointed to it. I could tell the colour, the direction it was facing, but Manur couldn't see it. He laughed again, the same, incredulous laugh. He didn't play tricks. He really thought I was wrong or pretending. Maybe I deserved the laugh. What was I doing pointing at a ship? It sailed up, somehow, into the conversation – or through a gulf in it.

We passed the revolving restaurant. It's on top of a column, a long way off the ground. Manur said, "I can't see it moving."

Like children, we gazed up, waiting for the whole thing to turn.

Greek for masturbators

When Manur got a room at the university, I went to see him. Someone else was there, a Greek student who spoke English. Eco's *The Name of the Rose* had been published recently. They both had opinions about it. I didn't say anything, except that I hadn't read it. Manur hadn't read it either. The Greek boy said he had started it in Greek.

"Why not?" he added, as if the point might disturb me. "It was written in Italian."

We moved on to girls. I say *we*. Indian girls and Greek girls were debated without insult, though not without censure, by the other two. It was a boys' party game, but all the boys weren't playing. The Greek addressed me again.

"What about Australian girls?"

I still didn't comment. To them, on the subject of girls, I knew nothing. To me, their ready chatter was like purring. I thought, *These two masturbate.*

Afterwards, we went for one of our strolls, Manur and I. There were two Greek girls on a patch of empty ground. You couldn't miss them: lavish mascara, black leather jackets and tight black jeans. Their clothes looked bonded to them. How did they get them off? I'm just wondering theoretically. The girls had seen us too. They were standing close together. They turned their faces in one movement, like a single predator, and stared ironically. When they saw we didn't want them, they laughed, and one of them said, "Μαλάκας" (malákas).

The irony would work in every case: if we wanted them and needed showing who was boss; if we didn't want them and needed dumping before we met; or for some other reason which only girls know. Manur was delighted with the female interest, the laughter and the talk. The fact that they had talked about us, not to us, and laughed at us, not with us, didn't seem to matter. Perhaps he missed the irony altogether. He grinned like a child. Clearly, he had never had a girlfriend. His eyes followed them as they walked away. All right, mine did too, but we were thinking different things.

An eye like Manur's, so sharp, so relentless, would be observing me as well. It was inevitable. With this observation came knowledge of my faults.

"You don't say anything," he said. He was tiring of me, the little Australian.

The last time he came up to see me, about a week later, Graeme was there. I'd invited them to dinner. Another grinding, all-male affair. I cooked a curry. It was a bad choice. Manur disliked spicy food – funny, isn't it? – and was honest enough to say so. Graeme disliked it too, but he went further. He questioned why chillies should exist. Here was a vision of the future, a post-vindaloo world in which I had no place.

Manur asked Graeme what μαλάκας meant. Graeme repeated the word, enunciating like an expert – in language, that is; he spoke Greek very well – then translated it with equal clarity.

"Masturbator."

When the meal was over, we stepped outside. A couple of teenage girls were passing. They lived on my street. They said hello, chanting at me brightly, as Greek girls tended to, "Γεια σου, Γραχαμ!"

Manur was amazed. He looked at them, at me and back at them, then he burst out laughing. The girls had walked on, but they must have heard. *And <u>he</u>'s dumping <u>me</u>.* His eyes followed them. After a few seconds, eyes still following, he said softly in his purring way, "Nice girls."

Silence and Pause in Pinter

Kay took Manur and me for a ride in her car. I forget where. We talked about Australia for a while. I was born there. Kay had taught French in the same city. Manur was in a chatty mood. He actually told a joke, albeit an old one.

"Someone met an Australian and asked him when he'd come. The Australian answered, 'I came today.' The other chap said, 'I asked you when you came, not why.'"

He smiled his little smile. Manur understood his own virtues – humour, in this case – if, for the most part, he liked to conceal them. He understood mine, too. Was I smiling? Was I saying funny things? I had no sense of humour. On the other hand, he affected Kay. When he told his joke, something happened to her. She looked surprised (though she often did), gave one of her tense chuckles and went on peering at the road.

"What's your thesis about?" she asked after the dip in the conversation. Manur's thesis was on silence and pause in Pinter. He'd told me when we first met, enthusiastically, as if no one else had dreamt of such a topic.

"It's fascinating," he'd said, "how much meaning you can find in a pause."

When Kay asked, she glanced over with polite interest, briefly, I'm glad to say, as she was driving. She must have thought her question couldn't fail. As a rule, authors aren't slow to discuss their work. Manur gave the title but no more. Kay persisted. She wanted to know, for politeness' sake, what he'd done. He'd been talking freely. She assumed he'd keep talking, if only to be polite, like her. But he didn't. She was confused. Was it his old, reserved self, or was there some other reason? Let's be honest. It was just another thesis which didn't matter, which didn't interest Kay or anybody else. She wasn't about to steal his ideas. She needed words to fill a silence.

She asked again. Still no answer. In fact, he had written nothing. He didn't tell me. It was obvious; not to Kay, however. She was irritated when he didn't answer, and he was irritated when she kept asking. Eyes on the road.

Even I, who lacked his funny bone, could appreciate the humour. I smiled my little smile – at her perplexity, at his discomfort. The thesis was meant to examine silence. It was doing that already. It was the equivalent of pause, a masterpiece of absent sound. But silence is something. His thesis wasn't anything except a title. *Silence and Pause in Pinter.* It seemed impressive, but no one made him write it, so he didn't. And he wouldn't talk.

Silence.

In Kay's cramped car, we all examined it, one Sunday afternoon a long time ago.

Gandhi's house

Manur didn't mention his thesis anymore. One day, he went back to India, to Ahmedabad, where he lived with his mother. He looked at ease. That's right. I was still dropping in, and I could still annoy him.

We were sitting on the sofa. I told him the BBC was going to broadcast a story I'd written. He went stiff for five seconds – it was a long time – then jerked his head towards me as if I'd insulted him. He told me that he wanted to write (his eye for detail, remember), but being bilingual made it difficult. As for my story, he missed the broadcast. He said he was in bed.

There are more important things than words. I needed clean water. The liquid from the tap was poisoning me. It was raining, so I took a bowl from the kitchen and put it on the roof, hoping it would fill overnight. I think I asked first or simply did it while Manur and his mother watched. It was an ordinary bowl, stainless steel and shiny. In India, such things are beautiful. You can buy them here in London, imported, but they lose something – not their shine, their context.

We sat there, Manur and I, listening to the rain, thinking about the bowl in our different ways. He was anxious. He said it was acid rain.

He pondered what the acid could do – to the bowl, not my stomach. Although he didn't tell me, and his mother didn't say (not to me, at least), she was upset. It wasn't my bowl. It was hers. Judging from his face, the acid was too.

Next morning, I retrieved the bowl. It was full to the lip. I could have used a larger one. He told me not to do it again.

Rajiv Gandhi became Prime Minister when his mother was killed. I told Manur it was the Gandhi name that got him elected. It was self-evident. I wasn't trying to offend him, but he was cross. It didn't reflect well on the country.

My trip to the Mahatma's ashram didn't help. Manur was concerned about my clothes. I should wear something better, he said. I replied I'd be a target for thieves. He laughed incredulously. As it turned out, I was a target anyway. The ashram was a short bus ride out of town. On the way back, a bony young man picked my pocket. I know he was bony because he jumped on me from behind as I was getting on the bus, and wrapped his arms around me. There was no door. Before we'd travelled very far, he dropped off like a full leech onto the road and was gone. A passenger remarked, "You'd better check your wallet."

The young man was surely disappointed. He only got the travel clock in my left pocket. He couldn't reach the other side. When I told Manur, he was speechless. No sympathy. He was annoyed again. It didn't reflect well on the country.

He had a job producing TV commercials. His current project was a petrol advertisement for a local company. He took me through it. His catch phrase pleased him the most, *Put a tiger in your tank*. He smiled and waited for my approval. It was, of course, the Esso slogan from the 1960s. Had no one else noticed that he'd stolen the line? Or, if they had, did no one care? I said nothing. There was nothing I could say. For Manur, it was another dreadful silence.

I hadn't changed, but he hadn't, either. He was very enthusiastic about his new job, the way he had been about his thesis. And he was still smiling, still observing.

"The actresses are fascinating. They never stop acting."

He paused for a moment and wondered at the actresses who never stopped acting. He recalled their tricks and charms, shaking his head gently, while I recalled nothing. I wasn't a TV producer. I didn't know any actresses. But I wondered something too: what actresses were doing in a petrol advertisement.

Old Town, Salonica

A consul in Salonica

In my first year in Salonica, I decided to go to Mt Athos. You need a special permit, a *diamonitirion*. Nowadays, they're granted by the Pilgrims' Office in Salonica. Back then, you had to arrange it through a consulate. There was no Australian consulate in Salonica, so I used the British one. I was lucky. It meant meeting Terry. I'll call him that, but it's not his real name.

He was sitting at a great desk on a great armchair, both solid wood, polished, as befitted Her Majesty's consul. There was an ordinary chair for me. As soon as I sat down, he called the British embassy in Athens. I didn't understand. The phone call wasn't about me. Nor was he posing. A consul doesn't have to. In fact, when he spoke, he was self-effacing, with me and on the phone. When the switchboard answered, he didn't give his name straightaway – no rank-pulling from Terry – and when he did, he muttered it, just the surname, apologetically, like a schoolboy owning up.

His skin gleamed, though he must have been sixty. Perhaps he was sweating, but it wasn't hot. It was March, yet his face was sunburnt already. He had wispy blonde hair, not balding, and blue eyes that shone like his skin, weakly. I could see some excess flesh. He wore a tie and a bulky shirt with blue and white stripes. All he needed was a cap, and you'd have a British schoolboy, a big, old-fashioned one. More than anything, I was struck by his gentleness. This, too, may have been excessive.

The phone call was about a drugs arrest. A real boy had been really naughty, an eighteen-year-old, Terry explained when the call was over.

"He claimed he hitched a lift and the driver raped him. It was hard to believe. I said, 'You would have fought him off, a strong lad like you.'"

Terry fell silent and gazed before him as if he was looking at the boy. The anecdote surprised me. It was consular business, no names, but I wondered why he'd told me. There was something intimate about it. I'd only known him for a few minutes. He also had a habit of repeating the last words I said, in a pensive tone. I didn't like it, but I liked Terry.

He described some of the drawbacks of visiting Mt Athos: poor transport, no women or meat. I said it didn't matter about the meat; I was vegetarian.

"Do you ever eat it?"

"No, I couldn't keep it down."

"Couldn't keep it down."

He nodded while he said it, like a man learning. As for the lack of women, he quipped that it didn't matter, either. He said they were jealous because they couldn't go, and took revenge by lounging naked on hire boats in front of the monasteries. He chuckled, but it was true.

He was planning a trip himself in his role as consul. He asked me if I wanted to join the official party.

"We'll get to use the jeep."

It was the sort of thing a schoolboy would say. I liked him even more. I said yes. There was an expat called Bryan who had also agreed to go. Terry was after one more person "to make up a decent party," as he put it; two pairs so you could walk side by side, when the narrow paths allowed, and no one would feel ignored. He asked me if I knew anyone. I thought of Manur. He was still in Salonica. In some ways, he was perfect: male, unassuming (on the surface) and unattached – there'd be no jealous woman left behind – and he fancied himself as a traveller. He'd flown from India, hadn't he? We'd also spent a weekend at Metéora, pillars of rock with their own monasteries. He seemed to enjoy that. The next time I saw him, I asked if he'd like to go to Athos. He said he would. I pulled out my travel stuff. I had some information about Athos. I also had two maps of the world, not much use on Athos, and I didn't need both. I offered one to Manur and let him choose. He opened out the maps side by side, compared them for a long while then took the better, more expensive one.

Mr David Manner

There are no two ways about it. Mt Athos is a fortress of discrimination. No women, for a start. I should stand with the oppressed and not go. In a sense, however, I am one of them. A hundred Greek visitors are permitted each day but only ten foreigners. Orthodox clerics from other countries are exempt from the quota, but they still need a letter of recommendation. There's a wrong type of Orthodox, too.

"You should be fine," Terry said when he signed my application. He meant my chances of admission. I was finer than he imagined. On a later visit, when I was there alone, I decided to stay an extra night beyond the four-day limit. I told the monastery I'd missed the boat. There was one a day. The extra night was illegal, literally, but they let me stay. There wasn't much choice since the boat had gone, though they weren't bothered. I could have stayed longer. All the same, Terry knew things I didn't. The mountain mightn't want you in the first place.

One morning, I took Manur to the consulate. Terry observed him (a few seconds too long, I thought) then put his reading glasses on and checked Manur's passport. I have an image in my head of his turning certain pages upside down to examine them more closely. This may be a fantasy, but Terry did peer at every page as if his job depended on it. After all, there may have been something, a stamp, a black cross, an empty space, which disqualified Manur and would make Terry look foolish if he didn't spot it. With his office work, Terry normally followed the rules, though he broke others, as I found out later. We all exaggerate, Manur included. His face was tight. The passport inspection had irked him. It got worse.

"Manur David Madyan."

Terry read out the full name (I've changed it slightly). Along with his official tone, there was a hint of doubt. He reflected for a moment then began writing on the application form.

"We'll make that David Manner."

He wasn't changing Manur's name forever, just for Mt Athos, for the permit, to make a better case for admission. He also put Manur down as British. It was another favour. I felt a laugh bubbling in my chest. When the application was done, Terry took his glasses off and sat back. He was pleased with himself. Manur had passed the interview, albeit in an altered form. Diplomacy is about compromise. He was now an Englishman and, implicitly, a Christian, not the right type for the monks, but as good as they usually got with a foreigner, and better – in their view and possibly in Terry's – than any non-Christian alternative. Terry didn't notice the humour. Manur didn't either. After the interview, as soon as the door closed behind us, he said, "I don't like him!" and quivered with disgust. "David was my father's name."

Terry meant well – he always did – but Manur's name wouldn't make any difference, or his race or anything else. We were all non-Orthodox, all damned. As long as you paid the fee, you got in. Mt Athos is unique, but it's rock and earth. We weren't applying for heaven.

When Terry listed the drawbacks of visiting Mt Athos, there was one thing he didn't mention: the rumours about the monks' sexual habits. Manur told me the next time we met. His Greek friends at the university had filled him in (gleefully, I expect) when he referred to the planned visit. If he went, he wouldn't just sacrifice his name, his country and his filial pride. He would part with his chastity as well. It was too much. He no longer wished to go. Manur disqualified himself.

Orthodoxy or Death

I told Jade and Joy I was going to Mt Athos with the British consul on an official visit. Joy was enthusiastic. Jade was thoughtful. She was a zealous Briton and a sterling girl. She also dreamed of going. Not only, as a female, was she barred from Athos, but I, the man who mocked her, was going there with the Queen's envoy, the man from Old Blighty, who had no idea she existed.

"You'll land on your feet," she mumbled jealously.

Terry was right about the jeep. One was waiting for us when the boat docked at Dafni. It took us up the hill to Karyés, leaving the lesser pilgrims in the dust. In a large, old building, our permits were examined. There was Terry, Bryan and a young man whose name I forget. An aide lowered his face to my ear and asked me softly in Greek, "Who is the consul?"

I pointed discreetly. I was flattered. The aide had asked *me*. I was, in his opinion, the person most likely to understand – or the one least likely to be the consul.

We were heading to Esphigmenou. The jeep took us as far as Vatopedi. At that point, the track became a path, and we had to walk. Even from a distance, Esphigmenou looked unwelcoming. It was prison-grey and dreary. We got closer. On the roof was a flag like a skull and cross bones and, on the wall, a massive banner with the words:

ΟΡΘΟΔΟΞΙΑ Η ΘΑΝΑΤΟC

Orthodoxy or death. Bold, as mission statements go, it wasn't just aimed at pilgrims. The monks were in a power struggle with the ruling body. They were used to a fight; in the old days, with marauding Turks. Terry had lost his job because of them, the modern sort, when they invaded Cyprus. He was the last British consul in Kyrenia. He lost his house, too.

"A pretty little town," he said wistfully. "There was a café on the waterfront. I used to drink ouzo and watch the sun set."

"Didn't the Turks invade because the junta in Athens was plotting a coup?" I'd heard this on the BBC. "They thought there'd be a massacre by the Greeks."

Silence. I had said the wrong thing; not wrong, perhaps, in terms of fact but wrong because it embarrassed Terry. I couldn't tell why. I wasn't siding with the Turks, though I might have seemed to be. His wife was Greek, but she wasn't there to hear me. Maybe he had no idea why the Turks invaded and could think of nothing to say. For us, of course, the reason didn't matter. The invasion did. Without it, he wouldn't have moved to Greece. I never would have met him, or Bryan, probably.

"Now, I have to move again," he lamented. The consulate was closing. There'd be an honorary consul instead, a Greek man, in smaller offices. It wouldn't cost so much. "I asked Geoffrey to have a word with Margaret. He said there's no point; he can't do anything with her."

The young man pricked up his ears.

"Geoffrey Howe? You know Geoffrey Howe?"

Mrs Thatcher's Foreign Secretary. Terry nodded but was silent. The young man turned to Bryan and asked him about his work. It had been for a UN body, reconstruction in Europe or something.

"An important post?"

"Yes, I suppose it was."

More silence. The young man didn't turn to me.

That night, before sleeping, I rinsed my shirt to get the sweat out. There were several beds in one room. I draped the wet shirt on a chair between Terry's bed and mine. It was another mistake. In the morning, the shirt was dry, but there was a pool of water on the floor.

"It looks like pee!" he complained. He was serious. For someone as gentle as Terry, it was almost shrill. The pool was right next to his bed. He disliked the mess, and he didn't want the blame for what I'd done. Water wasn't pee, but it was inappropriate, not all the time, just now, in its current position. A bit like Terry.

We thought he was going to rape you

Terry asked me to find out when breakfast would be. He was aware I spoke Greek. He wasn't aware how little. When a monk came out of the kitchen, I translated the word Terry had used. Another mistake. I couldn't recall the monks' term. I should have just said *food*.

"When is breakfast?"

"Breakfast! Breakfast!"

The Greek word resembles a clucking noise. Shrieked indignantly, it's even better. In a fury, the monk returned to the kitchen. It was a dangerous thing to do. There was a roar. A flash of fire reflected on the wall. I said, "His beard's gone up in flames."

"Beard's gone up in flames!" Terry laughed. It startled the young man. He collected himself then managed a smirk.

When we were leaving, in the reception area, a monk appeared and called me over with his forefinger. Terry raised his eyebrows. I followed the monk. He knew what he was doing, if no one else did. He had a stoop and scuttled off in his black robes like a beetle on some key, insect task. It was only a few steps, to a tiny room with a table against the wall, nothing more, and no window. The monk shut the door behind us. The others waited, but they were in their walking clothes, with a traveller's air, keen to go. I was less than a minute. When I came out, I said, "He asked me for dollars."

"We thought he was going to rape you," Terry answered. He was chuckling, but he seemed relieved. Why did the monk choose me? Did I look the biggest tourist, the most likely to have dollars, or the least assertive, the most likely to follow? Or the most corrupt? Black market dollars. Whatever it was, the monk had a worldly eye. *We thought he was going to rape you.* You didn't think too long.

On the path to Vatopedi, we heard an odd noise. It unsettled Terry. "What was that?"

"I thought it was my stomach," I said. We'd had beans for breakfast. Terry had warned us about flatulence. He was only half-joking. Now, he stopped walking, turned (he always went in front) and beheld me fully from head to toe.

"You know," he said, as if to himself, though everyone could hear, "I think Graham's rather wonderful."

A lot can happen on a country walk. We saw a lynx on a high slope, escaping from view; an elongated cat with funny ears. The young man said, "They roam wild here."

"Roam wild here," Terry echoed. He turned to me again. "Graham, would you mind carrying my bag?" He watched me take it for a few steps then said, "You must be as strong as an ox! So thin, too."

Then he walked off with the young man, animated, as if their conversation was enthralling. I glanced at Bryan. He was hurt. Terry had forgotten us.

It was spring. That's something beautiful. I mentioned herbal tea. Bryan replied, "It's an abomination!"

We rested on a patch of grass, all four of us, and dozed off in the sun. When we woke up, I said, "I hope no one's been...interfered with."

"No, unfortunately," Terry chuckled as he always did when I made that type of comment. The young man was ready. He chuckled too.

Terry twisted an ankle on the path. It was his light, canvas shoes, Bryan said; they weren't appropriate for the stony track, for the mountain. He said it mildly – Bryan was never loud – though he disapproved.

Terry left on a kind of ambulance boat. The young man left too. There was no point in staying.

A kiss in the Hotel Tourist

I popped into the consulate before it shut down. I had my photographs of Mt Athos to show Terry. The prints delighted him, genuinely, I thought, so I gave them to him. I kept the negatives. When he moved to England, he showed the photos to some friends. They decided to go to Athos together. They'd travel to Salonica then continue to the Holy Mountain.

So, Terry came back to Greece like most people, on holiday, a plain citizen. The consul was no more. We met up briefly. He brought three friends – he liked his party of four – but one of them ruffled even Terry. When the others couldn't hear, he confided, "Gerald comes across too camp."

There was an air of expectation about them, as if they had a mission to fulfil. I pictured them at Ouranóupolis (city of heaven), assembled on the pier like schoolboys on a trip, then boarding the boat to Athos, a special boat that left the girls behind.

After they returned to Salonica, I dropped in to their hotel room. If I hadn't, there wouldn't have been a kiss in the Hotel Tourist, not one involving me. They were going back to England, and I wanted to say goodbye to Terry. At the end of the evening, when I was about to leave, he leaned his face forward – he didn't say anything – and kissed me on the left cheek. He was drunk; he was maudlin, though he mightn't have done it in front of Bryan. Three men stood next to us. They all saw the kiss, and they all condoned it. I think I did too. There isn't much else to say. It was very quick. A kiss in the Hotel Tourist – a chapter heading, not the title for a book; a thing you do with sadness as much as love, like a last sip of ouzo when you're leaving Greece and you aren't sure if you're coming back again. A kiss is like the person who gives it, and this one felt like Terry: gentle, spontaneous, not too wicked but not too innocent. There weren't any more. It was our final meeting. I didn't tell Bryan about the kiss. I didn't need to. I could guess what he'd do. He'd swing around with a touch of rhetoric then say, with a second touch, "Oh, did he?"

In every monastery, in the pilgrims' quarters, there's a sign on the wall, by the door. The wording varies, but the message, in several languages, is the same: no inappropriate behaviour, no disrespect to the Holy Mountain. Examples include noise and bare skin, ordinary things for most people. Nothing about kissing. If you break the rules, you risk being "cast out of the monastery." We used to smile at the signs, Bryan and I – at most things, in fact – when I knew him better. We imagined being thrown off the roof. A Greek hotel has signs, lots of them, but nothing like these.

A few years later, when I was living in Rome, I got a letter from Terry asking if he could stay with me "if things get too difficult over here." It was ominous. There were no more letters. Some months passed, a year perhaps. Bryan sent me the news. Terry's wife had divorced him. He'd been cast out again. First, it was a country, Cyprus, when the Turks invaded; then a mountain, Athos, when he sprained his ankle; next, a town, Salonica, when the consulate closed; and now his own home in England. As always, he adapted; he found another place, for the time being, anyway. He was living with a young man, Bryan said, adding, "It's not homosexual or anything like that."

Good old Terry. He'll be chuckling somewhere. He liked irony. The British consulate reopened, and the consul is a woman.

Old Town, Salonica

Higher than Olympus

Bryan lived on the sixth floor, the last but one, in his wife's apartment in Salonica. It was on the waterfront. The buildings there were all fairly new. The apartment had two small bedrooms and a kitchen. The living area was a big, open space with a window from ceiling to floor right along the side which faced the harbour. At least, that's how I remember it. I'm using the past tense because I don't go anymore. Not much will have changed, except Bryan and his wife aren't there. Watching the vast window, as you felt you had to, was like sitting close to a movie screen, one that was fixed on a single frame of light.

On a day of great optical clarity (Bryan's words), the mountains were visible in the distance. That wasn't very often. I saw them only once from his apartment. January, it must have been. It was like a miracle, given the usual haze. The peaks were very small. It felt as if you were looking down on them. You were higher than Olympus.

Bryan told me how a group of Englishmen had climbed the main peak. You can walk up without much effort. For safety – someone's idea of safety – they were all attached to the same rope. Entertaining in itself, but they had also been drinking. After a happy ascent, they finally stood on top, a flat space not much bigger than a dining room table. Then someone lost his balance, pulled the others with him, and they fell to their death.

Bryan's wife was Greek. She appeared very old. When she was a girl, the Germans came to her school and took away the Jewish children. One was a friend of hers. Each time Bryan had me round, she invited her own acquaintances. I thought about it. The two of them weren't competing. She wasn't belligerent. She didn't dislike me too much, as far as I could tell. And her English was perfect. When she knew I was coming, she simply imagined the result: she'd have nothing to say and no interest in trying; she'd feel left out in her own home. So she called her friends. Still, it was heavy-handed. I felt sorry for Bryan. What did they talk about when I wasn't there? Was she interested in *him*?

The two groups sat apart. Bryan and I had the dining room table; his wife and friends, the armchairs and sofa. Four old Greek ladies. They wouldn't have knitted the whole evening, but it seems like that now. They chattered above the needle points, never raising their eyes. One night, in a quiet voice, Bryan noted how they all spoke at the same time. It was true. They didn't merely ignore Bryan and me. They didn't listen to each other, not for a second. It was riveting.

Once, just once, we all had tea together, sitting at the table. Bryan passed on the news that the BBC was going to broadcast a story I had written. He was proud of me, I think. One of the old ladies asked how much I was getting paid. The question surprised me. I didn't think it was important. When I answered, she laughed. Another explained, "He's only a beginner."

Naked on the Mountain

When Bryan died, I talked about him with his brother-in-law. I remember saying this, the exact words, "He never said anything, but I think he saw me as a kind of son."

Let's keep him for a while, old Bryan, and I'll tell you about our final trip to Athos. We stayed the first night at Símona Petra. We'd been before. It was one of our favourite monasteries. As soon as we arrived, a monk brought a tray of coffee, loukoumi and ouzo, in small receptacles (as Bryan would say), along with some water in big glasses. We'd nearly missed it – a bed, too – as they were about to close the door.

"I couldn't manage without this," Bryan said, eyeing the tray.

"It's the only reason I come!"

Bryan glanced at me and smiled, wondering how much I meant it.

We didn't come to Athos for the food. It was poor and not enough. Once, at Símona Petra or one of the other postcard monasteries on the west coast, I offered my lentils to Bryan, and he took them. I wasn't expecting him to. He didn't like lentils, and he could see I had nothing else. He must have been starving. You could tell from the way he ate my dinner. As I watched, I felt like a parent. I was pleased for him and with myself. I also regretted it. I was hungry.

After the meal – Bryan's meal – we sat on a balcony overlooking the courtyard, a tiny space, and the church filled most of it. It's what the space was for. Monks don't walk dogs or play ball. There was a tree or two, a ring of cobbles and enough room to get into the church. I spoke abruptly to Bryan, a profanity (as he would say). I forget which, but it weighed like stone. Bryan didn't swear, and we were on a holy mountain, in a monastery; above all, a place of beauty, where you say nothing; you fast from words, even kind ones. I didn't do it again, but he never did it to me.

In the dormitory, I opened my knapsack. I had a few things, though we couldn't eat them. There was a yellow torch, a miniature for travel, which I'd bought in Greece. Bryan liked it. I still have it in my drawer. The chain is broken, but it works, or it did when I last tried it. There was a mirror from a street market in Jaipur near the Palace of Winds. It was round, about the size of my hand and very light, for travel, same as the torch. It had a plastic cover which opened out so the mirror could stand up by itself then fold back when you were finished. Bryan liked that, too. The monks don't have mirrors. They aren't allowed. He turned it in his fingers, carefully, like a piece of contraband. It's long gone.

Things can seem more valuable than they are; others, you don't ap-preciate. Bryan stroked my chin, the soft underpart, with a forefinger. We were sitting on his bed. Later, when he fell asleep, I changed dormi-tories, not because he stroked me – he snored. That night, I slept well. I had a whole room to myself. However, in the morning, when I walked back to Bryan, he looked at me strangely.

I bathed on a hillside, on a shady path, though it wasn't secluded. In those days, you couldn't wash in the monasteries. There weren't any bathrooms. We found a pipe sticking out of a rock, with no tap, so it never stopped flowing. The water came straight from the mountain. It was frigid. Bryan wandered off. He was being polite – I was naked –

but he came back too soon. He wasn't the kissing sort. He may have been concerned. If I took too long, the monks might catch me. I'm a slow washer. He probably just got tired of waiting. Or lost track of time.

We walked on, in sunshine now. The air was warm and felt warmer after my bath. Bryan was ahead of me. On a level part, he halted and said that I'd hear from his lawyer when he died.

He came out with it abruptly, as I used to do. It wasn't like Bryan. "There'll be something for you."

I'd considered death and Bryan but not together. I didn't want to discuss it. I assumed the 'something' was books. I really did. Years on, I realised it was money. Bryan planned. He had planned this, too, to tell me on the mountain. It was the right moment, a place we both loved, and the right path: exquisite, certainly; just sun and gorse, sea and stones, open to the world, yet private, between the two of us.

When he died, there was no money. I was disappointed. I couldn't help it. Maybe he ran out or changed his mind. I no longer visited. One year, he passed through London but didn't tell me until he'd gone. "I had some business to do." Did he rewrite his will? It's a tad dramatic. But when I had the thought, silly as it was, it stayed in my head, as Bryan does now. I'm still poor, still silly. Perhaps the lawyer died first.

A glass of ouzo

I have this memory of Mt Athos on the shore below Zográphou monastery, where the monks have their port or arsenal. There'd been a storm, but you wouldn't know. The sea and the sky were the same creamy blue, like milk poured in water then left completely still. Just looking at it made you want to sleep.

Once, when I went with Bryan, he wandered off. It was before a meal. He was probably thinking about something and forgot the time, or things like time didn't matter. I had to tell the monks so they'd leave some food out when he wandered back. They were annoyed.

"This isn't a hotel!"

On the hot stones outside the monastery, one of the monks interrogated me: how I knew Bryan, where we'd met, how long I'd known him. They were all important questions, but they weren't going to bring Bryan back. I felt like a small boy being punished. No one worried about Bryan. It didn't occur to us that he mightn't come back. An hour or so later, he reappeared as casually as he'd gone. I said nothing, but that night, while he was snoring, I punched him in the arm.

Years afterwards, Bryan went to Athos by himself. He asked me, but I didn't go. I *was* in England. It must have saddened him, though. He understood it would be his last trip. Now, I don't have a choice. If I go, it won't be with Bryan.

In Salonica, when Candy and Cassie turned up, they were desperate to go to Mt Athos. I told them about Bryan and our trips to the mountain. I repeated one of his sentences, and Candy said, "I don't want to know anyone like that."

They never met. You don't let your kittens play with the St Bernard.

Cassie, white as milk beside the local girls, even next to Candy, had a Greek boyfriend called Athos. They were getting intimate. Candy mentioned it one day when Cassie wasn't there. I couldn't help saying, "She's going to Mount Athos after all." I thought Candy would laugh, but she was irritated. I blushed like a child.

When their twelve months were up and they were leaving for England, both girls said they'd return.

"You won't come back," I said firmly. "No one ever does."

They were cross, vowed to prove me wrong, left and didn't come back.

Bryan comes back, his image, I mean. I see him at different places, but most often at Xeropotámou. It's high on a slope above Símona Petra, with views of the sea. The monks have a bench to sit on, and that's where Bryan is. An old cat jumps on his lap. In a telling way, Bryan peers at me. A whole monastery to sleep in, and she chose him.

There are shadows now. Better get down to Símona Petra before they close the door. Don't miss out on your welcome tray, your coffee and loukoumi, a glass of ouzo, a glass of water. Put water in the ouzo, and it looks like milk.

You might learn something

Candy, Cassie and I were all teaching English at the same language school. At first, Candy defended everyone I criticised. There were tests one week. Candy said some of the parents were very anxious. She said it with a chuckle, but she was empathising.

"How pathetic!" I replied. It made her cross.

When I said the school secretary was bovine, her face showed me who she thought was stupid. When I grumbled about the director and his holiday during term (two weeks at a Red Sea resort), she told me in her classroom voice that I should talk to him when he got back.

"You might learn something!"

He was an old chap. When he spoke to Candy and Cassie, he was very kind. His tone was paternal, like pampering daughters. But daughters have to do what they're told. They worked it out later, the secretary, too.

The two girls lived in an apartment provided by the school. They did everything together. One morning, they even phoned in sick at the same time. They must have been up the night before and couldn't get out of bed. Like Jade and Joy, they weren't actually friends. They formed a pair for protection. Candy described one adventure. They were on a bus. Some Greek boys were teasing them, the way boys do. The girls were at the front, near the driver. He took pity on them and winked or nodded or something. At any rate, the girls understood. At the next stop, they got off by the middle door, and the boys followed. The driver shut it behind them but opened the front door just long enough for the girls to jump back on. The boys were left on the road, shaking their fists and shouting.

Cassie was always sweet, and if Candy was cross with me, at least she still spoke. A young man from England was not so lucky. He came to stay with them. They'd all done the same teaching course, Candy said. During practice sessions, while one of them was teaching, the other students stood in the corridor, observing through a pane of glass. When it was the young man's turn, he didn't look comfortable. Imagine life like that, a kind of sealed room with girls at the window, watching.

Everybody passed the course. The two girls arranged work before they came to Greece, and the freeloader asked himself along. That's what Candy called him. He hadn't found a job.

"I bet he thought he'd sleep with one of us," she said. "Wait till you see his trousers." She smiled sarcastically then told me his pet phrase, "It's really wacky."

All this poison before we'd even met. She asked me around for dinner, introduced us and didn't speak to him again. In lots of ways, he was an ordinary young man. But she was right about the trousers, black, leather things that squeaked when he walked. The sort of trousers which might impress a girl. Awkward, though; each step like wading through oil.

She was right about the pet phrase, too. He (I don't recall his name) chatted for a while when I arrived. There'd been a funny incident on his way from England. I don't recall that, either. When he finished telling the story, he said, with a chuckle, not expecting silence, "It was really wacky."

There was another funny incident, during dinner. I discovered bendy straws. The girls had put them in our glasses. When the young man fled to the toilet, I held my straw up between a thumb and forefinger, examined it and said, "It's really...kinky."

The girls laughed, a loud flush of giggles. I wonder how it sounded to the young man hiding in the toilet. He crept back eventually. After that, no one laughed. Dinner was like a funeral; worse, a funeral where the mourners don't get on.

There are girls you don't get to sleep with. Candy and Cassie left the room and didn't come back. It's why I'd been invited: they dumped the freeloader on me. I decided to speak to him, which was treachery, so I kept my voice down, but they probably didn't care if I spoke to him or not, as long as they didn't have to. Again, I don't recall what I said. It was saying things that mattered, and the soft voice I said them with. It may have seemed kind. He'd been ignored for a while. He swung his head around as if I'd tugged him, and gazed at me, so grateful it was sad. It shows you what a few words can do, a few, trite things you don't remember.

Paul Paul's Pink Penis

I'd been having a drink with Cassie and Candy, at my place, but it was time for them to go. Their apartment was down by the harbour. We walked along to the arch to find a taxi. It was a cold, December night, and I had my coat on. I opened it like a flasher, suddenly, in front of the two girls then lay on my back on the road, arms and legs apart, pretending to be dead. Even now, I see their white faces in the darkness, turning about with laughter, framed by the stonework of the arch.

We walked through the arch and took the first road left. A taxi pulled up immediately like a sniffer dog. The girls were ready, but I couldn't let them go. I recognised the driver.

"He's no good," I said in a sober voice without explaining. They laughed again.

The road is level here, at the top of the hill, and follows the old wall. To the right, as we were heading, the ground falls away. If you walk down, it's so steep you feel like running. The twisting lanes carry you along till you aren't sure which one to take. They're lined with little houses, some new, some old, each touching the one next door. Windows open onto the street. At one, a face was sitting behind the glass, lit by a yellow lamp.

"It's Paul!" I said. "Quick!"

Paul Paul was an artist, a Greek American. I wasn't going to share the girls with him. By now, they were giggling all the time. The way I said *Paul!* and *Quick!* – urgently – was meant to make them laugh. They scurried on without knowing why, laughing without knowing why, which made them laugh even more.

Παύλος Παύλου. The name is more convincing in Greek. In the yellow light, his face was strange. When he saw us, it got stranger. There was recognition then a query, for an instant only, though long enough for Paul to look offended, before the slope and the laughter drove us on. Worse, when I said "Quick!", he may have heard.

Now I knew where Paul lived, I went to see him. His house resembled mine, though his walls were stone. In the Old Town, most windows are small, but each morning, when the shutters open, the Greek sun retakes the whole building, possessing it with light.

We sat down. His fly wasn't zipped. He had no underpants. I think it was a trend. The underpants, not the fly. Do expats wear underpants today? They're usually tight, you have to wash them and they bother you when you're getting dressed. I mean the underpants.

I tried not to stare, but his penis was so cosy, curled up as if it was napping. I don't remember much about the visit. It's not surprising. But I remember what he said half an hour on when he saw his penis.

"You should have told me!"

When he spoke, he was staring at his penis, though I could see his face. It had the same, indignant look. That's *Paul Paul's Pink Penis,* a still life hanging in my head.

Paul Paul and the Toilet

Paul needed money, so he held an exhibition of his paintings. To advertise, he was putting posters up in town. I bumped into him. He took a rolled-up poster out of his knapsack and gave it to me. It was an example of his work, presumably the best. It appeared to be a copy from a photo or another painting, a Monet perhaps, the garden at Giverny. A figure was in the foreground or was trying to be. Afterwards, I showed the poster to Candy and Cassie. When Candy spotted the misshaped person, she said, "It's not outstanding."

I had enough posters in the house. I fixed Paul's on a wall in my toilet, which was in the backyard – it still is, probably, unless it's fallen down – an old Turkish thing, a hole in cement that fed into an underground tank. There was a rudimentary cistern and chain. You had to watch your feet when it flushed. If you put paper in, the hole would block, so I used a shopping bag (I didn't want to empty a bin) and asked visitors to do the same. The girls from England weren't persuaded.

"I hope I didn't put anything down there I shouldn't have," said Cassie once in a best-girl voice. Candy refrained altogether.

One day, Paul dropped in. We talked about Mt Athos, the beauty of it and the awkwardness. In those days, the toilets on Mt Athos weren't even Turkish, just platforms on a monastery wall, balconies with holes in them. You didn't go at night. On a warm day, peering down, you noticed little flowers on the wall and gulls in the air between you and the ocean. In bad weather, the surf seemed miles below. It struck the rocks in miniature. They've put in toilets now. The monks deserve their comforts.

I brought up the rumours I'd heard, to see what Paul would say. I was sceptical.

"They're true!" he replied. "I was propositioned."

I believed him. He was thirty or so but looked younger; well-built, with a fair complexion. An all-Greek-American boy, the type who could interest a monk. I was never propositioned and I went several times. A young monk at Hilandaríou asked me to stay. I don't know if that counts. He said I'd make a good monk.

Paul used my toilet. You can't tell someone not to, but I smiled as he went out. I wouldn't normally. When he came back, he said in a hurt voice, "You put my poster on the wall!"

He sensed that where it was expressed my opinion of it. Why else would I put it in the toilet? It was worse than throwing it away. I knew he'd be offended, but I didn't care. It was a lousy painting. Still, thinking back, I wish he hadn't seen it.

The exhibition was successful, apparently. People bought his paintings, and he made enough cash – so he said – to fly back to the States. Money for boys. He left some wooden frames with Graeme to post on later. Graeme left them with me. In the Old Town, expats did this a lot, let other people clean up after them. As for the holes in the ground, in Turkey they're called Greek toilets. I'm not joking.

That's Paul Paul, the artist who exhibited himself and then his paintings and was frequently offended.

Meryl's chickens

There was another expat who didn't work at the school, a Scot called Meryl. She was thirty or so and rented the hovel across my backyard. She used to live where I was, in the hovel on the street, then she moved to the rear. It was quieter, of course. It was also more discreet. She had visitors. One was a Greek called Iannis. He wore a jacket and tie. He was dressed up, I suppose. Nonetheless, he had a used air, like a travelling salesman. She referred to him only once, with a raised eyebrow. He came several times "to get his bald spot polished."

She didn't say that. I'm quoting myself. The phrase popped into my head when I first saw him. I thought I'd coined it, though I may have heard it somewhere. I told Candy and Cassie about him. There was no need. I just wanted to repeat the phrase. They glared back crossly. I'm not sure why. Perhaps they didn't like the smugness. I obviously felt it was clever. I was being nosey, too. Perhaps they objected to that – it was the neighbour's affair, so to speak – or to the levity. I don't think it was a moral view. I should have asked, but I didn't. They weren't looking very chatty. I was also embarrassed.

People just called her Meryl. It wasn't her real name, though it was similar; a corruption, as it were, one that suited her in people's minds. Like the local men, it followed her around. With Meryl, it was one mess after another. She had taught in a school on Corfu but was never paid. Then, there were the parties she gave, the drunken young men, and the chickens – hens, actually, along with a rooster. She couldn't control those, either. She built a fence in the yard or, rather, assembled what you need for one then failed to fix it in the ground. The ground was concrete. She knew that before she got the posts and wire, before she got the chickens, but she got them anyway. It didn't make sense, though it did if you knew Meryl. She left the fencing scattered around. Hens don't care too much. They picked their way across it, raising their feet primly and putting them down again as if it wasn't there. They clucked as they always had, without irony. I didn't go to any more parties.

There was always one more party. Once, some guests knocked on my back door, three or four young men. They must have seen me through the window, ignoring the merriment. Perhaps they were being friendly, or the snub affected them. Anyway, they weren't so drunk that it no longer mattered. One of them invited me over.

"I don't get on with the lady," I replied.

"The chickens?"

I nodded. When I didn't speak, someone added, "They make a mess inside?"

I nodded again, gravely, as if the chickens had won, but who lets chickens win, apart from Meryl? Not a single bird had entered my house, let alone relieved itself there. As I nodded, I stared at the floor where the young men were standing. They followed my eyes down and ruminated. That's a word I've not used before. When they looked up, something had changed. They were on my side.

Not Meryl's puppies

Meryl and mess went together. What she did and what she didn't, it all ended badly. The worst thing involved a litter of puppies a few weeks old. She was minding them for someone – someone who didn't know her very well. They entrusted their puppies to Meryl. Then she went on holiday and forgot them. A big mess that was.

An English girl rescued them. She was a regular at Meryl's. I'll call her Mary. She remembered the puppies and broke into the house. I wasn't home, across the yard, so I didn't see it. She told me afterwards, all about the yelping, the smell and the dog food. She bought a lot of tins. I recall her face when she said the number. It mattered then, to her and to the puppies, but it doesn't now. The dogs are dead – from old age, I hope, a long way from Meryl.

Mary mentioned my absence from the latest party. For expats in the Old Town, nothing was more important than a party. I thought she'd say something false, as people do, that it was a pity I hadn't gone. But she didn't. She said everyone left early, then laughed at my weak joke.

"When I didn't turn up, there was no point in staying."

Meryl had suggested that she join her on the holiday. Mary declined.

It was good news for the puppies and, no doubt, for her. Mary confided, "She's not the sort of person you go on holiday with."

She didn't explain. She didn't have to. We were talking about someone who let hens riot and puppies starve. Mary was on my side, and she wanted me to know. There were other secrets. Until the summer, she had taught English at a 'cram' school, the kind of place I worked in myself. She had planned to go back in October for the new school year but changed her mind. I'd considered working at the same school and had an interview with the assistant director. He stressed the importance of honesty, of being reliable. He said he had trusted a young woman who promised to return but never did.

"She told me she'd fallen in love!"

They're the words he used – announced, rather – without much need in an interview. When a teacher quits, it's bad news for the school. It upsets the management, including the assistant director. But I sensed something else. For him, the reason she gave was the real problem. *She told me she'd fallen in love!* She didn't just let the school down; she betrayed him personally, or that's how he felt. Perhaps she fell in love with the wrong person.

I told Mary about our conversation.

"I think he gave you as an example of shoddy behaviour."

"Poor Michaelis!" she said. "He never forgave me for leaving at the last moment."

I don't know how much she liked him. I thought he was conceited: he had a job, I didn't, and he could decide. It was painful talking to him. If I worked there, I'd have to do it every day. The job no longer appealed. He sensed he was losing me.

"The director likes you," he encouraged. It was too late. He had said too many irritating things, like "You're very quiet. A teacher needs to act!" He put a flourish on the final word, smiled and moved his chin as if he knew about acting. Again, I reported it to Mary, along with my reply.

"I said I hadn't come to the interview with the purpose of acting."

"Oh, that would have hurt him!"

A taverna near the waterfront, Salonica

Candy the witch

"Candy the witch! That's what he said. Candy the witch!"

Melly had invited us around. She was an old Greek lady who taught English at the school. She banged her glass down and sat back gloating.

"I did not," I said coolly.

"Yes, you did!"

"I didn't."

"I bet you did," said Candy reproachfully.

"Yes, I did."

Candy wore black. I added the hat and broom, that's all, and passed it on to Melly. The old girl was glowing. She liked telling tales, and she took her triumphs seriously. The girls glared at me, their mouths open, then burst out laughing.

We often drank together, but that night was special, the night of the witch, the night of Cassie's hand. I was on the sofa next to her. Melly and Candy were sitting opposite. Cassie asked me to pass her a biscuit and at once held out her hand. Melly shifted from her seat, which distracted Candy. Instead of a biscuit, I put my fingertips on Cassie's palm and stroked it. A young woman's hand, whiter than most, less silky than it could have been, though not rough, either. There was a tautness in the skin which kept me stroking. But it lasted seconds. I hardly stroked at all. After I stopped, she left her hand in the air, as if she still wanted something. I gave her a biscuit.

How much emotion was there? Regarding me and Cassie, not a lot, maybe not any. We did it because we could, improvised a stroking. It wasn't meant to hurt the other girl. Candy didn't see, and we didn't want her to. But we did it in her presence. It was cruel. There's something else which made it even crueller. Candy had a crush on me. Not deep, and only for a month. By the night of the witch, it was half over. But a crush has meaning. You know when someone latches onto you, however slightly. I didn't encourage her. It was something I stumbled on, like a car crash, a minor one; you slow down, see it's not so bad then motor by.

Cassie must have known about the crush, no matter how limp it was. When I stroked her, and she allowed it, we laughed at Candy, like conspirators, with imaginary laughter. If a hand needed stroking, it was hers. The stroke was our revenge. Mine, for the cross words – there'd been a few from Candy. It was Cassie's revenge, too. They didn't get on. They argued. I remember thinking, *Cassie's winning now*.

She wasn't winning in the classroom. Cassie had a group of nine-year-olds. She wasn't cut out for it. She said so herself.

"There's little Ángelos. He lies on the floor all lesson. Someone asks a question. Teacher blushes."

The girls flew home to England for Christmas. I went to the airport with them. Just before they left, Cassie kissed me on the cheek the way a child does. Then she stepped back, her face burning. Teacher blushes at the airport, too. Candy was annoyed. A worker grinned. There's always an emotion.

They came back to finish their year, but I was bored with them now and must have shown it. There were no more kisses, no laughs. A friend of Candy's turned up. I saw her looking at me disapprovingly, with a certain knowledge, and I knew what Candy had been saying. Candy the witch.

When they left for good, I kept in touch with Candy. We met up once in Pisa. She was still teaching English. She took me to an old building, perhaps the British School. The man at reception asked if we were there together.

"Yes," I said, "unfortunately," intending a joke. She didn't get in touch again.

Smelly Melly
with the Plastic Belly

Melly told everyone I called her that, Smelly Melly with the Plastic Belly, but I didn't. I just called her Smelly.

We had a favourite taverna near the waterfront. It was close to the school, an easy walk when lessons were over. Not every night, but when we were out together, you'd most likely find us there. We ate and drank. Melly mainly drank. She poured retsina down her throat and scorn on her native country. Once, to show I was listening, I echoed one of her least offensive comments, as you land a catch of fish, huge ones, then toss a tiddler back into the water. Melly was shocked. She crushed her fist against her heart and said that only Greeks could bad-mouth Greece.

If she had enough retsina, she'd cry. She used to shake her head and say, "It's not the drink." One evening, she brought a letter from a friend whose mother had died of cancer. She opened a couple of wrinkled sheets and started reading, the saddest bit, I suppose.

"Her mother said, 'I don't want to spoil Christmas.'" Melly stopped reading and looked up. "I don't want to spoil Christmas!" She began to cry. "It's not the drink!"

When she wasn't sentimental, she was cross. Once, Liddie came with us. She'd arrived from England a few days earlier. I mentioned Mt Athos. You know that women aren't allowed, and that people laugh at what they can't do. Melly laughed at Mt Athos. She resented the fact that she couldn't go and that men could, but most of all she resented the men who lived there.

"Watch out for the monks!" I'd heard this before, the same words. Melly raised her voice. "Go to your Mountain Athos! You do whatever it is!"

"Smelly," I chided. Quiet but with a hint of mockery. "Smelly."

Liddie's head perked up. I turned to her.

"A monk gave me a strawberry. He was standing in a field. He picked it and held it out for me."

"Exactly!" Melly said.

I lifted my glass: "To Mountain Athos."

We drank on. Melly was in form. That morning, she had tried to use her ID card, but the man said the photograph was nothing like her. She pulled out the insulted card and banged it on the table like the proof that would trounce the prosecution.

On the card, under plastic, was a much younger woman. I thought it was a different person. It was nothing like Melly at all.

"It's obviously me!"

"Of course it is!" said Liddie.

The old Greek put the card away and went on drinking.

An exceptional girl

Liddie was exceptional in at least three ways. To begin with, she arrived in Salonica by herself. There was no Lily beside her on the plane. No Libby or Linda.

I normally liked the English girls who came out to Greece, but I didn't like Liddie. It was another thing which set her apart. From the time we first met, I felt there was something wrong with her. She wasn't unattractive. Perhaps I mistrusted her before she gave me any reason to.

She was also a liar, a much bigger one than usual. Even if she told the truth, it wasn't for the sake of being honest. She would have a sly motive. I'm being negative. When I said *exceptional*, you were thinking of all the talents a girl might have. Well, Liddie was an exceptional liar, and when I worked it out, I didn't like her any better.

It took me a while to catch on. The first thing she talked about, as I remember, was how men tried to get her into bed. She had no patience with them, Don Juans in general. I thought she meant it and was warning me. Why else would a girl talk like that? I nearly said, *You don't have to worry about me*, but (as Liddie knew) there was no need to tell the truth.

Her apartment was one of those which belonged to the school, to house the staff. It typically held two English girls but now contained only one. She still had a flatmate, Maya, a Greek secretary at the same school. Maya was about our age. She had a boyfriend. Liddie described him to me. He was very muscular. She finished her little piece with the words, "I don't like muscly men."

Now, I'm not someone you would call muscular. I sensed something. Did she mean she liked me? There was logic in it. But not much. There were lots of other reasons not to like me. I didn't respond. In the end, she got sick of waiting. She asked me over to her flat. Maya had gone out with her boyfriend. Liddie complained about her as soon as I walked in. The Greek girl occupied the bathroom for hours, putting on makeup. Liddie just wore mascara. She took me into the bathroom and showed me Maya's stash, the colours, creams and powders. It was fantastic. We could have played with all those pretty things. Maya never would have known.

There were candles wherever I looked, around the sitting room, like a scene from *The Bold and the Beautiful*. They were unlit. They never had been. Not a single wick was black, and the wax gleamed smoothly. They were brand new. It all seemed temporary. And it didn't feel like Maya. Liddie lit each candle. It took a while. There were so many. She was slow, anyway, careful, as you are with candles – so careful, though, as if they weren't ordinary candles.

We ate some food and drank some wine. Liddie got more personal. She began with family, asking about my parents. I said they were dead. I didn't ask about hers. She tried again: schooldays. I said I didn't like school. She told me she was inhibited, and gave an example. When she was seventeen, she had a crush on one of her teachers.

"He liked me too," she said, "but if he'd done something, I would have run a mile." The candles flickered; you can't say they didn't. "He just said, 'Liddie, what you need is a good fuck.'"

"I hope you followed his advice."

The intemperate Buddhist

There were some other foreign teachers at the school. Marvin and Mariam, like most pairs I knew, were English and had names that started with the same letter, but many things were different. They were a couple; they liked each other; they weren't both female; they weren't young, and they arrived separately. They were also Buddhists.

Marvin came first. It was important as he missed Mariam. He moped around, especially around Candy and Cassie. He kept dropping in on them. It was the holidays, and I hadn't met him. Candy told me in a tired voice. A week later, she invited me to dinner. Marvin was there. The girls sat me down, produced food and drink then withdrew. I understood what they were up to. They'd done it to me before at another 'dinner' – palmed off an unwelcome male. It was funny, but afterwards, when I mentioned it to Candy, she looked guilty.

They talked about Marvin behind his back, gloomily to begin with, then mockingly. He had an earring, the first man I'd seen with one (it was a while ago). The girls laughed. If it rained, he wore black wellies. More laughter. They were the right colour, given how the street dust turned to black slime, but it wasn't so wet. Everyone else wore shoes, the whole city, a million people. The earring, the wellies: they weren't his only excesses.

"Do you have a special day coming soon?"

Marvin asked me that. He meant my birthday. He was tentative, as if he was uncertain, but Candy or Cassie must have told him. Why hadn't I? He was clearly wondering. I had told the girls. Were they more important than him? He was frowning, too. His feelings were hurt. But they healed quickly as he gave a party. It's the word he used when he invited me, but it was dinner, really, at their place; just Marvin, Mariam and me. There was Graham bread and Graham's port, with after-dinner mints (he couldn't find any called Graham). It was how he did a birthday party. He wasn't going to miss out because he was in Greece or because I hadn't told him. He wanted the party more than I did. It sounds ungrateful, but I felt he was overdoing it; doing it more for himself than for me.

Marvin drank retsina. He overdid that, too. When he asked me if I liked it, I said it tasted like toilet cleaner.

"Oh!" he said and continued drinking. We talked shop. "I'm a born teacher," he declared. He had taught for a year at the Australian National University. It suggested he was clever. "We always leave before the results come out."

That was clever, and the bookshelves. He was proud of them, a few planks of wood set on bricks, easily made, he explained, and easily dismantled. But there were some things that Marvin didn't notice. He gobbled his food. He was a noisy, disgusting eater. The first time I saw it, I stared. Mariam was embarrassed. He also swore a lot. Marvin was a vain, greedy, hard-drinking, foul-mouthed Buddhist. That's what he said, without the adjectives.

"There should be a middle way."

I said that. I don't recall why. It must have been a serious discussion. Marvin was surprised.

"That's the name of the Buddhist magazine. *The Middle Way*. You're more of a Buddhist than I am!"

The last clever thing he said (it was February): "A light bulb can stop a room from freezing."

Now the last unclever thing. The school year was almost finished. Mariam had a problem with one of her classes. The teenagers weren't behaving. Marvin told the school director to sit in on the rest of her lessons.

"Or we resign!"

"You're an alcoholic," replied the director.

"Bloody Greeks!"

There's one more adjective for Marvin: short-tempered. He was sacked. He urged the staff to go on strike and, when we didn't, returned to England. Mariam stayed behind. I think she completed her contract, but the school owed Marvin wages. The director informed Mariam that if he wanted his money, he'd have to come back to get it. When she told me, her eyes filled with tears.

"I didn't know people could be so cruel!"

Lule and the flowers of rudeness

Then there was Lule, the last foreign teacher at the school. The director didn't want any more. She wasn't English. Lule means flower in Albanian. It's not her real name, but I can't use that. You'll see why. I chose the name Lule because her family was Albanian, it's similar to her actual name, and it's not too hard to say. There's something else. If you knew the real Lule, you'd think 'flower' was pleasantly ironic, not pleasant for Lule, of course, and not the only irony.

In those days, Albania was difficult, like its name in Albanian: Shqipërisë. The country was a police state, but Lule praised it. A lot. If there'd been a Shqipërisë tourist office – on Egnatía, say, or over on Tsimiskí – they could have used her. I didn't expect her to condemn the place, but she didn't have to glorify it, either. She asked me if I'd thought about visiting Albania. An ordinary question, perhaps, but she had grown up in Australia and had no intention of going there herself. That annoyed me. I said I'd just see model farms and plastic hotels. That annoyed her. Given her enthusiasm, it was a bit rude.

Have you noticed how certain people bring out the worst in you? Lule was one of those. She put me in touch with my inner rudeness.

Whenever we met, I said something or did something rude. I can give examples, but you won't like me. One night, I was sitting with her and Melly in the café by the school. I'd been to Turkey in the summer. I wanted to impress them, so I described my attempt to cross the border illegally.

The Evros River between Greece and Turkey. You had to cross by vehicle, but I tried to walk. I wasn't a spy or a smuggler. I was wondering what would happen – and avoiding the taxi fare. That's all it was, a stroll across the water but forbidden. Before I even saw the bridge, a Greek soldier stepped out from behind a bush a few yards ahead of me. He was about nineteen, in combat gear that was too big for him, holding a rifle that was also too big. There were twigs in his helmet with clumps of leaves, and dirt smeared on his face, like an illustration from a boys' annual. He'd done well. I hadn't seen him till he stepped out. Now, he was standing in my way. I stopped walking. He was, without doubt, hoping I would, though he didn't speak. He had a sheepish smile, like an apology. He didn't want to shoot me.

"Motherfucker,' I said. Not to him. I don't often swear like that, but I was sitting next to Lule. As far as I could tell, she never swore. Melly was an old girl with a mother complex. They both flinched.

"They have a hard time, you know," Melly said. There were stories in the news about conscripts who snapped and shot their officers. Too long behind a bush on the Evros River. Melly empathised but not just with young soldiers, with boys as a whole. I once saw her in the corridor at school, gazing up (she was very short) at the face of a male pupil, a strong, handsome one. He didn't see her.

"And their mothers wait at home," she continued. "Yes, they do!" though I hadn't queried it. Lule gave a mocking sigh then said, "We women have a hard time."

I liked the sigh, but it didn't go far enough – and I was sitting next to Lule.

"You're not women!"

Lule blossoms

I invited Lule up to my house on the hill. I must have been desperate. That doesn't sound nice, does it? I'm still being rude just thinking about Lule. The Greek sun followed her in, showing her plainness and her age. It showed mine, too, I suppose.

With most adults, I have no idea what to say. It was even more difficult with Lule. Happily, my shutters opened on the street. I didn't feel alone. She observed, with a little smile, how close the traffic was and the people walking by. I said I liked it; I could reach out and touch passing motorists. When I got to the word *reach*, I stretched my arm out toward the open window. Her smile went away.

In the Old Town, roads don't go far. There aren't many cars. Children run about, playing in the street. They call their adult neighbours by the first name, like friends.

"Do you really like living here?" Lule smiled.

"Yes," I replied. "In Australia, there'd be a man in a grey raincoat standing at the end of the road."

The smile went again. A child appeared at the window, a girl called Maria. She was twelve. I was fond of her. She often stopped to talk.

Each time, she said hello sweetly. "Γεια σου, Γραχαμ!" Most Greeks pronounce the *a* as in *bus* and put an *h* in the middle, cutting my name in half. Maria did too. I can hear her thin voice. She was very pretty. When she came that day, Lule raised a palm and dabbed at her hair. She never dabbed for me. I had two guests now, one on the chair in front of me, the other on my left at the window. What was I doing sitting there with Lule?

I said a few things to Maria. Up there, no one spoke English. I had my own brand of Greek. I thought Lule might laugh, though she couldn't speak a word. In any case, I didn't want her watching. I turned my back on Maria. I hadn't done that before. I didn't say goodbye. I simply turned. It would have hurt her. I hope she's forgotten. She probably has – it was decades ago – but I haven't. Something rude was always going to happen. I was sitting with Lule.

Lule kissed one of her students. Liddie told me. It was all she said, apart from the boy's name. I had to guess the rest. Lule must have told her. The lucky boy was nineteen, doing Proficiency in English and acquiring it in other things as well. He was squat and solid, with thick-rimmed glasses, black, curly hair and eyebrows like wire brushes. Liddie didn't say all that. She only referred to the kiss, and she did tell lots of lies, but this time I believed her. Lule had feelings too, and the pupils liked her (some of them). She didn't set essays as she hated marking, and she wasn't so good at grammar. In Lule's class, it was mainly conversation. She was good at oral work.

I'd taught the boy myself, different things from Lule. He was clever, and he laughed at my jokes, but his face was hard to look at, in my opinion. Now Lule's lips had been there, I scanned it more closely. In my head, I kept seeing the kiss. It was a Lule I didn't know, a romantic flower. I'm being cautious. Tricky subject, pupil amour. You need the right words. She initiated, or he was drunk and groped her. Either way, it doesn't sound pretty. The language of love. It's not English. They would have kissed in that.

Lule and the party pooper

I saw Lule in the street with half a dozen students, all boys. They were outside her flat, standing on the pavement. There was a kind of shape about them, this little, male clump and Lule. I thought they were going somewhere. A boy said they were going up to Lule's. It was the student she had kissed. He suggested I come too. It was nice of him.

Lule hadn't mentioned the party. It's one of my clearest memories, her face when he told me. It's the reason I went, along with the kissing business. We sat in the living room, Romeo on one side and Lule on the other, carefully apart, if there'd been a kiss. Perhaps there hadn't. Liddie could have made it up. If she did, it was her best lie ever. The boy was more at ease than anyone. So confident. It's why you kiss a boy, or what a kiss can do, not just kissing Lule. But she didn't speak to him, not once, even when she stopped being cross. If her eyes came close to his, they skipped over. It wasn't accidental. Still, she did the same to me. Had *I* kissed her?

We were drinking heavily. With a warm giggle, Lule pointed out that Albanians liked a drink. Someone brought up the police state. She pointed out that Albanians were happy.

"No one leaves," she said.

"They're too drunk to find the border."

It's the only thing I remember saying. The Greek boys erupted. The one Lule kissed laughed loudest. I can see his shaking face, the wire brushes bouncing up and down. She was cross again. I began to enjoy the party.

At the cram school, complaints were being made about Lule. She wasn't teaching anything. The director asked me to talk to her. He was concerned about losing students. He was also a coward. He should have talked to her himself. I was a coward too. I should have said no.

When I told her, she was surprised. I don't know what surprised her more, hearing that her students had complained or hearing it from me. It wasn't fair on Lule. She was teaching things. It must have been the girls. Anyway, she didn't listen. There were more complaints. I mark pupils' work. I'm bad at correcting women.

Lule was sacked. She booked the coach to Athens. A small group formed to see her off, no students, mainly teachers. A Greek man was there. I'd never seen him. He was older than her students, an official lover, by the look of it. To the end, I was learning about Lule.

They spoke confidentially until the coach arrived. Then he walked over to another teacher, an English girl, and started chatting to her. She seemed surprised. I don't think they'd met. Lule had her suitcase, ready to board. He could have waited till she'd gone. He could have been sad, kissed her till the last moment, done what lovers do. But when the coach left, the girl would too. He mightn't get another chance. Feigning warmth for Lule was no use now. He would lose them both.

I didn't want Lule to pine. You never know. She might have been the pining sort. He wasn't worth it. I said, "He's not wasting much time."

Of all the things I said and did to Lule or to someone else when Lule was there, this was the cruellest.

"I don't blame him," she muttered.

Protestant cemetery, Salonica

A cup of coffee and a sweet

I couldn't see Mt Olympus from my window even when the air was clean enough. A Byzantine wall was in the way. I could see the house where Olga lived, a roof and sides made of tin and wood, stuck like a barnacle to the giant masonry. It was perfect, the sort of thing that tourists photograph. There were Germans around. Olga lived by herself. She was very old. She must be dead now. Olga was her real name. I wouldn't use it, but I don't think she'd mind.

Our houses eyed each other across the road. It was narrow, with space for one car. People mainly walked. Olga used to sit at her window and watch mine. If I went to see her, she'd tell me what I'd done in my room, like a real-time biographer. For the English girls, she was just a nosey neighbour. But Olga would have liked them. *Ela!* she called – *Come!* – when she had some news or wanted company. I always went.

Inside her house was perfect too. You can do that to the place you live in. I don't recall much: lace and cleanliness, and knowing it was perfect. I loved those visits. I felt she was looking after me. She had her rituals. My favourite was coffee in a tiny pot and syrupy fruit from a jar. Each time, she did the same things in the same order. The fruit would change, that's all. While I sat watching her, I couldn't think of a place I'd rather be. Once, when we'd finished drinking, she turned her cup over and knocked it on the table so the grounds fell out. Then she read her future. She urged me to do it with my own cup. It's the one thing we didn't do again. There was no need, was there? We knew the future.

Our conversations were also the same. I couldn't speak much Greek, and Olga only enjoyed certain news. The detail would be different, like the fruit. Normally, she talked about the past.

She told me when a girl put her fingers on my head; a Greek girl who said she was seventeen. I'm not sure why she touched me. Perhaps she wanted me to kiss her. There might have been a mundane reason – who makes love in front of an open window? – but it looked romantic from across the road where Olga was sitting. She described what had happened (it wasn't much), showing me, as far as her hip allowed, as if she was a girl again, although she didn't touch me. She placed her fingers in the air where my temples would have been. I remember that as clearly as the girl.

The last time I was in Salonica, I walked up to the Old Town to see if our hovels were still there. I just stood at the end of the road.

Where are you?

If I rang Bryan, his wife always answered the phone, always in Greek, in a loud, public voice. "Εμπρος!" (Embros!) She was Greek in Greece, but I thought, *No one rings Bryan*. When she knew it was me, she would ask in English, softly and privately, "Where are you?"

She was warmer on the phone than when I saw her. Once, she said, "You never come!" She was right. We lived in the same city. I could have visited more often. But I wasn't important to her. Why should she care? She was thinking of Bryan. He must have gone on about me; he missed me. She was caring for him. When I understood, I liked her a bit more. They were fond of each other, but they married old. They had little in common. She wanted company. He wanted a place to live. She had friends; he didn't. I kept away because she annoyed me. At the start, Bryan annoyed me too. He talked about steam trains and vintage cameras, like a young boy who loved what was old. He was a man of tradition.

"I don't like those programs that make fun of priests."

An allusion to *Father Ted*. But he didn't seem religious. Some mischief, he approved of, the 'moonlight flit,' for example. He liked that term. It evoked his Bohemian days, the adventures of youth. He had his own traditions. He related his best stories again and again, like the Spanish landlady who crossed herself before she lit the boiler. They used to explode, the boilers and the landladies if you didn't pay the rent. In Salonica, Bryan did nothing unwise, or if he did, I never found out. He didn't travel anymore and he wasn't renting. Moonlight flits were no longer needed. On the other hand, he followed my own transgressions with a smile.

When I left Greece, I thought about keeping the house, renting from afar. Romantic but expensive if I wasn't living there, and the landlady annoyed me. (I get annoyed easily.) I decided to move out. I told Bryan one evening at the dining room table.

"I'm letting the house go."

He glanced across in his pregnant way. For both of us, it was a big step, a deeper farewell. The old ladies didn't hear. They went on knitting as if I wasn't there, as if I'd gone already.

I gave Bryan my shortwave radio so he could listen to the BBC. He offered to pay, but I refused. He put me on the coach to Italy with my 'Turkish' carpet, as he called it. He wore a silk scarf on his neck, elegantly, like a gentleman abroad. He offered me money again, reaching in his pocket as if for his wallet, though he left it there. I refused again. It was a wet day. He looked at the beating rain and said what he always said at such moments.

"It'll wash away a lot of sins."

We weren't saying goodbye, not yet. I was coming back for the rest of my 'Turkish' possessions. It was sad enough. A cold wind was blowing, the Vardar, from the mountains of Yugoslavia, another old thing. He'd been there and the rest of the Balkans. It was a wild place, I think, in his mind, the barbarian north, if you live in Greece. He didn't say much – he never did – but when a north-westerly blew, he referred to it.

"The Vardaris."

The name meant something, especially the way Bryan said it. He was feeling the past, not just a wind.

A bad smell

The smelliest visitor I've ever had was my Greek landlady. She was also the noisiest. She had her opinions on rent and everything else, proclaiming them in a loud voice. The noise, like the smell, informed the whole house. For a long time, she was merely the landlord's daughter. Then he died. In Greece, there's a period of mourning. For forty days, you're not allowed to wash. The more you smell, the sadder you appear. People sympathise. In fact, they suffer with you.

She had always smelt a little, even when the old boy was alive. She came instead of him, bustling in and out, a practised rent collector. She used to bring her son. Nine-year-olds don't smell. Saturday was bath day, Mikey said. Every four baths (before the old man died), they stood in front of me, knowing something good was going to happen: the magic of a pile of drachmas. When she got the cash, she squeezed the boy and cuddled him as if he was a baby. Some mothers don't have sons; they have accomplices. I thought, *How does he put up with the smell?*

Bath aside, you don't stop doing things when people die. It's not so hard, is it, holding out your hand for money? She came up all the same. The money had a keenness, like the grief, which she hadn't known before. Now, she didn't just collect it. She got to keep it, too.

I liked the old man, but when he died, he wasn't thinking about me. The first rent day after his death, his daughter smelt bad enough. But rent day falls every month. On her next visit, she was still in mourning. She also brought a lawyer. She wanted to increase the rent. It was very low, but the house wasn't worth any more. And she'd put it up a few months earlier. That stank too. I told the lawyer. He glanced at her sharply.

I was tired of them. I said I was moving out. Mother and son, they turned to each other like jackpot winners. They saw a queue of tenants, fat, generous ones, all desperate to rent their rotten hovel. Whenever he came, Mikey was thrilled to see me. He was thrilled sick to see me go. He'll be the landlord one day. Perhaps he is already.

If the sun was out, and it often was, Bryan liked to walk up the hill. The slope is difficult, so you wander left and right, unless you're hurrying. Bryan had no reason to hurry. When he made it to the top, he kept to the ancient wall, picking only paths and lanes. After I left, he still went, but when he reached my house, he didn't knock. He just checked if it seemed occupied then walked on. If he had some news, he wrote to me. For a while, there was a tenant and a mattress on the roof, which amused him. That was years ago. It may be vacant now. A nice thought, really.

You've been a real friend

A few months after leaving Greece, I returned to Bryan's and picked up my things. It was almost four years until I saw him again. I didn't go to Salonica straightaway. I flew to the island of Skyros, via Athens. I told him I was going, but I didn't invite him. It was cruel. Bryan was bored at home. All those sewing evenings. He snored, though, and wandered off when we travelled together. The boredom had knitted into him.

On Skyros, my first morning, I ate sweet *bougatsa*, walked empty roads and smelt the wild sage. A farmer gave me a lift on his tractor, a mile or so, but when I got down, I felt I knew him. Bryan would have liked all this. I was looking for Rupert Brooke's grave. Bryan had mentioned it. I can hear his soft voice. Tris Boukes. His lips moved deftly. He couldn't speak Greek and never tried, but these two words pleased him. The grave was worth a visit, he said, though it was hard to find. There were no signs. That wildness again. In England, there would have been a trail. Perhaps there is now. The neatness might spoil it, but you'd find the grave. He passed on some tips. I never found it. If he'd been there, he would have shown me. But he wasn't. I hadn't wanted him. Brooke was long dead, and now Bryan is too. I'm not very good at graves.

If I had to be buried in a hard place, I'd choose Tris Boukes. I've seen a photograph, stony ground ringed by olive trees. I got close. I remember stony ground and olive trees, just not the right ones. Brooke rested there with his party, that April, when the sage was flowering. It is, indeed, a lovely place; not worth dying for but lovely nonetheless. We like a dead poet more than a living one. The Greeks like Brooke; more than the English, ironically, considering what he wrote: a foreign field being forever England. Maybe they haven't read his poems.

In Salonica, I went to see Bryan. I apologised for going to Skyros without him. He swung his head around and peered at me mournfully. I made an excuse about the timetable and fully-booked flights. He wasn't convinced. He thought I didn't care enough. Perhaps I didn't.

When I left, he was standing in the entrance to his apartment block, facing the road. I noticed the lines near his mouth then caught his eye and wished I hadn't. He'd read my mind. *You're old.*

"You've been a real friend," I said. It was true, if banal. It touched Bryan, though. His eyes misted. He meant a lot to me, but I meant more to him. Without our knowing, it was the last time we met.

His apartment block was on a corner at the edge of the paralía. For some reason, it had two addresses, one for each side of the corner, though the entrance was only on one. The addresses were written above the door, to prevent ambiguity, I suppose. That was the intention. He advised me to put both of them on the letters I sent.

"If they don't get to me at one, they will at the other."

I did what he said, but now he's not at either.

To get to Bryan's, I usually took a bus along the paralía. Sometimes, I chose a different route, the number 6 on Vasílissis Olgas. From Bryan's stop, you walk down narrow lanes between apartment blocks. They mute the traffic. It's not far, but it's so dark and dusty you might be underground. When you reach Bryan's, you reach the sun; you feel, even here, in drab Salonica, the dazzle of the islands. Walking back, it's not so nice. The lanes are the same, but the harbour's vanished, and Bryan isn't waiting on the other side. On my final walk, I heard a man yelling. I turned around. Two women were jogging towards me. They didn't look Greek. The man was waving his fist at them, like a scene from a movie. They must have stolen something, money, probably, but there are other things. It was theirs now, whatever it was, safe beneath a shawl. As they drew nearer, I could see they were smiling. They hardly jogged, and then they walked, like me. He was too old to chase them.

One last spin across the border

Bryan's Greek relatives showed me his ashes, or the box they were in, parked by a wall in the living room. It's not something you want to trip on. They offered to unpack the urn. I said not to.

Cremation had just been legalised in Greece, but there was nowhere to do it, so he went to Bulgaria instead. One last spin across the border. His wife had gone a year earlier. Bryan scattered her ashes in the Aegean, off Mytilene, the island she was born. I don't know where he was standing, a deck or shore, but I see him at the railing of a white ferry, high above the ocean, that Greek blue. Cremation's fine but packed off in a fridge then back in a cardboard box with labels on? His wife's brother paid. He complained about the cost – there, in front of Bryan.

I'd been to Greece already that year. Bryan wasn't answering my letters. I was concerned. I hadn't seen him for nineteen years. I didn't see him then. He died four hours before I got there. I didn't know, of course. I walked in, expecting Bryan. His wife's brother was sitting at the window, the sky behind him and his face in shadow. I thought he was Bryan. I said "Hello, Bryan!" with a bright voice, when Bryan was dead, dead a few hours but dead all the same.

I returned two months later, looking for a grave but found his ashes. They were about to sail. I missed that, too. I was flying back to England. Before I left, I bought some pies in the market, loukoumi and a bigger, stronger bottle of ouzo than you can get in London. I thought Bryan would approve. I also took a few of his treasures. The camera I was after, the Leica – he'd often talked about it – was not in its case. His wife's brother said Bryan might have taken it to be repaired, then forgotten it. I chose a different one (Bryan collected them) and put it on the sofa next to me along with my other pickings.

"That belonged to my father."

Brother-in-law again. I found some precious maps (one of Mt Athos) and put them in my bag. Brother didn't care about those.

I stopped at a café near Bryan's apartment. It was near the school, too. I used to go with Melly. I put the bag of treasures on a chair where Bryan might have sat, had ouzo and olives then went to the cemetery, the 'Protestant' one, though he wasn't there, either. It's tiny and has a lot of spare ground. You'd find a grave without any trouble. Bryan took me once to show me where he'd be or thought he would. He could have been there, where I'd expected, like the shadow at the window, but he changed his mind. He was in a box instead – in the living room, of all places. I wish I hadn't seen it. Wherever you are, there's not much right with dying.

It was sunset. The cemetery was closing. I passed through the gate, an old iron thing that shut with a padlock and chain. You don't want the living. Like a tourist, I walked down the hill, past the Rotonda, the Arch of Galerius and on to the waterfront. To my left, the White Tower; along the harbour, Bryan's apartment. Tourists don't come for that. I couldn't see his window – it was too far away – but I knew it was there, pointing at the ocean. You want the dead. I glanced at the tower. The Greek flag was flying. There was a ladder on the side with a figure at the top, a man in uniform. He stepped onto the parapet. Next moment, the flag was whisking down. Another man appeared, and they folded it between them. I had my ceremony at last.

An X through the middle

The boat to Mount Athos. A breeze pushed up little waves, white-crested, like tips of rock. Monks sat by the railing, motionless. They didn't watch the coast. When the spray forced itself above the railing and burst like diamonds on their black robes, they still didn't move. There was a barrel of brown eels on the deck, live ones. They never stopped moving, squirming in the sun. There were baskets of silver fish, piles of thick rope and other things I can't remember, things you find on real boats on a real sea.

A crowd of gulls followed us, shrieking and thrashing their wings as if they were drowning. A single bird came down, low and languid, over the deck. A monk reached out for it, as lazy as the bird. If he'd caught it, he would have been surprised. The bird would too.

I got off the boat at Dionysíou. So did the monk with the lazy arm. He began talking. A Dutchman, he had come to study the form and intricacy of prayer – his words. The monastery had a reputation. For a gang of men, there are worse things than prayer. He took me through a courtyard, up some stairs to the reception room and rang a bell. A monk brought sweets and ouzo and tiny cups of black coffee. The

Dutchman had lived there for three months, but he wasn't settled. His eyes darted. The laziness had gone. I mentioned the Dutch woman who had been arrested on Athos for masquerading as a man.

"In my country," he replied, "anyone can pass for a man."

He knew a place on the mountain, not going far, but I wouldn't find it alone. A path runs up, more stair than path, by the monastery garden. The land is so steep the garden is in tiers, each with a stone wall, like pools of soil. There were vegetables, fruit trees in blossom, and tanks of mountain water. You can climb from the bottom, from the sea shore, but look up when you start, and you'll wonder how.

The Dutchman walked ahead, breathing heavily. His neck and hands shone with sweat. He paused several times, although (he was right) it wasn't far. There's a ledge of rock above the monastery, with flowers in spring, just coloured spots, really, and a bench to rest on. When you look down, all you do is stare: the slate rooves, the court-yard, the church inside – a stone bird in a stone nest – and beyond that, the ocean.

We sat on the bench. He pulled a cigarette from his robe.

"You're not Orthodox, perhaps not even religious. Here the Greeks will tell you of the true faith. They may convert you. The mountain needs new blood." I must have said things, but I've forgotten. "I have a book about the saint. You might like to see it."

He mainly used the present tense, sometimes the future, never the past. While he smoked, he left the matchbox on his knee. There was a woman on the label in old Greek dress. Someone had circled her in red pencil and put an X through the middle.

"We must go," he said. "They'll be eating soon. Today is a saint's day, and a special meal is planned."

He reached down, stubbed the cigarette on a flat stone then lifted the edge, revealing a stash of butts. He added the new butt, replaced the stone and stood up.

A gull fluttered from the slope above us, composed its wings then made a smooth arc around the monastery.

Doing violence to the fruit

August in Belgrade. The streetlamps were glowing. Dust which at midday was flat and thin seemed soft now, like grey foam.

I'd met an American girl. She was eighteen. I wasn't much older. We were changing trains, both travelling to Greece for the first time. It was midnight and we had to wait till morning, so we strolled around. In a bar opposite the station, men were perched on chairs like a spaghetti Western. When we got inside, it felt wrong. We walked back to the door. I was behind her. A hand reached out and caressed the fair curls on her right cheek. It was expert and looked loving. We kept walking. Outside the bar, she glanced at me knowingly. I didn't tell her, but another hand had pinched me in the anus. It was expert too, if not so loving.

On the train from Paris, there was no room. I'd reserved a seat, but a very big lady was sitting in it, and she refused to move. She didn't say anything. When I showed her my ticket, she simply didn't move. The girl – I think her name was Vinnie – had no reservation. We were standing in the corridor and started talking. A friend of hers ran a ballet school on Paros. She was going to see him. Then she spoke to another passenger. After that, she told me, "He's the nicest person I've met on this train." I turned my face to hers. A little silence. "No, you're the nicest person."

Some soldiers were in the corridor. We tried walking to the buffet car, but one of them picked Vinnie up by the waist and held her in the air. It wasn't ballet. She wriggled hard, waving her bare limbs like a child. The soldiers ignored me. They were younger than the men in the bar, just boys. Again, I walked behind her. Again, I did nothing.

There was a fruit stall near the Clint Eastwood bar. I bought some red grapes. Vinnie asked if I chewed the seeds or swallowed them whole. I said I chewed them. She had a friend who swallowed them whole. She only mentioned male friends. He had told her that chewing did violence to the seeds. I might have seen it coming. I nodded but thought, *What could be more violent than eating something?* I didn't say it, though.

In the station square, Vinnie unrolled a sleeping bag, pushed her thin body inside then lay back with her face to the night sky.

"You can get in if you like."

It took me by surprise. I said I was okay.

We left in the morning. When our train pulled into Athens, it was several hours late.

"Can I come with you to Paros?"

Vinnie or whoever you are.

I hadn't washed the grapes. There was nothing to wash them with. I paid for it now, taunted by dysentery, on the dock at Piraeus after she was gone.

www.ingramcontent.com/pod-product-compliance
Lightning Source LLC
Chambersburg PA
CBHW060514160726
47991CB00001B/36